Shattered Glass in Birmingham

SHATTERED GLASS
IN BIRMINGHAM

My Family's Fight for Civil Rights, 1961–1964

Randall C. Jimerson

LOUISIANA STATE UNIVERSITY PRESS)|(BATON ROUGE

Published by Louisiana State University Press
Copyright © 2014 by Louisiana State University Press
All rights reserved
Manufactured in the United States of America
First printing

Designer: Michelle A. Neustrom
Typeface: Ingeborg
Printer and binder: Maple Press

Library of Congress Cataloging-in-Publication Data
Jimerson, Randall C.
    Shattered glass in Birmingham : my family's fight for civil rights, 1961–
1964 / Randall C. Jimerson.
        pages cm
    Includes bibliographical references and index.
    ISBN 978-0-8071-5437-3 (cloth : alk. paper) — ISBN 978-0-8071-5438-0
(pdf) — ISBN 978-0-8071-5439-7 (epub) — ISBN 978-0-8071-5440-3
(mobi) 1. Jimerson family. 2. Jimerson, Randall C. 3. Civil rights movements—Alabama—Birmingham—History—20th century. 4. African
Americans—Civil rights—Alabama—Birmingham—History—20th century. 5. African Americans—Alabama—Birmingham—Biography.
6. Birmingham (Ala.) —History—20th century. 7. Birmingham (Ala.)
—Biography. I. Title.
    F334.B653J56 2013
    323.1196'0730761781—dc23
                                                        2013022657

Dedicated to:
    Ann, Paul, Sue, and Mark

and to the next generation:
    Laura and Beth Jimerson
    Maria and Vanya Klein
    Emma Jimerson
    Ruthy, Efrain, and Ismael López

CONTENTS

ACKNOWLEDGMENTS

Although told primarily from my own perspective, this is truly a family memoir. It incorporates stories and memories from my mother and father, my sisters Ann and Sue, and brothers Paul and Mark. I thank each of them for allowing me to retell their stories through my own point of view. Ann truly deserves credit as coauthor of this volume. We have both been thinking about our time in Birmingham for fifty years, building and shaping memories of life-changing experiences. More than a decade ago Ann tried valiantly to get her siblings organized and motivated to write our recollections of Alabama. Each of us wrote one or two such vignettes, but we never matched Ann's optimistic plans.

Finally, in 2011 I decided to take on the project myself, with contributions from Ann, Paul, Sue, and Mark. I had already done research on the civil rights activities of my father and his colleagues and associates at the Atlanta University Center archives, the Birmingham Public Library archives (BPL), and the Birmingham Civil Rights Institute (BCRI) in 2002. In December 2011 I made another research trip to Alabama. Ann joined me to conduct research and tape an oral history interview at BCRI about our childhood experiences in Birmingham. As I began writing this memoir, Ann provided encouragement, moral support, and editing suggestions for my rough drafts of every chapter and for later revised drafts. She also composed the "Questions for Discussion" available on the press's website. Mark also generously offered valuable editing and stylistic suggestions, as did Paul and Sue. I am especially grateful to the four of them for writing eloquent personal accounts of how the Birmingham years affected each of their lives.

As I conducted research for this memoir, many archivists and librarians provided essential assistance and exemplary service. During my trips to Atlanta in 1988 and 2002, Karen Jefferson and Cathy Lynn Mundale of the Atlanta University Center's Archives and Special Collections helped me locate my father's papers in the Southern Regional Council records, and made nearly four hundred pages of photocopies for me. At the Birmingham Public Library Department of Archives and Manuscripts during my research visits in 2002 and 2011, Jim Baggett lived up to his outstanding reputation among civil rights researchers, and Don Veasey provided generous and quick assistance in securing copies of photographs in 2013. In 2011 Ed Bridges and Norwood Kerr of the Alabama Department of Archives and History in Montgomery offered expert advice and permitted Ann and me to examine unprocessed papers of Charles Morgan Jr., which proved very useful. Elizabeth Wells of Samford University Special Collections provided valuable information about Howard College and Homewood.

The staff of the Birmingham Civil Rights Institute has been particularly helpful in providing information and research assistance. Archivist Laura Anderson, in particular, has become a collaborator on my project. I also thank BCRI president Dr. Lawrence J. Pijeaux Jr., founding president Odessa Woolfolk, and archivist Wayne Coleman. Jan Ballard of the American Baptist Historical Society and Lisa McNair, daughter of Chris McNair, provided permission to include two photographs for the book, and I deeply appreciate their assistance.

One of the special joys of this project has been to reconnect with family friends from our Alabama years. Eileen Walbert and David Walbert have earned special places in my heart for their continued commitment to the movement and its legacy, as well as their warm hospitality. It was a special privilege to introduce Reverend Robert E. Hughes when he received a humanitarian award from the Whatcom Peace and Justice Center (Bellingham, Washington) in 2010, and to interview Bob and his wife Dottie at their home in Issaquah, Washington, in January 2012. Sadly, Bob passed away before I could complete this book or help him write his autobiography. Bob's nephew, Rev. Paul Hughes of Birmingham, provided valuable insights into his uncle's career and, during our visit with him in 2011, he even offered a prayer for the research project Ann and I were conducting. Ann and I have enjoyed visiting with Bette Lee Hanson in Washington, D.C., and Ann is currently conducting a series of oral history interviews with her. I have also had the honor of meeting two former civil rights colleagues of my father, Reverend Fred Shuttlesworth in 2002 and Ambassador Andrew Young in 2005.

As I began writing this memoir in 2012, Bob Zellner graciously agreed to be interviewed by telephone from his new home in North Carolina. Connie Curry, whom I first met at a history conference in 1997, provided valuable suggestions on my first drafts of several chapters and told me that my father had a reputation among civil rights workers in the 1960s as being very effective. I want to thank Andrew Manis for sending a copy of his oral history interview with my father to Ann and me several years ago; it has been very helpful in filling in some details and gaps in my father's story. Diane McWhorter has provided encouragement and advice at several key points along the way. I also want to thank Brenda Banks, Kerrie Cotten Williams, Mary Jensen, Gary McKinney, and Casey Kelly for assistance and advice. My brother-in-law, Rev. Dr. Peter Moon, who has been active in setting up a civil rights museum in Farmville, Virginia, offered valuable suggestions and encouragement as I began revising the manuscript.

The Research and Sponsored Programs office at Western Washington University provided travel funding for my research trip to Birmingham and Montgomery in 2011. Almost twenty years ago my supervisor at the University of Connecticut, university librarian Dr. Norman D. Stevens, assisted me in obtaining funding to transcribe interviews I had conducted with my father in 1992. I also want to thank my colleagues in the Department of History at Western Washington University for support and collegiality, especially Department Chair Kevin Leonard, George Mariz, and staff members Jennie Huber and Willie Smith. My students, past and present, have heard some of these stories, and have helped me in learning how to talk about my own experiences.

I also want to thank many friends who have listened, offered encouragement, and helped me in many other ways: Tom Connors, Terry Cook, Daria D'Arienzo, David Garnes, Verne Harris, Beth Joffrion, Tony Kurtz, John Lancaster, Tom Nesmith, Ruth Steele, and Helen Samuels, among too many others to list. If by some chance my Birmingham friends Gregg Beasley, Mike Ham, or Tony stumble across this, I hope they will contact me to renew our acquaintance.

At LSU Press, Rand Dotson has patiently guided me through the editorial process and offered just the right combination of advice, encouragement, and reassurance. The anonymous reviewer selected by the press offered an exceptionally good critique of my first draft, prodding me in ways that greatly improved the manuscript and saved me from an embarrassing number of careless errors. I also want to thank Lee Sioles and other LSU Press staff, and Stan Ivester, a compassionate and generous copyeditor.

In this process—as in every facet of my life for the past forty years—Joyce has made it all worthwhile, keeping me grounded and providing love and support. Our daughters, Laura and Beth, give me encouragement about the future. It is my hope that they will find this story of the past interesting.

Of course none of this would have been possible without my parents. Although Dad did not live long enough for me to complete my ambitious plans for more extensive interviews, his example of commitment to civil rights, world peace, and social justice left a lasting legacy. Mom provided a model of love, compassion, and integrity that I only hope I can live up to. If dementia had not weakened her once brilliant mind, I know she would have helped me make this family story richer. I offer this family memoir in tribute to my parents, in gratitude to my brothers and sisters, and with optimism to our children, the next generation.

PROLOGUE

Jesus has no face. Looking at the damaged stained glass window, this detail shocks him. Most of the church windows have been blasted out completely, but in this tall centerpiece window only a few bits of glass have been shattered, including the face of Christ.

Almost as soon as he notices this, he shifts his focus back to the wider scene of devastation. As he crosses Sixth Avenue from the park, he notices a confusion of people and vehicles. Police cars and fire trucks fill Sixteenth Street, which is littered with debris. Several mangled cars sit askew, with broken windshields, crumpled front hoods, missing doors.

Helmeted policemen hold carbines at the ready in front of their chests. They warily survey the crowd on the sidewalk, both looking tense and feigning boredom. Firemen in hard hats and rainproof slickers trudge back and forth. Some police and fire personnel are piling blocks of stone and bricks to clear the area near a large hole in the lower side of the church basement.

Across from the church, crowds of onlookers, black and white, seem to be thinning out. Those who remain huddle in groups of three or four, anxiously watching. They speak in hushed voices, a soft murmuring of southern accents. The brick-throwing that followed first news of the bombing no longer troubles the eerie quiet.

Reaching the sidewalk across from the church, Jim sees that the debris consists of broken stonework, bricks, mortar, concrete, splintered wood, and shattered glass. All are coated with grainy white dust, pulverized bits of the Sixteenth Street Baptist Church.

He scans the black faces in the street and on the sidewalks. "Where is Cross?" he wonders. He starts to ask a police officer, but thinks better of it. He notices a few other white men not in uniform. White shirts and ties, holding a camera or a notepad. Journalists, reporters.

Nearby he sees an elderly black man still wearing his Sunday suit and tie. He is coated in white dust. "Sir, excuse me," Jim says. "I'm a friend of Reverend Cross. Do you know where he is?" The old man stares straight through him. He shakes his head slowly.

"Might still be in the church," says a younger black man standing nearby. He points across the street. His suit is clean, but his white shirt shows damp sweat marks around the collar.

Jim turns to look. Through a blasted-out side window he can see someone inside the church office. A small desktop fan sits atop a filing cabinet. The man is speaking on a telephone. From this distance Jim can't make out whether it is Reverend Cross.

The back door to the church has been obliterated by the bomb blast. Jim circles around to try the front entrance. He averts his gaze whenever a policeman looks at him or starts to move to intercept him.

As he climbs the broad stone steps to the sanctuary, Jim remembers his last time here. During the demonstrations last spring he came to a mass meeting to hear King and Abernathy and Shuttlesworth exhort the crowd.

Jim walks into the sanctuary. It is quiet as a tomb. A breeze blows through holes that until a few hours ago had been elegant stained glass windows. In one remaining window he sees daylight where Christ's face should be. The Savior stands in a familiar pose, holding a shepherd's staff and knocking on a sturdy-looking wooden door. His body leans slightly as though listening for a response.

To the right, in one tall window frame a dislodged section of the stained glass window tilts precariously, resting against the sill on only one sharp corner of its framing. The windows to the left of Christ have been completely blasted out.

Shards of stained glass and granular dust cover the pews, the floor, and the raised pulpit platform. In front of and below the pulpit sits a carved wooden communion table, with its familiar engraved beckoning, "This Do in Remembrance of Me."

To the right of the pulpit, he opens a door and finds his way to the church office. The assistant minister tells him that Reverend Cross has gone home. Jim asks him to tell Reverend Cross that he stopped by to express his concern, and that he will contact the families of the victims. They shake hands, and Jim turns to leave.

As he walks down the front steps, he looks across the street to Kelly Ingram Park. His mind flashes back to the images of police dogs and fire hoses used to subdue the demonstrators several months before. He pauses at the bottom step.

Instead of leaving he turns left, walking along the side of the church. A helmeted policeman holding a carbine with bayonet attached is looking at a small group of blacks, not at him. Firemen walk by, oblivious to a dark-haired white man in a faded suit, wrinkled white shirt, and narrow tie.

Jim steps gingerly over bricks, cut-stone blocks, broken glass, and spears of wood. He stops twenty yards from the jagged gaping hole near the northeast corner of the church—the hole through which four lifeless bodies and several wounded victims had been carried only hours before.

At his feet he sees several panes of mangled stained glass amid the debris. He bends down and picks up one section of a broken window—twisted lead holding together small pieces of colored glass—some fragments broken and missing. "Someone should save this," he thinks. "In remembrance." He picks up another rosette of stained glass, and then a handful of smaller shards.

He surveys the street, both directions. No one is watching him. He takes off his blue suit coat, and wraps it around the shattered pieces of a stained glass window. He walks gingerly along debris-littered Sixteenth Street, across Sixth Avenue, through Kelly Ingram Park, back to his waiting car. Carrying stained glass mementos.

Shattered Glass in Birmingham

1

A Difficult Decision

"But Daddy, if things are really that bad, we *have* to go!"

When Ann said this, I knew we would be leaving Virginia. She was only nine, almost ten, and Dad couldn't say no to her. For several months, November 1960 to March 1961, Dad and Mom had been debating whether he should take a new job in far off Alabama. Now Dad had Ann on his side.

I didn't like the idea. It would mean tearing up roots again—roots that were just beginning to feel strong. I would have to start over with a new school, new house, new neighbors, a new church, and—for me—another slow process of making friends.

The whole discussion about Alabama began just before the Kennedy and Nixon election. One afternoon I was cutting up the head of Ann's discarded doll to make a beard for my Halloween costume, as General Grant, when Dad came into the family room holding up the *Hopewell News*.

"You must be proud to have a famous father!" he said. "Look at this!"

He pointed to a small headline: "Ministers Plan Workshop on Social Change." The article said that ministers and laymen from Hopewell and Petersburg would speak at a workshop next Tuesday at Fort Lee Chapel, on "Preparing Our People to Face Social Change." The event was organized by Reverend Eugene Ensley and Reverend Norman C. Jimerson, chairman of the Social Action Committee of the Petersburg Ministerial Union and chaplain at the Federal Reformatory.

"We're trying to improve relations between the races," Dad explained.

Mom called out from the kitchen: "Jim! Supper's ready! Kids! Wash your hands."

As I sat down at the kitchen table, Mom was dishing up spaghetti. "I hope it's OK," she said to Dad. "I can't keep the sauce from sticking to that pan."

We couldn't eat until someone said grace. It was Ann's turn. She went on and on, as if she wasn't hungry at all. I could smell Mom's spaghetti sauce, and I could feel it getting cold.

While we ate, Ann and I had to tell what happened at school. "Nothing," I said. But a lot had happened in fourth grade, according to Ann.

When Ann finished, Mom turned towards Dad. "That's good news about the workshop, Jim," she said. She dabbed her mouth with a napkin. "Do you think many men will attend?"

"Last year there were about twenty or thirty. Probably about the same next week," he said. "We have some good speakers, both white and Negro."

"I'm glad you and Gene could work together on this," Mom said. "I always enjoy it when he and Bonnie come over to play bridge."

Dad said, "I just hope this workshop will do some good." He ate another forkful of spaghetti. "This is fine, Mel. A little burning just adds flavor," he said. He sipped some iced tea. "A lot of men are afraid to speak publicly about race. Maybe this will give them courage to be good Christians."

He looked around the table and smiled at Susie. "Who wants dessert?" We all chanted: "I scream, you scream, we all scream for ice cream!"

Mom looked at Dad. "Did you remember to stop at A&P, Jim?"

"Oh, I thought there was something—." He looked at our disappointed faces. "Who wants a cookie? It's a special treat."

The day after Halloween, Dad was late for supper, but after a while Mom let us start. "I'll eat with your father," she said.

We had just finished when we heard the station wagon in the driveway. Dad came into the kitchen from the screened porch. He gave Mom a kiss on the cheek, and said, "Smells great, Mel! I'm starving." He smiled at Susie and Ann. "Now, how are my little sweethearts?" He rubbed Paul's short hair: "Hey, Butch! How's tricks?" Then he punched my shoulder. "Any news from sixth grade?"

Dad looked at Mom again, but she had already started reheating the fried chicken and mashed potatoes. He waited until she turned to look at him.

"What do you think about moving to Birmingham, Alabama?" he asked, smiling his how-can-you-say-no smile. But his eyebrows arched uncertainly.

"Not very much," she said. She rolled her eyes, which spoke for her: here we go again—.

Dad quickly, smoothly changed the subject. "So the workshop went well," he said. "After the meeting, some of us stayed to put away the chairs and tables. Paul Rilling was there from the Southern Regional Council in Atlanta.

He said that the head of their Alabama Council had been forced to leave the state." He paused, looking down at the table. "They can't find anyone to take the job."

Mom turned to check the stove. She wiped her hands on her apron, not smiling.

She looked at us and said, "You kids are excused." It sounded like an order. We left the table quickly. Ann started her homework. Susie rubbed Spitzy's tummy, in the living room. "Good doggie," she said. Paul took his coloring book to the family room. I sat on the steps near the kitchen to look at my baseball cards. I wanted to hear Mom and Dad.

Dad was talking: "Rilling said, 'Why don't you apply, Jim? You have the right experience and maturity.'"

"Oh, Jim," Mom said. "Please, no!" She paused. "I don't want to pull up all our ties again—."

"I just said I'd think about it."

All I could hear after that was the harsh clinking of silverware on dinner plates.

"Randy, time to do the dishes!" Dad called out a few minutes later. He supervised while I washed, telling me to do the silverware faster and to use hotter water to rinse. Then he corralled us all into the living room.

One of the problems of having a minister for a father—even if he was a prison chaplain, not a real church preacher—was having to sit through "family devotions." It seemed like every night, but was probably only two or three nights a week. Family devotions began with a prayer. Then we would read a Bible verse that Mom or Dad selected, or sing a hymn. I didn't mind taking my turn reading. At least it was easier than making up a prayer.

When we were all together in the living room this time, Dad gave a short prayer, and asked Ann to read a Bible verse, in Corinthians. It ended, "And now abideth faith, hope, charity, these three; but the greatest of these is charity." Dad said charity is an old word that means love.

"One thing I hope you kids are learning in church and Sunday school is to love all people, and to do the right thing, even when it might make you unpopular."

"That's two things, Jim."

"OK. But I want you all to know what I've been doing." He looked at each of us. "The meeting today was about race relations between Negroes and white people—about loving people even if they look different from you. Right after that, three or four of us were sitting around talking. One of the ministers said he knew segregation was wrong, but he wouldn't be able to say anything for ten years."

Ann asked, "Why couldn't he talk for ten years?"

"That's when the church mortgage will be paid off." Dad shook his head. He laughed. "It sounded so bizarre! Worrying more about the collection plate than saying what's right!"

Mom said, "But ministers do have to think about money, if they want the church to survive."

"OK, but where do you draw the line?" Dad replied. "Do you worry about losing your job? Or follow Christ's teachings?"

"Remember when you preached about race?" Mom asked.

Dad laughed. "I didn't even mention integration. I talked about commitment to Christ."

Mom looked at Ann and me. "The minister who asked him to speak was a friend, even. He needed someone to preach when he was out of town."

"He thought he was helping me!" Dad laughed. "He said, 'I know you just moved here from up North, but it wouldn't be appropriate to mention race—at all."

Mom added: "It sounded as though he was *warning* you."

Ann said, "What did you do, Daddy?"

Mom sighed loudly and shook her head. She looked at Dad, then at Ann. "Just like him—he talked about race relations!"

"I didn't tell them what to do. Just to look to Christ for answers."

Mom looked at each of us. "That caused a big hubbub! Your father was supposed to speak again Tuesday at the men's group supper—."

Dad interrupted: "I was ready to leave the house when the minister called. He'd just gotten back in town, so they didn't need me." He laughed and shook his head.

Mom said, "I told him, 'I think he got upset about your sermon on Sunday.'"

"So I called him up," Dad continued. "He said, 'We felt it was inappropriate to say anything about segregation.'" Dad shrugged, then laughed. "I told him I didn't say what they should do. But he said, 'I know, but you shouldn't even bring it up.'"

Mom said, "He did have a point, though, Jim. You have a federal job. None of the other ministers has that security. For them to speak out would put their jobs on the line."

Dad said, "Yeah, in my job I'm expected to oppose discrimination."

"What makes it hard for you, Jim, is that you always want *everybody*—100 percent—to like you. At least personally. But then you insist on doing things that upset people."

"Guilty as charged!" Dad grinned. "But I'm getting better." He looked around at each of us. "If somebody is promoting segregation and he doesn't like me, at least he knows where I stand. I'm not going to change. As one minister said at the workshop, 'I'm proud of my enemies—most of the segregationists in town.'"

Ever since the Supreme Court decision in 1954 that segregated schools— "separate but equal"—were against the Constitution, White Citizens Councils had arisen in Virginia and throughout the South. In Hopewell, race relations were quiet, but in nearby Petersburg and Richmond, massive resistance campaigns opposed school desegregation.

"It just seems obvious to me that segregation is wrong and un-Christian," Dad told us. "There isn't any question that a Christian should take a stand for integration."

In the weeks after the race relations workshop, Dad kept asking: "How'd you like to move to Birmingham?"

"Oh, Jim, not again," Mom complained. "Just when I finally have some close friends. I can't leave Ann Leake, and Bonnie, and the church women's group!"

"I didn't say we're leaving—" Dad replied.

"But things are going fine here. The children are settled in now. Randy is enjoying Little League. Ann is doing well in school, and has some close friends. Paul and Susie are happy here. We're finally beginning to feel like a normal family."

"Well, let's just think about it—."

Mom frowned. "Another move would be hard to take, for the family. What about the church? The PTA? I can't just drop everything and leave every time you—." Her voice trailed off. She choked back a sob.

"I don't know if I would even want the job," Dad said. "It's just that they are having trouble finding anybody to go to Alabama."

"They can just keep looking."

It took a long time for Dad to convince us—and himself—about Alabama. You could tell that he thought he should apply for the job as executive director of the Alabama Council on Human Relations. He was trying hard to soften us up, to get Mom to agree, and to make us all accept his choice. But even he sounded unsure if this was what he should do.

From the start, Dad must have known this would be a tough sell. They had been married for thirteen years, and had lived in eight different places. Before that each of them had lived in the same house from birth until leaving home for college. Dad was always looking for something new, somewhere else. Mom said she would have preferred to stay in Beaver Falls, Pennsylvania, her whole life. Or at least close by. But even though she complained, she seemed to enjoy the excitement of going new places.

After Dad started talking about Alabama, our family devotions seemed like a civics class. Week after week, Dad told about things he had heard about the Deep South. News stories. Crime stories. Mostly about black people being beaten, killed, mistreated. In segregated Virginia, we had very little contact with black people, and certainly no black friends. Alabama sounded exotic and remote, like China or Africa.

One evening, after lighting the logs in the fireplace, Dad said: "The reason that the Alabama Council on Human Relations doesn't have a director is that the Methodist Church forced Reverend Bob Hughes to resign. He had given information about race relations to a *New York Times* reporter named Harrison Salisbury, and Birmingham officials put him in jail when he refused to talk about it."

"What's 'race relations'?" Paul asked.

Dad said: "Well, it means how people get along. White people and Negroes. Some white people don't want to rub shoulders with Negroes."

Mom said, "They call them 'coloreds,' or use bad words like 'nigger' or 'Sambo' to show they don't think they are as good as white people. Just because their skin is dark."

"But Aunt Marian loves Negroes," Ann said. "She's a missionary in Nigeria."

"That's right, Annie," Dad said. He poked the logs, sending up a shower of sparks. Then he turned back to us. "So, anyhow, the Alabama Council needs to find a new director."

"No wonder!" Mom said, turning around to rejoin the discussion. "If Bob Hughes going to jail isn't enough to scare off people, I don't know what *would* be. The news is *full* of stories about how dangerous it is down there."

"It isn't *that* dangerous," Dad said. "For whites. Hughes wasn't injured. Only forced to leave."

Mom changed the subject. "Ann? Randy? Have you done your homework?"

"Yes, Mommy," said Miss Goody Two-shoes.

"Yeah, I guess so," I mumbled. It was almost true. I had looked at my social studies book, so it wasn't really a lie.

"Go upstairs right now, young man, and finish your homework!" Mom ordered. "Susie and Paul, it's after eight o'clock! Time for bed!"

For a couple of months there was no more news about Alabama. The flowers began to blossom, and the grass grew long enough to mow. I pushed the hand mower back and forth, stopping to back up and clear the blades when they clogged. I had to stop every minute or two anyhow, to sneeze and blow my nose. Mom said hay fever came from her side of the family.

Then Dad started talking about Alabama again. His stories got scarier and scarier. The evidence of hatred piled up, week after week, in our living room.

"I've been reading leaflets and articles about violence against Negroes," Dad began, one evening. "Black people who speak up or complain about mistreatment and inequality are being tortured or killed. One black man was castrated by a group of whites who went around planning to attack the first Negro they came across."

"What does that mean?" Paul asked.

Dad thought for a minute. "Hmmm," he said. He paused. "Well, it means having your private parts cut off."

"Yikes!"

"Most of the time the local police are on the Klan's side," Dad said. "Often the police are members of the Klan." He frowned. "If a Negro gets 'uppity,' the police or Klan will drag him out of his house and beat or kill him. They want to teach other Negroes a lesson. This is what happens if you cross the color line."

Mom said, "I hate to think that people can be so cruel."

Dad told us more about the Alabama Council on Human Relations. This was one of twelve state divisions of the Southern Regional Council, an organization set up to promote peaceful race relations.

"So of course they are denounced as radicals and communists," Dad said.

Bob Hughes began in 1954 by setting up an office in Montgomery, the state capital. One of the young black ministers he recruited as an officer of the local Montgomery chapter of the Alabama Council was Martin Luther King Jr. During the Montgomery bus boycott, in 1955 and 1956, Hughes provided support behind the scenes.

Dad said: "That was when I first heard about King. I was studying psychology and religion at Boston University when the bus boycott began. King had graduated from BU a few years before, and one of my professors had taught him."

After the Montgomery bus boycott, Hughes moved the Alabama Council headquarters to Birmingham. "It was—still is—the most segregated city in the United States," Dad told us.

When the Klan learned about Hughes's civil rights work, they targeted him for harassment. One evening Hughes heard a commotion in front of his house. He looked out to see a group of hooded men raising a wooden cross on his front lawn, dousing it with gasoline, and setting it on fire.

Hughes went outside and brought the garden hose around to put out the flames. He saw a line of cars, filled with Klansmen, slowing driving by. He decided to show them that they could not intimidate him. Before the cross stopped burning, he turned the hose away, so it could flare up. Water and fire, on and off. He kept this up until the cars drove off, one at a time.

Dad said: "That takes guts!"

"Sure does," I agreed. "I'd have been scared about getting *shot*."

"People who burn crosses or shout insults are usually cowards," Dad said. "You just have to call their bluff. You have to show you aren't afraid."

"But what if you *are* afraid?" asked Ann.

We couldn't afford to go out to eat very often. But when Dad was able to preach early at the reformatory, he could come to church with us in Hopewell. He liked Reverend Bob Stevens. They shared preacher stories and jokes. On the Sundays when Dad came to our church, if we had been behaving well, he sometimes took us out to eat on the way home.

My favorite was Elmo's Restaurant on Fifteenth Avenue, just off City Point Road. They had the best barbecue around. When the weather was nice we could sit in their screened-in back room.

One Sunday Dad said we could go to Elmo's after church. I could already taste the sweet barbecue sauce. We were all dressed up—sport-coat and tie for the boys, pastel dresses and patent leather shoes for the girls.

Dad parked the station wagon, and we walked to the front door. But as Dad reached to open Elmo's screen door, he stopped. "I'm sorry, kids, but we can't eat here." He paused and looked back at the car. "Let's go to Howard Johnson's!" He tried to make it sound exciting.

"But you promised," I said.

"What's wrong?" Mom asked.

"Look at this sign," Dad said. "I must have never noticed it before. Or else it's new."

On the screen door we saw a small metal sign, white with black letters and a black border around the edges: "WHITES ONLY."

"Melva, take the children back to the car. I'm gonna talk to Elmo."

"Oh, Jim, please don't make a scene," Mom said. "Let's just go."

But Dad went into the restaurant, while we complained and poked each other in the car. After a few minutes—it seemed like forever—Dad came out, scowling. He forced a smile. "Who wants a milkshake?"

He drove away, staring out the windshield without talking. "Well, I gave him a little lesson in what it means to be a Christian," Dad said, after several minutes. "Almost as good as going to church to hear a sermon. Maybe better." He chuckled. "But Elmo says the sign is staying up. I told him we won't come back until he takes it down."

"You mean I can't have barbecue ever again?" I asked.

The next night we had family devotions after supper. After the prayers, we talked about Elmo's sign. This was part of something called "segregation," Dad said. White people didn't want Negroes to go to their schools, or their restaurants, or churches. He said these things made him think the job in Alabama might be important.

"It's hard to know what I should do," Dad said. "But the more I think about it, I wonder if maybe God is calling me to do what nobody else wants to do."

Mom said, "Why doesn't God tell you to think about your own family?" She held her face between her hands. "Why do *you* have to save the world?"

"If regular people don't speak up against this segregation, it won't ever end," he said. "All it takes for evil to triumph is for 'good people to do nothing.'"

He looked at us, trying to smile. "Your mother and I have been talking about Alabama," he began. "I know you kids don't like the idea of moving again. But I have been praying about this decision."

He glanced at Mom. She was quiet, frowning. "Ever since we came to Virginia, newspaper reports and editorials have condemned integration. It's what the White Citizens Council calls massive resistance. Prince Edward County—just a little west of here—even closed their schools so white children won't have to mix with Negroes."

Ann said, "There aren't *any* Negro kids at *our* school."

"Last year a new boy came to our class," I said. "His skin looked dark. I thought it might be the start of integration."

Dad said, "Did anyone talk about that?"

"No. I knew some of kids would be angry about a Negro kid," I said. "But nobody said anything, so he must just have a suntan or something. Maybe he's Italian, like the neighbors' kids in Waltham."

Dad looked at Mom. She nodded without speaking. "Your mother and I want you to know what's happening." He paused while his mouth opened and closed quietly. "Nothing has been decided yet. But I accepted an offer to talk about the job. I'm flying down to Birmingham tomorrow."

I looked at the cake crumbs on my plate.

Dad said, "This doesn't mean we'll move. They just want to meet me and discuss the situation."

Mom tried to smile. She said, "This might not be the right thing to do. But if your father doesn't at least look into it, he would always regret it."

I said, "But I don't *want* to go to Alabama."

Dad looked at me. "We might not have to. They might not want *me*."

Mom added, "Or they might find someone else, closer."

Dad said, "Now, while I'm gone, you kids be good for your mother. Do what she tells you and don't give her a hard time." He looked at me and Paul. Then he looked at Ann and Susie. "And pray for me to do what's right."

"I will, Daddy," Ann said. Then we each mumbled, "Me, too."

Mom just said, "Oh, Jim—" and looked away.

After Dad came home from Birmingham, he talked with Mom for a long time. Then he asked us all to come to the living room.

"I want you kids to know what happened at the interview," he began. "I met with the board of the Alabama Council and we talked about the job. There were three men on the committee: a young lawyer named David Vann, an elderly black minister named Reverend Wilson, and another board member. What was *his* name?

"Anyhow, David Vann came out to the airport to meet me. He took me out and bought me a steak dinner. He said, 'Do you like filet mignon?' I said, 'I don't know what it is.'" Dad laughed real loud, as though this was one of his big jokes.

"So he said, 'Try it. You'll like it.' And I did. But it's hardly cooked at all, so it's kinda bloody."

"Gross!" Susie said.

"It must have taken me over an hour just to eat that piece of meat." Dad laughed again. "But we had a long evening to talk."

"And Vann was friendly, warm. He seems like a nice guy. He's a young white lawyer, probably late twenties. He works for a large, very conservative law firm. He's 'liberal' on race, but hides it as much as he can from his colleagues. Kind of a closet liberal."

Dad cleared his throat and swallowed hard. "The meeting with the board started at ten o'clock the next morning. Two young fellows were going to be interviewed first. I was third. In the interview we were friendly. They talked, and I talked. I thought I was the only person crazy enough to want that job. When I got down there and found that I was *not* the only applicant, I thought, 'Well, you don't need me.'

"We talked about the Alabama Council and what they want to do. The council's letterhead has the words—kind of their motto—'Alabama Council on Human Relations. An organization to promote equal opportunity for all people through research and education.' Which is a subtle way of saying to promote integration and racial equality. I think 'through research and education' is quite distinct from demonstrations."

"Does that mean you won't have to sit-in at lunch counters and bus stations?" I asked. "Like those college kids?"

"That's right. My job would be to work behind the scenes, not to cause trouble. To get people to talk together and work together. Whites and Negroes," Dad replied.

"There are three main responsibilities. One is to run the organization, help local chapters, send out a newsletter. Two is respond to any crisis. If a black person gets injured or killed, or whites threaten them, or whatever happens, I would try to reduce tensions and smooth things out. Third is travel the state, doing 'research.' That means keeping your eyes and ears open, to know what's going on.

"After the interview, four times—from the time we broke up—I tried to call David Vann in his office, and tell him I decided that I didn't want the job. That was from the airport, and when I got to Atlanta. And when I got to

Richmond. And each time I was told by different people that Vann wasn't in the office. So I couldn't talk to him."

Several days later Dad said, "I got a letter today from Father Foley, president of the Alabama Council. They offered me the job." He glanced nervously at Mom. "Now I have to make a decision. I mean, *we* have to." He bit his lip and squinted. "Soon."

"We're not sure yet," Mom added. She heaved a sigh, and looked at the floor.

Dad said, "I've struggled with this decision for six months, and still don't know what to do."

"Your friends do," Mom said. "Practically everyone who has heard about this asks, 'Why would you want to do something like that?' They think you'd be crazy to take this job."

Dad said, "Another thing is: I've just been offered an opportunity to get six months' training paid by the federal government—along with my salary. This would mean a promotion—more money, more prestige. Maybe a job at a larger maximum security prison."

"Like Lewisburg," Mom added. "Then we'd be closer to my family."

Dad said, "But the Alabama Council job seems like something exciting. Doing what nobody else wants to do."

"There isn't anything going on where you don't want to get involved," Mom said. "When bad things are happening, you want to solve the problem."

"Well, that's what the Alabama Council is trying to do," Dad told us. "They hope that getting whites and Negroes to talk about this will help stop the beatings, the lynchings, and the hatred. It really is dangerous to be a Negro—to have dark skin—in Alabama. It's like South Africa, with apartheid."

Ann said, "But Daddy, if things are really that bad, we *have* to go!"

Although he clearly wanted to accept the Alabama job, Dad still found it difficult to make a final decision. Trying to get a firm commitment, the Alabama Council board asked Dad to come down for another meeting. They talked on May 4 and worked out a compromise on the salary. This time Dad said yes. Two days later, at its annual meeting at Talladega College, an all-black school east of Birmingham, the board unanimously voted to offer the position of executive director of the Alabama Council on Human Relations to "Rev. Norman C. ('Jim') Jimerson."

When he came home, Dad told us: "After I accepted the job, I told David Vann that a month earlier I had tried four times to call him and say I wasn't interested in the job. He said he had been in the office all that time. He had no idea that I was trying to call him. So maybe this is what was supposed to happen."

If God really does want us to go to Alabama, I thought, he got what he wished for. But Mom didn't.

On May 12, Father Foley wrote to Dad, saying he was glad Dad had accepted their offer. "It is a great relief for us to know that a man of your experience—army background and years as a Federal Civil Servant—will be the head of our operation here in Alabama," Foley stated. "I have asked everyone to keep this confidential so that your move to Birmingham will be quiet and unaccompanied by any publicity that might interfere with the smoothness of your adjustment to life in the 'Magic City.'"

This should have been a warning of what was to come.

Two days after Father Foley wrote this letter—and before Dad received it in Virginia—Birmingham was the center of national headlines. On Mother's Day, May 14, Freedom Riders seeking to integrate public transportation in the South were brutally beaten in Birmingham, while the police looked the other way. Earlier that day another Freedom Rider bus had been attacked and burned in Anniston, sixty miles northeast of "the Magic City."

2

Yankees in Virginia

I had just gotten used to Virginia when Dad decided to drag us all to Alabama. One evening I was lying on the family room floor, propped on my elbows, watching TV. Mom was behind me, ironing a basket of shirts and dresses. Balanced on the end of her folding ironing board was a glass Pepsi bottle with a metal sprinkler head for keeping the clothes damp.

The screen door in the kitchen banged loudly. "Don't let the door slam!" Mom yelled. "I can't hear Perry Como with all that noise." Spitzy raced in, her long brown ears flapping and her short legs moving fast. Susie was right behind.

I kept quiet. In front of me the 1941 *Rand McNally World Atlas* showed the peculiar shape of Alabama. It looked like a big domino balancing on one leg. Without the Florida panhandle, it would tip over into the Gulf of Mexico. Birmingham was a big yellow oval in the north-central part of the state. South and a little east was Montgomery, the state capital. The other large city was Mobile, way down on the lopsided leg near the Gulf of Mexico.

Another new state. A wobbly looking place, I thought. What will it be like?

I counted on my fingers. Five states already. Alabama would be six. I was born in Ann Arbor, Michigan, the only state I couldn't remember, in 1949. When I was two months old, Dad graduated from the university. Mom told me we spent that summer at Granddad and Monty's house in Beaver Falls, Pennsylvania (state two). We went back there every summer, so it seemed like my real home, sort of.

In the fall we moved to Newton Center, Massachusetts (state three), so Dad could study at Andover Newton seminary. Mom said we lived in a third-floor apartment, with no water. For cooking or to use a bathroom they had to go down to the second floor. For a whole year. With a small baby (me) and dirty diapers. Then we moved to Needham, where Mom and Dad bought their first house. Ann was born while we lived there, just before I turned two.

After finishing seminary, Dad became minister of the Community Church in Hudson, New Hampshire, my fourth state. Every time we went to the brick church, all the white-haired ladies swarmed around Ann and me. "Aren't you cute?" they asked. I tried to hide behind Mom. She was holding Ann. This happened every week. I didn't like going to church. When I was almost five, Paul was born.

After three years in Hudson, Dad decided to get a PhD in psychology and religion at Boston University. We moved to nearby Waltham, where I finished kindergarten. Soon after, baby Susan was born. Now I had two sisters and one brother. Halfway through second grade, in February 1957, we moved to Virginia, my fifth state.

Dad said he was going to be chaplain at a federal reformatory near Petersburg, Virginia. He had to explain almost all of those words. A chaplain is a minister, but not in a church. Some chaplains were in the army, but he would work at a prison for young men. That's what "reformatory" meant. A place where people could learn not to break the law. Not steal stuff. Not write fake checks. Not sell moonshine. (That meant illegal drinks that could make you act crazy or mean.) And federal meant it was run by the United States government. It was the whole country, not just one state.

"When I came out of the Army after World War Two, I decided that I wanted to become a prison chaplain," Dad told us. "Not many ministers want this kind of work, but I do. It's important and I should do it."

Before we left Waltham, Mom told Ann and me that Virginia was going to be a different kind of place. People would talk strangely—with a southern accent. And they would think differently about some things. Like manners, or what was right and wrong. They might call us "Yankees."

"What does that mean?" I asked. She took me to the public library. We got a book about the Civil War, with lots of drawings of soldiers in blue and gray uniforms fighting each other.

"Read this," Mom said. "It will tell you about the North and the South. People from the North are called Yankees. People in the South call themselves Rebels."

Mom knew everything. Dad said she was valedictorian in her high school. That means she was the smartest student. But Mom said it was just a small class, so it didn't mean much, really.

Dad drove us to Virginia in our aqua-colored 1955 Ford station wagon. We stopped in Washington, D.C., to see the large government buildings and the castle-like Smithsonian museum. Trolley cars rattled by on the streets. Mom told us that when she was little even small cities had streetcars because most people couldn't afford to buy a car.

This was my first visit to the South. As Mom had said, people sounded strange. Their words mushed together, and everything they said sounded like a question. It was hard to understand what they were saying.

After we crossed into Virginia, I noticed something odd about the gas stations. They all had three restrooms, marked men, women, and "colored."

"Do all the colored people have to use the same bathroom?" I asked. "Boys and girls together?"

"Yes," Dad said. "People here won't let the black and white people mix together. It's called segregation. And they don't want to pay for four restrooms."

"But some gas stations only have two restrooms," I said.

"Yes, and then the Negroes have to hold it, or go out back behind some bushes."

"Yuck," Ann said.

"That's not fair," I said.

When we got to Petersburg, our house wasn't a house at all. It was one of four apartments in a long white stucco building. People who worked at the reformatory lived in a neighborhood of small houses, close to the prison. It was way out in the country, not near any town or city.

Dad liked to drive by the reformatory farm and moo at the cows. He would stop the station wagon near the fence, roll down the window, and bellow, "Mooo-ooo-wahhh, Ah-mooo-waaahh." If the cows looked up, he grinned like all get-out.

He said this reminded him of when he was a boy. His father taught shop at the high school in Corning, New York, but in summer the family moved to their farmhouse near Hornby. Dad loved summers on the farm. But when he was only ten, his father died. He was repairing an old refrigerator and cut his hand. Then he went to clean the barn, without bandaging the cut. When he got sick, the doctors couldn't tell it was lockjaw at first. By the time they knew, it was too late. Nobody told Dad his father had died. They thought it would be too hard for him. Or for themselves. So he found out by reading the obituary in the newspaper. He never got over it.

On my first day walking around the neighborhood, I found out I was a Yankee. I stopped to talk with a boy a few years older than me. "You're a Yankee," he drawled. "I bet you're from Boston. You have a Boston accent."

"No I don't. You're the one who talks funny," I responded. "And I'm from Waltham. You have to drive or take a train to get to Boston."

"You're still a *Yankee,*" he said.

I learned even more about being a Yankee when I went to Prince George County School. It was an enormous building spread out in all directions. Everybody in the county—except kids from Petersburg and Hopewell, which had their own schools—came here. At least the white kids did. There weren't any black kids in the big school. It included everyone from kindergarten—Ann's class—through the end of high school.

My second-grade teacher said she was glad to have me join the class, but I would have to see what I needed to do to catch up with the other students. "I hear y'all are from up north?" she said cheerfully.

"Yes," I muttered.

"Yes, what?" she said.

"Yes, . . . from Massachusetts," I explained.

"Young man, you need to show some manners!" she bristled. "Around here we don't just bark out 'yes' or 'no.' We say, 'yes, ma'am' or 'no, sir' when we address our elders."

"OK," I said.

She got mad again. It kept getting worse. This was confusing. It was hard to remember everything.

When the last bell rang I had to find the right school bus. Ann looked scared. She was quiet on the bus. It had been a long day in a strange place. When I got home I went up to the bedroom, which all four of us kids shared. Mom and Dad had the other bedroom.

Later, Mom called us for supper. I said I wasn't hungry. And I felt sick. Too sick to go to school tomorrow.

After supper we had a long talk in the kitchen. Mom said I needed to learn how to get along in the new school. If the teachers expected me to say "ma'am," I had to remember to say it. I must show the respect they demanded. There were new rules in Virginia. I needed to follow them.

Jimmy Riggsby lived in the apartment at the other end of our building. We were the same age, almost. I was two months older, but I tried not to brag about it. We weren't in the same class, so I didn't see him much at school. But after school and on weekends we roamed all through the woods behind the apartment building.

There were paths that went all the way down to the Appomattox River. It was a slow brown river. Jimmy said it started in the mountains and flowed down to Hopewell. There it became part of the even bigger James River. If you threw a stick in it here, it might go all the way to the Atlantic Ocean.

Jimmy said that one of the workers at the reformatory was swimming when he was bitten by about a dozen cottonmouths. Some people called them water moccasins. They were almost as poisonous as copperheads. The man was saved because he stayed under water with only his nose showing. That way the venom couldn't get under his skin. Finally the snakes all lost their grip and he escaped. But he was cut all over.

Jimmy said this was a true story, but I wasn't sure. How could he swim with snakes biting and hanging all over him? How could he stay under water that long?

In the fall I started third grade. School was a challenge for me, but eventually the Sears Roebuck catalog arrived, and I began making my Christmas wish list of toys and games. Dad decided I was old enough to take part in the church service at the reformatory.

On Christmas morning Dad and I walked in the main door of the large main building. Dad said "Merry Christmas!" to the guard, who picked up a big metal ring with lots of long thin keys. He unlocked a heavy gate with metal bars and walked in with us to unlock another big gate. Each time a gate clanged shut behind us it made me shiver. Then he said goodbye.

Dad knew just where to go. He came here every day.

We saw inmates wearing the same gray uniforms. Some were carrying mops and buckets. Others were digging in the prison yard or carrying stones. There were almost as many black men as white men. They all seemed to stare at me. I held Dad's hand tightly. Some of the men smiled and said, "Hey, preacher!" or "Merry Christmas, Chaplain." They didn't look dangerous, but you never knew.

I had been practicing reading the Christmas story in Luke, chapter 2. When the church service started there were gray uniforms scattered along the pews. I sat next to Dad on the raised platform near the small altar. There were no stained glass windows, just clear windows with heavy bars.

After everyone sang "O Little Town of Bethlehem," I walked to the podium. I tried not to look at the inmates or the iron bars. I opened the big Bible and started reading: "And it came to pass in those days, that there went out a decree from Caesar Augustus, that all the world should be taxed." It went okay for a few lines. I got through "espoused wife" and "swaddling clothes." Then I read: "suddenly there was with the angel a multitude, suddenly there was with the angel a multitude. . . ." I had read the same line twice. I could feel my face getting warm. Should I stop and do it over? I decided to keep going. Now I traced the words with my finger and kept my eyes close to the Bible. When I finished I closed the Bible and walked back to my chair.

Dad preached a short sermon about the baby Jesus and following his example. After another hymn, the service was over. They never passed an offering plate.

"Your boy did a good job," one of the inmates said.

"Pretty good for only eight years old," Dad said. "His first public speaking job." He was smiling his big-toothed smile, ear to ear.

My smile was inside. I wasn't afraid of the inmates now. Maybe Dad would ask me to do this again.

After the holidays Dad told us we were moving again. Not far; just to Hopewell. He and Mom were buying a house with lots of bedrooms and a big yard. We would go to a new school, but it was close enough to walk.

Our new house was white with a red-shingled roof. I got my own bedroom on the upper floor. The Driscolls lived straight across the street in a tall yellow stucco house. David was two years older than me and about five inches taller. Johnny was even older and bigger. They were from Boston, so we weren't the only Yankees on Prince George Avenue.

The Baby Boom meant there were always lots of kids around, riding bikes, playing marbles, trading baseball cards—ready to join a baseball game if someone brought out a bat and ball.

Hopewell was a sleepy town, not like Waltham. It was like Hudson—only bigger. The streets were paved, but only the downtown streets and main roads had sidewalks. The most interesting thing about Hopewell was that you could always tell which way the wind was blowing. If it smelled like rotten eggs, it was coming from a paper mill on the south side. If it smelled like skunk, it was blowing past the Allied Chemical plant on the north side. If it smelled like cow poop, it was coming from the farms to the west. And if you couldn't smell anything bad, it meant the wind wasn't blowing at all.

Right after we moved, Ann and I started at DuPont Elementary School. It was the middle of the school year, and on the first day Mom took us to the school office so Ann and I could get into the right classes. It was a two-story brick building, very old. Mom said it was built when she was still a baby. That's how old it was!

To get to school, we crossed City Point Road and walked down Stonewall Avenue, across Grant and Lee to get to Jackson Street. The other streets nearby were Gordon, Pickett, and Clingman—all of them named for Confederate generals, except for Grant Street.

There were two other elementary schools in Hopewell, plus a high school closer to downtown off City Point Road. Dad said there were separate schools for black children, but we hardly ever saw that part of town.

Before long I had some new friends. Mike Hammond lived on Jackson Street in a small dirty-white house. We played baseball together, and he showed me his baseball cards. I started buying some for myself, and we traded duplicates with other boys. His grandparents were in Chicago, so he was a Cubs fan. Another friend, Mark Butterworth, lived in a tall brick house with a side porch and a tennis court. His father owned a furniture store.

Besides reading, the school subject I liked best was history. We spent a lot of time talking about the Civil War. Lots of battles took place in Virginia. Teacher said the Yankees were cruel and tried to force the southerners to obey them. "Yankees call this the Civil War, but it *should* be called the War Between the States, or the War of Northern Aggression," she explained.

I decided that since I was a Yankee, I would call it the Civil War.

My birthday came on April 9. I was nine now. "Do you know this is a very important date, Randy?" the teacher asked. "Do you know what happened on April 9, 1865?"

"No," I answered. "I mean: No, ma'am."

"Why, that was the day that General Lee surrendered to General Grant, at Appomattox," she explained. "That ended the War Between the States."

"During the war there was no Hopewell. It was called City Point, because it was where the Appomattox River flowed into the James River. The Yankees captured City Point in 1864. It was their headquarters during the siege of Petersburg. President Lincoln even came here near the end of the war to meet General Grant."

When we were walking home, Mike said that Lincoln was the best president the South ever had.

"But he was the Yankee president—for the North," I said.

Mike said: "No, he was the best president ever. He *had* to be on our side." He thought for a minute, looking both ways as we crossed Stonewall Avenue. "Just like Robert E. Lee and Stonewall Jackson. . . . Besides, Teacher said Lincoln was in Hopewell!"

Ann was in second grade when she came home scared to death. She ran in the front door, crying. "Mommy, help!" She was shaking. "I was going to play with Sally, but when I got near Darlene's house there was a big crowd of colored people. They were laughing at me!"

"Negroes, Ann," Mom said. "But why were they laughing at you? Did they try to hurt you?"

"I don't know, Mommy. They were standing on the sidewalk, so I couldn't get to Sally's house. There were lots of big men and women. They were talking loud and *laughing*! I saw them look right at me!"

Mom looked in the telephone book and then dialed the heavy black phone in the hallway.

"Ellen? This is Melva Jimerson. My daughter Ann is a friend of Darlene's." She repeated what Ann had told her, then stopped to listen. "Thank you, I'll tell her. Good-bye."

When she hung up the receiver she was smiling. "It's OK, Ann," she said. "Those Negroes were not laughing at *you*. They were just talking to each other. Mrs. Johnson's maid had just left their house and her friends were picking her up. They probably didn't even notice you."

"But Mommy, they were *scary*!" Ann said.

Mom said: "Just because people look *different* from you doesn't mean they would *hurt* you, Ann." She hugged Ann and smoothed her blond hair. "There's no reason to be afraid of Negroes." Ann sniffled, and lowered her dark eyebrows. She looked like she might start sobbing again.

Mom took her hankie and wiped Ann's cheeks. She said, "It's OK to feel scared, but *most* people are good inside. We *all* need to learn to get along with people who seem different on the *outside*."

When it got to be spring, my friends all talked about Little League. Mike and Mark went to tryouts, and I went with them. I was picked for the Optimists, but not for the regular Little League team. So instead of getting a uniform and a red cap with a big "O," I would be on the Optimists' "farm league" team. Not even good enough for Little League! The one good part was that the farm league teams played every morning, Monday to Friday, instead of only two evenings a week.

Every morning in summer, I rode my old red bike down Prince George Avenue, to West Broadway and into town. My glove bounced up and down in the wire basket on the handlebars. The baseball field was next to the stone wall around City Point National Cemetery, where Civil War soldiers were buried.

After the games, we rode our bikes to the drugstore on Broadway. Sometimes we bought Cokes, but we always bought a pack of baseball cards. The hard flat stick of pink bubblegum in each pack took a while to soften up before we could blow big pink bubbles. The cards were neighborhood currency. I traded duplicates for my favorite players on the Pirates and Red Sox.

That summer, 1958, when we visited Monty and Granddad, Granddad took Dad and me to Forbes Field in Pittsburgh for my first major league game. I've been a baseball fan ever since.

Our first Christmas in Hopewell was the best ever. I got my first three-speed bike, shiny black and chrome. Just as we finished opening our gifts, Dad said, "I forgot something. It's in the garage." When he came back to the family room, he was holding something under his coat.

"What is it?" Paul asked.

Dad's coat began to move, and then a small brown face appeared above his coat zipper.

"A puppy!" Susie squealed. "It's a puppy!" She was only three, but she knew all about pets. "Thank you! Thank you!"

The puppy was reddish-brown, with a black nose, shiny dark eyes, and hard black toenails. She had a red bow tied around her neck. "She's a long-legged dachshund," Dad told us. "Some people call them wiener dogs. They're the perfect shape to hunt badgers in their tunnels." We took turns holding her.

Dad said, "This is a German dog, so we should give her a German name." He was studying German with a tutor in Petersburg, trying to get his PhD in psychology and religion. When he left Boston University, he had completed everything except learning German and writing his dissertation.

His tutor suggested the name Spitzbub. It sounded like "spits boob." That made me laugh. Dad said it meant "little dickens." That's what this puppy was, all right. All of us enjoyed playing with the new puppy, but Spitzy and Susie became inseparable. They practically grew up together.

Next to Christmas, my favorite holiday was Halloween. In sixth grade I decided to dress for Halloween as my favorite Civil War general, U. S. Grant. It was 1960, and Civil War Centennial events had already begun.

For my costume, I wore a blue sports coat, with aluminum foil wrapped around the buttons. Mom made epaulets for the shoulders. I had a blue Civil War Centennial hat that looked like the one General Grant wore in old photos. Ann let me use one of her old dolls that had a broken arm. I cut the head, trimmed the doll's hair, and tied it onto my chin as a beard.

Mom asked, "Randy, are you sure that's the costume you want to wear? Don't you think you might get in trouble?"

I said, "If I'm going to be called a Yankee, I'll be the general who *won* the Civil War!"

My Grant costume attracted a lot of attention. "Honey, you won't guess who's at our front door?" one lady called back to her husband.

Some people scowled at General Grant. Others laughed, and said that General Grant had a lot of nerve to trick-or-treat in Virginia.

In the fall of 1960, there was a lot of talk about the election, Kennedy against Nixon. Mom's family had been Franklin Roosevelt Democrats, but they didn't like the idea of a Catholic president. Dad grew up in what he called "God's Country," upstate New York. He was a Rockefeller Republican, he said. His mother was a life-long Republican, and didn't hide her feelings about Democrats. She said the only good thing about her son, Harry Truman Jimerson, dying young, was that people wouldn't think she named him for a Democrat.

At school, students plastered bumper stickers on their blue three-ringed notebooks. Some said Nixon-Lodge, others Kennedy-Johnson. I couldn't imagine anyone but Eisenhower as president. He seemed like a friendly grandfather.

For my parents, both raised as American (Northern) Baptists, John F. Kennedy's Catholicism was a serious issue. "He would have to do whatever the Pope says," Mom explained.

During the campaign, Senator Lyndon Johnson came to Hopewell for a Democratic rally. Even though she didn't support the Democrats, Mom took Paul and Susie (Ann and I were in school) downtown to see the hoopla. Walking through the crowd, LBJ bent over and shook Paul's hand.

"Who knows?" Mom said at dinner. "Maybe someday Paul will be able to say he shook hands with the vice-president."

We watched the Nixon-Kennedy debates on our old black-and-white TV. In January, my sixth-grade teacher brought a TV into the classroom so we could all watch the Kennedy inauguration. I had heard about Robert Frost, the New England poet, so it was exciting to see him on TV. But when the wind blew too hard and he couldn't read the poem he had written, I felt sorry for him.

By then, Dad had already begun talking about Alabama. By May he had decided to accept the job as director of the Alabama Council on Human Relations. Now we had to prepare for another move. One that I dreaded.

3

Heart of Dixie

All that summer, when I wasn't thinking about baseball, I was thinking about moving. Dad would start his new job in Alabama on August 1, 1961.

By the end of the school year in June, Mom had already begun the familiar rituals of cleaning, sorting, discarding, and packing. This time I was old enough to help. I took sheets of newsprint and carefully wrapped the good china—dinner plates, salad plates, serving dishes, and a gravy boat. Then the good glasses, kitchen pots and pans Mom didn't use often, and more.

I didn't know anything about Birmingham except the frightening stories of violence and prejudice against black people. What would it be like for me? I tried to imagine going to a new school, trying to make new friends, learning the streets and houses of a new neighborhood. I was nervous about moving. I worried that I wouldn't have any friends in Alabama.

Meanwhile, I had joined the Boy Scouts the previous fall and went to troop meetings in our church basement. I read the *Boy Scouts Handbook* and *Boys' Life* magazine. I learned to tie all kinds of knots and tried to advance from Tenderfoot to Second Class. Dad and his brothers had been Eagle Scouts. That's what I aimed for.

Just before school ended, our troop went on a campout. Dad came with us to help the troop leader. We slept in a pup tent, lashed sticks together to make a table for preparing food, and cooked meals over a campfire. The next day we had archery practice and a nature walk through the woods.

In the station wagon on the way home, Dad said: "I know you don't like the idea of moving to Alabama. It's even a little scary for me. I have to talk like it's nothing, so Melva—your Mom—won't worry. But it could be dangerous."

"So why do you want to go there?" I asked. "Why can't we stay?"

"Well, I've seen how much discrimination Negroes face. I think white people need to do something. If not me, who else? If I really believe what Jesus taught us, I need to act like it."

"Even when it makes Mom upset?"

He said, "I don't like to make life hard for her. But ever since we came to Virginia I've seen how bad things are for the Negroes. When I became chaplain at the reformatory, I got active in the Ministerial Association. There are several black ministers who come occasionally, and two regulars. Wyatt T. Walker is one of them. He asked me to preach in his church. Do you remember that we went to his house for dinner, with the whole family?"

"I guess so."

"Well, for the last two years I have organized these workshops on race relations. It made me think this is something I can do, and make a difference."

For about ten minutes he drove without talking, looking around at the woods, hayfields, and small country churches. Then he told a couple of his favorite jokes.

"Did you hear about the sailboat race? Two boats: one Russian, the other American. The Americans won. But the Russians told everyone, 'We finished second, and the Americans were next to last!'" He laughed loudly.

"Do you know why ducks have flat feet?"

I had heard the same jokes over and over, so I didn't laugh.

Dad looked at me, and clicked his tongue. "You know, one of my favorite things—. What happened was, when you were about three or four—it was in Hudson, I remember—I told you a joke and you just looked at me. You were just a little kid. And you said, 'Gee, Dad, that was almost funny.' What a line! I laughed all day about that. 'That was *almost* funny.'" And he laughed again.

Just as we pulled into our driveway—I could see Spitzy stretched out in a sunny spot near the forsythia bush—Dad stopped the car and turned off the engine. "Randy, you're old enough to understand what's happening in this country now, especially what I will be doing with the Alabama Council. That's why I want you to know what's going on. I'm counting on you to help the younger kids, and to make life easier for your mother. OK?"

"I'll try," I said. This was going to be my new responsibility, something I could do for Mom. It didn't make it easier to leave Hopewell. But I was proud that Dad thought I was old enough to help him.

One thing I couldn't help with was buying a house. It turned out to be more difficult than Mom and Dad expected. They had to buy two houses.

Before starting his new job in Alabama, Dad wrote to Paul Rilling in late June, asking for money to attend a two-week human-relations workshop at

Fisk University, an all-black college in Nashville. Father Albert Foley replied, saying the Alabama Council would pay for his travel expenses and the forty-dollar fee to attend the workshop. This would be a valuable orientation for his new position.

Since Dad was about to leave for two weeks, when Mom heard that her sister, Aunt Eileen, was driving north from Florida, we went with her to Beaver Falls. I always enjoyed summer vacations at Monty and Granddad's house. They lived on seventeen acres in the country, at the end of a long gravel driveway lined with pine trees. All the way from the main road ran a narrow, rocky creek (they called it a "crick"). It was a great place for building dams, catching crayfish, and splashing around on hot days.

The long side porch overlooked a small pond in front of the house. We all got to take turns in the rowboat, back and forth, from the lily pads at the shallow end, where a pipe from the creek fed the pond, to the concrete box at the deep end, where a spillway sent water back to the creek.

Mom said we could stay at Monty and Granddad's while she left on the train. She met Dad in Nashville, and they both went on to Birmingham to buy a house. David Vann showed them around and introduced them to a real estate agent. They found a southern-style house with a large front porch, on the south side of Birmingham, and put down a deposit.

But after we all got back to Hopewell, the realtor called and told Dad the loan didn't go through. He would return the earnest money.

"That's too bad," Dad said to Mom. "That really seemed like a good house for us."

"Jim, I think they don't want us living there," Mom said. "Don't take everything people say at face value. I bet they don't like the idea of somebody in your job buying that house."

So Dad called back and talked to the realtor. He asked for an explanation.

"You were right," he told Mom when he hung up the receiver. "That guy said they weren't going to sell a house to a communist. He said, 'I don't know if you know it but that is a communist organization. That Hughes fella was one of *them*. We can't do business with anybody working with that group.' I had to bite my tongue."

The second time they went to Birmingham to buy a house, Granddad and Monty insisted on driving down with them. Granddad wanted to see where they were going to live. We had returned to Beaver Falls for another vacation. While Granddad drove the four of them down to Alabama, Ann, Paul, Susie, and I stayed with Mom's sister, Aunt Eileen, and her brother, Uncle

Doug. They lived a block apart in a small neighborhood in Chippewa, near Beaver Falls.

After the problems with the first house, the Alabama Council hired attorney Charles Morgan Jr. to help with arrangements. Dad and Mom also talked with David Vann and Roger Hanson, president of the Birmingham chapter of the Alabama Council, to decide on a good location to bring up a family of four children. They suggested that there would be less danger if we lived in a middle-class white neighborhood. Suburban Homewood, just over Red Mountain south of Birmingham, would be less likely to be targeted by the Klan.

They found a house they liked, and could afford, on a tree-lined street just off Route 31, the main road to Montgomery. This time there was no problem with the loan or the sale. Morgan drew up papers to close the transaction.

While Mom was still unpacking from the trip back to Hopewell, one of the neighbors on Prince George Avenue knocked on the door. She looked very upset.

"What's the matter?" Mom asked. "Tom didn't have another heart attack, did he?"

"No, he's fine," the young woman stated quickly. She scowled at Mom. "But it's all over town that y'all are selling your house to *Nigras*!" She looked up and down the street, taking in all the neighbors' houses. "We-all aim to do something about it!" she blurted out.

She said that word had gotten around that we had moved out, never to return. That Mom had taken the children with her, and that Dad had left at night so he wouldn't be "caught." One of the neighbors had seen Dad leave early in the morning, before daybreak. For two weeks the neighbors had been terrified that blacks would be moving in.

Mom was angry. She said, "Did you really think we had moved out and left behind all our furniture? That we would leave without saying goodbye?" She thought for a minute. Then she explained that she had taken the children to see their grandparents. Dad had left a few days later on an early morning plane, for a business trip. She also remembered that before Dad left a black soldier stationed at Fort Lee had come to the house one evening to get help with some problem.

"Someone must have added two plus two and gotten seven," she said. The woman looked confused.

Mom told her: "We are selling our house to some good friends from the Baptist church. We didn't even show it to any Negroes." She didn't say that they would have been glad to do so, if asked.

"Oh, Melva, that is such a relief!" the woman exclaimed. A smile brightened the face that moments ago had been dark with fear and hostility. "I am so sorry that I even *thought* you would do such a thing! Everyone will be happy to hear this."

Friends and co-workers tried to talk them out of going to Birmingham. When Dad told his colleagues at the Federal Reformatory about his new job, they voiced all kinds of objections and warned him about the dangers of speaking out about civil rights in Alabama.

"What color roses do you want on your grave?" they asked. Their demeanor was hostile, almost threatening.

After the Freedom Riders had been attacked, and their bus burned, friends asked Mom and Dad, "Do you *still* want to go?" Others said, "Is Jim crazy, putting his whole family at risk?"

Granddad had been angry that this do-gooder preacher would put his daughter in such a dangerous situation. He went with them to look for a house, mainly so he could see for himself how bad it would be in Birmingham.

Grandma Jim worried that her youngest son was going to lead people astray and she would be held responsible.

While Dad was attending the Human Relations Workshop at Fisk University, he tried to learn what he would need to know in his new position. He asked all of the civil rights people there, "What would you do if you had this job?" One of those he asked was Thurgood Marshall, the NAACP attorney who had spearheaded the *Brown v. Board of Education* lawsuit that overturned "separate but equal" school segregation in 1954.

"What would you do in my situation?" Dad asked.

"I'd get the hell out!" Thurgood Marshall replied. These were blunt words from a courageous civil rights leader, who would later become the first African American Supreme Court justice. But Dad didn't think this was very helpful advice.

Meanwhile, we kept packing up clothes, lamps, tools, and household items. I could tell Mom was scared, but she wouldn't rebel against Dad's decision. He could be hard-headed when he thought he was doing the right thing.

"If God wants him to do this with his life, then that's what we'll do," Mom said. "I knew from the start that once he began talking about Alabama it would grow on him." She carefully wrapped a lamp and put it in a tall box. "There isn't much I can ever do when he decides that God is calling him to go somewhere."

Mom said that another candidate had turned down the Alabama Council job when his wife put down her foot. "At least I'm not guilty of *that*. I'll just play the good wife."

One day when I was helping Dad with chores, he told me, "Women want a man to be strong and make the decisions." I didn't try to argue.

On July 25 Mom and Dad signed the papers to buy the house in Homewood and sell our house in Hopewell. Dad told us, "Tomorrow the moving van will pick up all this stuff, and we'll be ready to go."

The following morning a large green and yellow Mayflower moving van backed into the driveway. It seemed odd to me that a company named for the famous ship that had brought Pilgrims to Massachusetts, where we used to live, was taking us even deeper into the South. "Guess we can't avoid showing everyone that we're Yankees," I thought.

The men spent all day loading everything into the Mayflower truck. After the moving van turned the corner onto City Point Road, we climbed into the station wagon. Dad honked the horn loudly as we pulled away, and we waved good-bye to the home where I had spent a longer time than anywhere else in my life: three and a half years. Mom and Dad said it was too late to start the long drive, so we stayed at the Evergreen Motel.

On our long drives to Beaver Falls, Dad had shown me how to read the Esso road maps, and help him decide what routes to take. Now I had another chance to use those skills. Early the next morning, as we left Hopewell for the last time, I opened my small yellow spiral-bound memo book and wrote on the first page: "July 28th. Started: 8:10 a.m. Mileage: 83531.7." We headed southwest, through Danville and into North Carolina—Winston-Salem, Asheville, and finally Cherokee, deep in the Smoky Mountains. "Arrived: 6:50 p.m. Mileage 83934.0." We stayed at the Mountaineer Court motel in Cherokee.

After supper we went to an enormous outdoor theater and watched a pageant called "Unto These Hills." We sat way up high, but could still see the bright-colored costumes and hear the dramatic story about the Cherokee people, and how they were forced to leave their homes to go to Oklahoma in the 1830s. Many died on the long trek, called the "Trail of Tears."

The next day the road out of Cherokee seemed to go straight up into Great Smoky Mountains National Park. Steam came out of the hood, and we had to pull over and wait for the engine to cool. We headed up the steep mountain road and then back down into Tennessee.

Ever since we left Hopewell we had seen barn roofs painted with big letters, "SEE ROCK CITY." Mom said a company painted the barns for free, if farmers would let them paint this advertising sign on the roof. So when we got to Chattanooga, we drove up Lookout Mountain. Rock City was built along the rocky ledge of the mountain, with old rock formations, beautiful flower gardens, and a viewing platform. Dad kept putting coins into the big silver viewing machine so each of us could enjoy the "See Seven States" panorama.

Then we drove through the Civil War battlefield at the north edge of Lookout Mountain. Far below was Chattanooga, hugging a curving brown river. Yankee soldiers had climbed the steep cliffs to attack and defeat the surprised Rebel defenders. That was almost a hundred years ago.

The road from Birmingham to Homewood curled up the slopes of Red Mountain to a low pass, just below a large statue of Vulcan, the Roman god of fire and the forge. Then it plunged down the south side of the mountain and became Eighteenth Street, the main shopping section of Homewood.

Following the Montgomery highway out of Homewood, we turned right at the top of a small ridge, on Saulter Road. Our house was a quarter of a mile down, on the left side.

Dad pulled over to the left curb. A black mailbox with the number "1905" stood next to a railing leading downhill.

"I don't see any house at all," I said. "It's like the edge of a cliff."

But as we stretched out of the station wagon, we could see first the roof and then the front of a one-story house with faded green wood siding. It was L-shaped, with a big picture window in the middle, and a small porch at the corner formed by an extension jutting out on the right. In front of this "ell" was a large magnolia tree with long glossy leaves. This would be our new home.

"It's tiny," I said.

"I think it's cute," said Ann.

"Home, sweet home," Dad said. Mom looked at us and tried to smile.

The last entry in my memo book, dated July 30, was: "Arrived: 8:30 P.M.

Mileage: 84281.1." The trip had taken three long days, covering 749.4 miles. But the distance—both in miles and in time—between Hopewell and Homewood would soon seem far greater than that.

The next day, while the Mayflower movers unloaded our belongings, a girl about Ann's age walked over to see the excitement. She asked a lot of questions, and then took Ann to her house near Montgomery Highway. "This is where I live, with my Diddy," she said. "Do you want a Co'-Cola?" Hearing this strange accent, Ann thought, "This really is a different kind of place."

Homewood turned out to be about the size of Hopewell, but with prettier streets, nicer houses, and better stores for shopping. It wasn't as fancy as Mountain Brook, the ritzy suburb just to the east, also buffered from Birmingham by Red Mountain. The small neighborhood of Rosedale, near the main shopping area, was predominantly black. The rest of Homewood remained exclusively white.

Saulter Road was part of the Windsor Highlands development, south of downtown. The entire neighborhood was shaded by trees, mainly tall southern pines. Streets curved around the hills in a complex pattern that made it easy to get lost, both when riding bikes or walking. There were creeks and paths leading through the woods. We had almost a full month to explore the new territory before school would start.

All four of us would be attending Shades Cahaba Elementary, a short walk away. Homewood Junior High was not big enough to handle three full grades of Baby Boomers, so I would go to Shades Cahaba for seventh grade. Ann was in fifth, Paul in second, and Susie would be starting first grade, all at the same school.

On Saulter Road our Virginia license plates marked us as new arrivals. The Alabama license plates proclaimed "Heart of Dixie" as the state motto. Cars only had to have one plate, in the rear, so people could personalize their cars with a decorative front plate. Some front plates, I noticed, had religious messages or short Bible verses. Some University of Alabama alumni displayed "Roll Tide" plates, while Auburn supporters countered with their "War Eagle" slogan.

But by far the two most common front car plates carried references to the Civil War. Since this was the centennial, that seemed natural. The most popular was a large Confederate battle flag. Right behind that was a plate that showed a gray-bearded old soldier in a torn gray Confederate uniform. The slogan underneath read, "Hell, no! I ain't fergettin'!"

At age twelve, one of my biggest worries about moving to Alabama was not fitting in. In Virginia being called a Yankee had set me apart from my friends and neighbors. I did not want to start off on the wrong foot in our new hometown.

Of course I knew that my new neighbors and classmates would soon find out that I was an outsider. But I wanted to delay that if I could. I didn't want to be introduced as a Yankee. I would disguise myself as a southerner. I would always say, "Yes, ma'am" and "No, ma'am." I would try to drawl out my words and end each sentence on a higher note, as though even a simple statement of fact were a question. I would fit in.

So when I met Mike Ham, the boy my age who lived right next door to us, I was ready. As we were introducing ourselves, Mike asked, "Where *you*'all from?" Instead of saying I was born in Michigan or grew up in Massachusetts, I drawled out, "We came here from *Virginia*."

Mike replied, "Whoa! That's *way* up north. Y'all are damn *Yankees*!"

4

A Challenging Job

Moving a family of four young children 750 miles away from their support network of relatives and friends must have added tremendous stresses to my parents' lives. Mom had never liked the abrupt uprooting of frequent relocations. Now she was in a distant and dangerous new state, a two-day drive from her parents, brother, and sister. She had left behind in Hopewell a close circle of friends, as well as leadership positions in the Baptist Church and school PTA.

Even before arriving in Alabama, my parents had been refused a mortgage for the house they hoped to buy in Birmingham, accused by neighbors in Virginia of planning to sell their home to blacks, and warned of the violence and intimidation that could greet their arrival in the "Heart of Dixie."

Despite these premonitions of danger, our first greeting in Homewood was friendly, an example of true southern hospitality. An older woman and her son saw our Virginia license plates and stopped to introduce themselves.

"Hello? I'm Mrs. Long and this is my son, Dale? We want to welcome *you*'all to the neighborhood?" The four adults shook hands, and smiled politely.

Dale looked back and forth from Mom to Dad, and at the four children darting in and out. "I'm Dale Long? I'm an instructor at Howard College? It's right up the hill behind you?" In Alabama every statement sounded like a question.

Two of Mrs. Long's daughters attended the Hopewell First Baptist Church. They had written to tell her that we were moving to Homewood. Mrs. Long said they spoke very highly of Mom's service as a Sunday school teacher for adult women, and as president of the Women's Missionary Union.

Mrs. Long said, "The girls asked me to look out for you? We live just around the corner? On Windsor Drive?"

Mom said, "Thank you so much for stopping by! It's good to meet some friendly people here."

Mrs. Long said, "Let us know if we can help with anything, y'hear?"

Dad said, "Thank you. We will. Nice to meet you."

While Mom focused on the chores of unpacking, organizing a new household, and addressing the needs of her four young children, Dad had only one day to prepare for his new job as executive director of the Alabama Council on Human Relations. We arrived in Homewood on Sunday night, and he had to be at his new office on Tuesday morning.

Several years earlier, Reverend Bob Hughes had moved the Alabama Council office from Montgomery to Birmingham, in a small suite on the twelfth floor of the landmark Comer Building. The office secretary, Mrs. Annette Cox, greeted Dad and showed him the few files that remained from Hughes's abrupt departure almost a year earlier. The office had been closed for two months, awaiting the secretary's return from maternity leave and the arrival of a new director.

The Alabama Council director reported to the Southern Regional Council's field representative, Paul Rilling. Nine months earlier, he had first broached the possibility of Dad applying for this position, during the Petersburg Ministerial Association workshop on human relations. Rilling sent a lengthy letter for Dad to receive upon his arrival, with detailed suggestions about how to begin: "The strength of the ACHR is the loyalty of its membership, the confidence of the Negro leadership in the state, and a fairly efficient organizational structure built up by Bob Hughes over the last six years. The weaknesses of the Council are in its small size, approximately 450, the fear of sympathetic white persons of any identification with an organization so clearly in opposition to the prevailing political leadership, the scattered and varying nature of the local groups, and the difficulty of raising sufficient financial support in Alabama for such a cause."

Rilling added, "The ACHR has been virtually the only channel of communication between white and Negro citizens in the state of Alabama." The council had given local black leaders the support of an interracial constituency, and demonstrated that at least one group that included white members would stand up against massive resistance. In crisis situations, the council offered assistance to victims of intimidation. It had also been invaluable as a channel for information and interpretation to the national news media.

He advised Dad to begin by visiting each of the local and district chapters in the state, to learn about the organization and to meet its leaders. Second, he should inform himself about the current racial situation in Alabama. "In traveling about the state I would also urge that you make almost immediate and personal contact with the chief Negro leaders in the state," Rilling suggested.

The third step should be to help the local chapters develop program activities for the coming months. This might include fact-finding studies, publications, or workshops: "Are there current spots of particular crisis or tension, or spots where such crisis is likely to develop this fall? If so, is there any way that the Council or some of its local groups can be relevant to these areas?"

One warning, in particular, showed the potential dangers faced by anyone working in race relations. "Be quite careful about the security of your office and your records. Any correspondence being discarded should be torn up in small pieces before being thrown into the waste basket. All papers and data should be under lock and key each night."

Dad didn't tell us all of this, at least not at once. He didn't want Mom to worry. "I got a letter from Rilling with some good suggestions," he said.

Mom asked, "What did he say?"

"Just the usual advice: how to get started." He laughed and gave Mom a hug. "This is going to be interesting." He looked around the living room at Ann weaving multi-colored potholders on a small metal rack, Spitzy asleep on the rug. I was organizing my baseball cards. We could hear Paul chasing Susie through the dining room and kitchen, both giggling.

Dad smiled at Mom. "It's a challenging job. I can't wait to get started."

Virginia summers were hot, but nothing compared to Alabama. The asphalt became soft and sticky. The grass turned golden-brown, and the house felt like an oven. Not even the commercial-size fan built into the rear hallway ceiling could vent enough hot air into the attic to make a difference. We drank iced tea and Kool-Aid almost continually. Even Spitzy panted painfully, her pink tongue hanging out, after a short run chasing Susie around the yard.

Walking along the side streets curving downhill from Saulter Road, we began to meet other kids in the neighborhood.

Mike Ham quickly became my best friend. For a long time, he was my only friend. He lived next door, in a white house even smaller than ours. Mike had an older brother, Lamar, a high-school student. Their father was a manager at The Club, an exclusive private club atop Red Mountain, not far from the statue of Vulcan.

Mike didn't play baseball or collect baseball cards. But we rode our bikes into town, and he showed me the underpass below Route 31 leading to Shades Cahaba School. We stopped at Melrose's, across the street, for ice cream or Cokes at the soda fountain. At V. J. Elmore five-and-dime store on Eighteenth Street, the main shopping area, we dreamed about toys we wished we could afford. We drooled over the shiny new three-speed English bicycles at Homewood Cycle & Hobby Shop.

One way to beat the summer heat was going to the public swimming pool in Central Park. Dad drove us down Oxmoor Road, past Our Lady of Sorrows Catholic Church. The park had a small picnic area, shaded by tall leafy trees, with a lazy creek meandering through. The pool was up a small slope, with a parking area in back. We changed into our swimsuits in a cinder-block building, then spread our towels on the concrete near the shallow end of the pool.

"Brrrrr!" we said. "It's too cold!"

Mom said, "It just feels that way because the air is so much hotter."

"You don't know what cold water is, until you swim in Lake Seneca," Dad said. "When I was a boy, you could practically see icicles at the ends of your fingers!" He smiled, remembering his childhood in upstate New York—Corning and the Finger Lakes. "That's *God's* Country!" he said.

Dad dove in at the deep end and swam vigorously back and forth before playing with Susie and Paul in the shallow water. He let them stand on his interlocked hands and jump into the water. Standing in waist-high water, he stooped down so Ann and I could climb on his shoulders and dive off when he stood up straight. Mom never went to the deep end, but paddled around, keeping her head above the water and blinking at the splashing drops.

If we behaved ourselves, Dad might give in to our begging for a stop at Jack's Hamburgers. Jack's was a new walk-up stand with a slanted roof and vertical orange and yellow stripes on each side of the small building. The big sign, on a dividing strip between two rows for parking, spelled out "J A C K'S" in five white rectangles on five tall poles.

We picked up our order and ate in the car. "This is the life," I thought.

"I have to go to Huntsville tomorrow," Dad said. "How about coming with me?"

Less than a full week after starting his new job, Dad was already beginning to visit the local chapters of the Alabama Council. Since school was still weeks away, I could go with him on his first road trip, even on a Monday.

The drive to Huntsville took more than two hours—through Birmingham, then straight north on the new divided highway, Interstate 65. The highway ended at Cullman, and we took US Route 31 to Decatur, then northeast across the wide Tennessee River to Huntsville.

"People tell me there's a big difference between northern Alabama and the rest of the state," Dad explained as we reached Cullman. "It's always considered kind of an aberration. Different from what you'd expect."

"What makes it different?" I asked.

"Not as many big slave plantations in this part of the state, before the Civil War. So around Cullman there were a lot of Union volunteers. The whole northern third of the state is still generally more liberal than the rest of Alabama. About race, at least."

In Huntsville, we stopped at a traffic light. We heard a car screeching to a stop.

"Did you see that?" Dad exclaimed. "That car just hit a woman! She went flying through the air!"

By the time I could say, "No," Dad had pulled over and jumped out of the station wagon. He ran across the intersection and knelt beside a woman lying on the ground. Soon an ambulance came to take her away. Through the windshield, I could see Dad still talking to some policemen. After several more minutes he came back to the car.

"Looks like she'll be all right," he said.

"But why did *you* have to go over there?" I asked.

"That's what I *should* do—help people with problems," he replied. "If I can give someone comfort, well, you know. . . ." He grinned, showing his horsey teeth.

I said: "But it's hot in the car. I didn't know what to do."

At the Huntsville chapter meeting Dad met local people interested in civil rights, and found out about recent problems in the area. He spent time talking to Reverend Ezekiel Bell, a young black Baptist preacher, who told him about a group of young men who were trying to work out community problems in their neighborhood. Despite this, Bell was discouraged that the black people in Huntsville showed little interest in civil rights or even in bettering themselves in other ways.

On the way home, Dad said, "This is great! Getting acquainted with people. Finding out what's going on. That's what I need to be doing."

That was Monday. On Wednesday, during supper, Dad said he had an interesting day.

"Last night a young Swedish student came by the office," he began. "He said he wanted to meet Reverend Fred Shuttlesworth, so this morning I took him to Shuttlesworth's house." Shuttlesworth was the leading civil rights activist in Birmingham. While we were still in Virginia, Dad had told us about Reverend Shuttlesworth being beaten with chains for trying to enroll his daughter in a white high school.

While Dad and the Swedish student were visiting, Reverend Shuttlesworth received a call from a nineteen-year-old white girl who had attended several meetings at his church, Bethel Baptist, in northeast Birmingham. Her parents were forcing her to leave home. The phone call was interrupted, and she called back a little later. Her father had come home from work and pulled out the phone wire. Now she was calling from a drugstore.

She said that last evening the police came by her house. They told her parents that she had been seen getting into a car at Terminal Station with two colored men. They also warned the parents that five cars of Klansmen were following her around town.

"We arranged for her to meet me at my office," Dad said.

When she arrived at the ACHR office, the young woman said her name was Connie Bradford. She went to school in New Orleans, was active in CORE—the Congress of Racial Equality, which had organized the Freedom Rides last spring—and was out on bond for disturbing the peace. She told Dad she wanted to stay in the South, to work in civil rights, but also hoped to continue her college education.

Shuttlesworth came by Dad's office to meet with them. Connie was worried because Sergeant Cook of the Birmingham police wanted to talk with her. Her father told her that he didn't care what happened to her, but that he was concerned about the family. She was sure that her parents would not let her stay another night. Her clothes were packed, ready to be picked up.

"I found out that they live a block or two from us, in Homewood," Dad told us. He looked at Mom, whose eyes had opened wide, eyebrows arched. Warning flags.

Dad said, "At first I wondered if she should immediately get out of town." Mom pushed her chair back quickly, and started clearing the table. She didn't look at us.

Dad kept talking: "She knows Margaret Long's daughter and said she thought she would like to go to Atlanta to stay with her."

Mom stopped and turned around. "Oh, Jim, this is getting too close to *home*!" Mom looked worried. "*Please* be careful."

Dad quickly said, "I will." But his voice was shaky. "Shuttlesworth told her definitely not to mention my name or the organization. That should protect us." He tried to smile reassuringly.

Reverend Shuttlesworth and Dad decided that Connie Bradford should stay at the YWCA, call her parents, and try to smooth things over. They advised her that it would be best for her to stay in town and face possible harassment here rather than trying to run away from these problems.

After this conversation, Dad said he went upstairs to have coffee with Chuck Morgan and tell him about the case. Morgan said he would meet with Connie.

"He's concerned that the Klan might attack her," Dad told us.

Mom said, anxiously, "And I am concerned they might go after *you*—or our children!"

"I know, I know. That's one reason I'm going to stay out of the spotlight." He hesitated, and smiled weakly. His voice became quiet: "As much as I can."

One figure in Birmingham always stayed *in* the spotlight. Vulcan, the giant statue of a Roman god, stood on a tall stone pedestal atop Red Mountain, visible for miles in each direction. At night powerful floodlights illuminated the statue. Curious to see this iconic landmark up close, Dad drove us up the winding entry road from Eighteenth Street.

At close range, the figure of Vulcan seemed misshapen, with a contorted, bearded face. With his left hand holding a hammer balanced on a large anvil, Vulcan raised his right arm and looked up at a lighted torch. If there had been a traffic fatality in the area within the past twenty-four hours, the torch glowed red. If not, it was green.

Looking north toward the steel foundries of Birmingham, Vulcan turned his back on Homewood. Clothed only in an open-backed smithy apron, Vulcan actually seemed to be mooning our quiet suburb. We learned that a radio DJ got some local residents to start a petition to have the statue's naked buttocks covered. They even talked about how much fabric it would take. I didn't know if they were serious about this, or just joking.

Before we entered the stone tower to climb metal stairs to the outside viewing platform just below the statue, we read signs telling the history of this landmark. Birmingham's business and government leaders wanted to advertise the local steel industry and the state of Alabama to the world by entering an exhibit in the 1904 St. Louis World's Fair. Birmingham's rapid growth, since its founding in 1871, led local boosters to call it the "Magic City." They commissioned Italian artist Giuseppe Moretti to cast a large statue of the Roman god of fire and the forge, made from local iron.

After the 1904 World's Fair, the statue moved from place to place. During the New Deal, the Works Progress Administration developed a park site on Red Mountain, and in May 1939, Vulcan finally found a permanent new home atop a stone-walled pedestal.

Mom read: "It's the largest cast iron statue in the world."

Ann said: "It's the *ugliest* statue in the world."

"Where are his pants?" asked Paul.

We started up the steps. From the platform, Birmingham twinkled with millions of colorful bright lights. We looked up at the giant silver statue.

"What a peculiar symbol for this city," Mom said. "You would think they could have found something more appealing. Something *artistic* at least."

Summer didn't last forever, but it seemed as though the hot weather would. The four of us walked, separately with our own groups of friends, to Shades Cahaba Elementary School. Along busy Route 31, through the underpass, and into the 1930s.

Even compared to old-fashioned DuPont Elementary, this school seemed more like the schools Mom and Dad told us they went to. Ancient wooden desks, anchored to the floor, still had round holes for inkwells, even though there were no ink pots. Letters of the alphabet circled above faded slate blackboards. Dingy faded green and blue walls cried out for fresh paint. The uneven wood floors showed scuff marks from generations of small shoes.

The teachers and their teaching styles seemed ancient. Ann said that Mrs. Allen (*Miz* Allen) scheduled everything in fifth grade very methodically. They had to memorize a poem each month. Ann said, "Probably the same ones for thirty years!" After lunch, Mrs. Allen made them all rest their heads on their desks while she read aloud from a book for half an hour.

Ann and I laughed when we told Mom how out-of-date everything seemed. But for Paul and Susie, Shades Cahaba was a scary new place. They didn't know how to adjust. Mom had to console them, and reassure them that they would soon get used to the new school.

"I don't want to," Susie whined.

"I know what you mean," I told her. I wanted to make her feel better. "I felt that way when I went to first grade, too."

In seventh grade, I had my own adjustments to make. Although we had to go to the elementary school, we followed junior high rules. That meant going to a different classroom for each subject: English, math, social studies, literature, science, art, and band. I was still trying to learn how to play the trombone—which I had started playing in fourth grade—without actually practicing. Elementary school recess gave way to physical education, with more oversight of our exercise time on the playground.

Still naturally very shy, I once again had trouble making new friends. Mike Ham remained the only boy I spent time with away from school. One day we rode our bikes down the hill behind our houses. Mike showed me a dirt road that led uphill to the recently built campus of Howard College.

Howard was a Southern Baptist college, founded in 1841, that had moved to Homewood in 1957. A sign said so. The campus consisted of seven or eight buildings, all looking the same: orange-red brick, white framed windows, small cupolas on the roofs. They looked like the Sunday school building in Hopewell. Mom said this was the Georgian Colonial style of architecture. She had been an architect, so she would know.

The college buildings seemed exposed and isolated from each other. There were only a few small, newly planted trees on campus. Mike said this was because, when they cleared land for the college, someone messed up. One person marked the trees to be cut down, and the other workers left those, and cut down everything else. To put the buildings in the right places, they had to cut down all the rest of the trees. This sounded like a made-up story, but Mom said she had heard the same thing.

In September, Dad had to organize a meeting for the Alabama Council Board of Directors, at the A. G. Gaston Building on Fifth Avenue North. This was the office of Birmingham's only black millionaire. Mr. Gaston owned an insurance company, a motel, and other businesses. Dad told us he was conservative and cautious, especially on race issues. Reverend Shuttlesworth didn't seem to trust him. He kept trying to get Gaston to use his money and influence to help the civil rights movement.

Holding an interracial meeting in a black-owned building could still be risky in 1961. In his memo announcing the board meeting, Dad wrote: "Each

Board member is requested to be very careful not to take a taxi or any public transportation to the Gaston Building. Those arriving by bus, plane or train are requested to come to the office at 1224 Comer Building on Saturday morning and private transportation will be arranged from the office to the Gaston Building. With this precaution there is feeling in Birmingham that this city will be a good place to meet."

This was not the only problem with safety and security. Two weeks before the September 30 board meeting, Dad received a letter from the Legislative Reference Service of the Library of Congress. A congressman had requested a statement of the history of the Alabama Council, copies of the materials produced by the Alabama Council, and the list of its board of directors. This sounded a like a fishing expedition, similar to the earlier demand that Bob Hughes turn over his files to the grand jury.

Dad wrote to Paul Rilling: "Vann and Morgan suggested that an attempt be made to find out who was asking for this information."

The police had regularly taken down license-plate numbers of cars parked outside Alabama Council meetings. Spies reported to the police details about who attended, who spoke at the meetings, and what they said. This request from a congressman simply took such investigations to a higher level.

One day in October, Dad brought home the first newsletter he had put together for the Alabama Council. This was an important part of his responsibility to promote communication with the local chapters. Dad smiled proudly when he handed it to me.

"I wrote it, and your mother made some drawings to add something visual."

The newsletter had a letter from Bob Hughes, in southern Africa. He said that with a new director the Alabama Council could look forward to a new period of progress. "I've had the privilege of talking at length to Jim and I can say with confidence that it will be more than a renewal of State Office activity, but a needed fresh new start."

Dad said to Mom, "That was kind of him. Maybe it will help people accept me."

Another newsletter item explained the group's purposes and activities. Dad read it aloud:

The Alabama Council is actively encouraging the development of local solutions to local problems through increased communication and through research and education. For example, the State Office seeks to encourage local chapters to keep the lines of communication open between races. Programs for the local chapters provide a forum for discussion and debate. . . .

Influential white leadership and responsible members of the colored community meet together quietly to discuss means of promoting the welfare of the colored people. Many people are benefiting from such activities without realizing the efforts involved. Such groups are working to get the job done without seeking publicity or credit.

Dad looked at Mom. "That means I'm working *behind* the scenes. Staying out of trouble."

She replied, "Since when did *you* try to stay out of trouble? Remember when you spoke out against Joe McCarthy in Hudson?"

Dad didn't answer. He looked at Susie and grinned. "Why do ducks have flat feet?"

"I don't know!" Susie smiled.

"From stamping out forest fires!" he said. "Why do *elephants* have flat feet?"

"From forest fires!" She giggled.

Dad said: "No!—from stamping out flaming ducks!" Susie laughed. I groaned. Another stale joke.

Mom frowned. She said: "Jim, you always try to *joke* your way out of problems! This is serious."

Now Dad *did* look serious. "You do enough worrying for both of us." He started to smile, then changed his mind. "We'll be OK. Trust me."

Dad was beginning to realize that one of the greatest challenges of working for a civil rights organization would be fund-raising. The newsletter had to go out, and with every newsletter there was an appeal for money. For the first two or three years while Bob Hughes was director, the Ford Foundation funded the Alabama Council. But the Ford Foundation got scared off after Hughes worked with Martin Luther King Jr. on the Montgomery bus boycott. The council had become too controversial.

A smaller foundation, the Field Foundation of New York, provided some funding, but the Southern Regional Council and the separate state councils still had to do a lot of scrounging for money. By 1961 the Alabama Council relied primarily on membership dues. At five dollars a year, from 450 members, this didn't go very far. Dad would have to raise outside contributions or grants in order to cover most of his own salary and expenses. Most civil rights leaders were ministers or held another regular job, doing civil rights activities on their own time. But Dad was the only white person in Alabama paid for full-time civil rights work.

The Alabama Council launched a fund drive early in 1962. To meet its $16,000 yearly budget, ACHR would receive up to $5,000 in matching funds from national foundations, through SRC. Despite a "tremendous amount of energy" from several board members, private donations of less than $4,000 still left the organization needing to raise $7,000 to continue operations.

The ACHR secretary, Annette Cox, often had to write to Atlanta asking the Southern Regional Council to send their quarterly grant so she could pay the bills. In one such letter, she stated: "As of this date, we do not have enough funds in the checking account to cover our expenses."

By June 1962, Dad could report some progress in gaining potential support from a wealthy banker in the state, who said he admired the council's work. But a fund raising trip to Philadelphia and New York secured only $30.

"This was slightly short of my expenses," he reported, in a memo to other SRC state council directors. "I keep telling myself that Councils don't go out of business because of lack of financial support," he wrote, "or do they?" He joked that each of the other states should raise some money for the Alabama Council—an attempt at humor for which he soon had to apologize.

In a letter to Paul Rilling in August 1962, Dad stated: "It would all be so simple if Alabama would withdraw from the Union and have foreign aid instead of Federal grants. You might work on this."

That same week, John J. Brewbaker of Norfolk, Virginia—the SRC public schools consultant—reported on his recent visit to Birmingham and other parts of Alabama. "In talking with Mr. Jimerson, I found he was doing an excellent job making contacts and lining up influential citizens for the cause of open schools and desegregation," Brewbaker stated. "I found out that part of his tenseness was due to the poor financial condition of the Alabama Council. If would be tragic if he has to close for lack of funds."

As organizations deliberately staying out of public attention, working behind the scenes, both the Southern Regional Council and the Alabama Council lacked the name recognition needed to attract celebrity supporters and financial contributors. Fundraising would remain a significant problem.

An even greater challenge would be to bring together the white and black communities by encouraging interracial communication. Decades—generations—of mistrust grew out of prejudice and hatred among the white leadership of Alabama, and fear and resentment among blacks. Birmingham had already earned a reputation as the most segregated city in the South, the Johannesburg of North America.

Bob Hughes had to build trust with the black community, to gain acceptance as a white southerner. However, his soft, buttery voice evoked some common cultural heritage with southern blacks. As a white northern minister, Dad faced an added barrier to acceptance. He did not share a southern accent or a lifelong understanding of local culture, habits, manners, and language. The black community would judge him according to his actions, his sincerity, and his willingness to risk personal comfort and security.

It would be even more difficult to convince white community leaders to trust this Yankee outsider. The South's memory of Reconstruction and the destruction of its cherished cultural heritage made any northerner suspect. So too the bitter resentment still felt towards Yankee carpetbaggers, who symbolized for white southerners the worst elements of northern domination following the Civil War. Repeatedly, Dad heard the words "outside agitator," "communist," and "nigger-lover" thrown in his face, or whispered under someone's breath.

However, in some progressive cities of the South, white business leaders had recognized that insistent clinging to segregation had damaged both the South's international reputation and their own economic interests. On September 12, 1961, the morning paper, the *Birmingham Post-Herald*—typically more moderate than the conservative afternoon paper, the *Birmingham News*—reported on a statement by successful real estate proprietor William Engel. An assimilated Jew, regarded as a dependable segregationist, Engel suggested that massive resistance harmed the local community.

As Paul Rilling wrote from Atlanta, "This seems to be an important breakthrough in the power structure. Wouldn't it be wonderful if Birmingham could develop a concerned committee of businessmen to operate as they did in Dallas."

Dad responded, "There is a very small and very confidential group of businessmen in Birmingham that are attempting to develop a group similar to those in Atlanta and Dallas." However, he told Rilling: "Two business people that have told me about this group are unwilling at this point to even tell me who is involved. One of the men asked me to give him names of people that might be interested in working with this group, but not to tell them that such a group is actually beginning."

These businessmen trusted Dad, but only to a certain point. One advantage of being an outsider was that local moderates could confide their doubts about segregation to him without compromising their reputations among their peers. Since he did not walk in the same social circle, he would not let out their secrets. But he would have to prove himself more fully before gaining their complete confidence.

The October 1961 ACHR newsletter reported on the slogan being used to attract new business to the city: "It's Good to Have You in Birmingham." Dad wrote that it was ironic that some who had been actively involved in racial demagoguery were trying to make Birmingham seem attractive to northern businessmen and investors. He called it peculiar that local citizens have to be convinced that their own city is a good place to live.

On a more hopeful note, some business people in Birmingham now recognized that what is good for race relations is good for business. Dad reported: "Birmingham needs, now more than ever, to demonstrate to the nation's business community that it can and will face its racial problems in good faith."

In early November, James Head, president of the Chamber of Commerce's Committee of 100, circulated a letter to local businessmen, asking them to sign a bland statement calling for city officials to maintain law and order in Birmingham. This was an indirect, but clear, rebuke to local police and politicians, who had looked the other way while Klansmen and their sympathizers beat Freedom Riders, assaulted "uppity" Negroes, and tried to prevent school desegregation.

Head's committee sought to bring new industry to Birmingham. But by promoting even a lukewarm statement of support for the law, they risked alienating die-hard segregationists. As a moderate, willing to confront the extremists, Jim Head represented the type of local business leader the Alabama Council needed to reach.

When he heard about Jim Head's letter, Dad wrote to Paul Rilling: "It is hoped that some 200 businessmen will sign this very mild statement." Although the moderate business leaders did not reach this goal, they did secure 89 signatures. Not much, but a beginning.

In the fall of 1961, Dad optimistically thought there were signs of hope in Alabama.

For every sign of progress, however, there seemed a dozen indications of resistance. The leading opponent of integration and moderation had long been Birmingham's commissioner of public safety, Eugene "Bull" Connor. By

1961 Connor had become a symbol of intransigence and bigotry. In October 1961, Dad reported that Connor's aspirations to become Alabama's next governor had led to further deterioration of the racial climate in Birmingham.

The situation appeared to be moving rapidly in opposite directions, Dad stated. At the same time that moderate business leaders tried to create a more tolerant and stable atmosphere, Connor and his cronies stoked resentment and resistance.

In the months since the Freedom Riders were viciously beaten in Birmingham, Connor repeatedly ordered the arrest of the Greyhound bus station manager and a waitress for allowing blacks to eat there. This was a clear violation of the Federal Interstate Commerce Commission order that prohibited segregation in such facilities—the type of violation that the Freedom Riders had challenged.

In early November, the *Birmingham Post-Herald* carried a front-page story that an agent of the Civil Rights Division of the U.S. Justice Department was in Birmingham to inquire about these arrests. Bull Connor stated that, if anyone conducting the probe "violates any of our laws, we'll put him in Southside jail. Instead of probing Bull Connor, they'd better be probing the Communists in this country who seem to have more rights than we in the South." Connor vowed that even though segregation might be declared unconstitutional, he would enforce Alabama's segregation laws, as long as they were on the books.

Seeking to establish open communications on these public issues, Dad took two steps. First, he "dropped in" to talk with Dr. John Buchanan, referred to as the "great white father" among Baptist ministers, who claimed to have as much influence over Bull Connor as anyone in town. They discussed the efforts by local businessmen to create a more peaceful racial climate in Birmingham. Buchanan confirmed that, in Dad's words, "Bull Connor has an amazing spy system and knows everything that is going on that concerns him within a few minutes." This intimidated most people who considered opposing Connor's racist policies.

The second step Dad took was to visit the Greyhound station and meet with the station manager, whom Bull Connor had arrested four times for violating local segregation laws. On November 9, Dad and two companions ate lunch at the station, so they could assess the situation. Dad reported to Paul Rilling: "I talked with the manager and assured him that he had a lot of moral support." The manager stated that the police are all very nice to him when he is arrested. He just goes to the police station and signs an appearance bond. Dad concluded: "He seemed to take it all without being upset. He said he was simply 'between a rock and a hard place.' If he didn't serve Negroes, he would violate federal law. If he did, he broke local laws."

Despite the extreme tensions of confronting segregation directly, and risking the wrath of the notorious Bull Connor, Dad wrote to Rilling: "I am having a wonderful time with the Alabama Council."

As Dad encountered the hostility and intimidation that came with championing civil rights in the Heart of Dixie, he received much-needed support and encouragement, both from old friends and new colleagues. At the end of August 1961, as he completed his first month with the Alabama Council, he received two letters of support.

Herbert Gezork, the president of his alma mater, Andover Newton Theological School, offered praise and encouragement: "You are at the very frontier of Christian work, and your job is a truly prophetic one. I want to assure you of my earnest prayers. However great the obstacles may be, and however frequent the setbacks and discouragements may be, be assured that you are on the side of the future."

In a more personal and humorous message, Victor Sims of the Petersburg Reformatory wrote: "We all miss you and there isn't a day that goes by, that I don't have someone ask about you and whether you had been thrown in the 'Clink.' I assure them that you haven't and we all have a good laugh. Seriously, Jim, almost all of the men here admire your stand for what you feel is right and, inside, enjoy the feeling that they have met a man who stands by his convictions."

Mom and Dad received letters from other friends in Hopewell, including Reverend Gene Ensley, who had collaborated with Dad in planning the Petersburg Ministerial Association workshops on race relations. After Dad sent him the October 1961 Alabama Council newsletter, Ensley responded: "I read with interest the progress you and the Council are making there in Alabama. Rest assured that we pray often for your success there."

One of the Alabama clergymen who quickly befriended him upon his arrival was Father Brice Joyce, a white priest serving a black Catholic parish in Sheffield, one of the "Tri-cities" in northwest Alabama. As part of his first series of visits around the state, Dad looked up Father Joyce because his name appeared in old newsletters of the Alabama Council. On this first visit, he offered Dad a key to the rectory. He said, "You'll be coming through here sometime when I'm not here. There's a little room off to the right of the living room in front. That's your bedroom."

In November 1961, Father Joyce sent a handwritten message on Our Lady of Grace stationery: "Rest assured, Jim, that my prayers are continuous for you. Don't give up." After lamenting that churches were not doing their duty on race relations, he concluded: "When you get that sinking feeling in the pit of your stomach, remember that you aren't the only one with butterflies."

Within the first days and months of his arrival in Alabama, Reverend Norman C. Jimerson fully realized how challenging and potentially dangerous his new job would be. Words of encouragement, and letters of support, helped to counter the vicious hatred and ostracism he encountered.

As an ordained American Baptist minister, Dad assumed that he would find solace and reassurance through his church ties. Yet the effort to find a new church home in Birmingham led to the first—and perhaps most dispiriting— episode of rejection and vilification that he, and our family, would encounter.

5

Searching for a Church Home

"Tell us about how you met Mommy!" we would often ask Dad. The story became a family favorite, a romantic tale of love and destiny. We children understood that we would not have been born if Mom and Dad had not met, had not decided to join their futures together.

Dad would begin: "I went back to Ann Arbor to finish my degree, then took a summer job at Babcock & Wilcox, in Beaver Falls. One Sunday I visited the First Baptist Church. I asked a young fella next to me, 'Who's that good-looking brunette in the choir?' He said, 'That's my sister. Would you like to meet her?'"

"I thought he had a lot of nerve, walking right up to speak to me!" Mom said. "Even with Doug to introduce him. But he was handsome—dark wavy hair, big smile—and he was persistent!"

Dad said, "It took a while to get her to go out with me, but finally she agreed. Your Granddad was pretty skeptical about some stranger dating his daughter."

Mom said: "I had only known him for five weeks when he proposed!"

Dad explained: "I had to go back to college, and didn't want to leave her behind."

They married on September 12, 1947, seven weeks after they first met in church. After a brief honeymoon at Cook Forest State Park, they returned to Ann Arbor.

This story taught several related lessons: first, we should always go to church; second, a church family was the best place to establish one's own family; third, faith is the best foundation for one's life.

The other lesson that this story seemed to suggest—*not* part of the moral our parents intended—was that it was good to act on impulses, to trust feelings more than rational calculations. At least this was not an idea that Mom wanted us to learn. After all, that's what had brought us into the turmoil we faced in Alabama.

The Baptist church had always been a second home for my parents. Along with the essential support of family and friends, the church provided a valuable source of inspiration, reassurance, and acceptance. Wherever they lived, they quickly found a church home. In a new city, the local church offered a welcoming community and peace amidst the world's problems.

Having a minister for a father—even when he was not in a church pulpit—meant that there was no negotiation about going to church and Sunday school. Unless we had flu or measles, we had to cover our coughs and sneezes with a handkerchief (hankie for the girls) while fidgeting on the hard pews. Many of my early memories centered on church activities: Sunday school, hymns, vacation bible school, Christmas pageants, Easter services (sometimes with trumpets to accompany the triumphal hymns of resurrection).

As soon as we arrived in Alabama, Dad and Mom searched for a new church home. They knew that participating in the civil rights movement would pose dangers of harassment, intimidation, perhaps even violence. The church would provide sanctuary—in the double meanings that word conveyed—and comfort. However, as Mom would later say, "I fully expected harassment from the Klan, but not from the church! It hadn't even entered my mind."

Someone had told Dad that a fellow Andover Newton seminarian, Reverend John Wiley, served as minister of Vestavia Hills Baptist Church. Within a few days of our arrival in Homewood, Dad phoned him and received a friendly welcome and an invitation to come to church on Sunday. Wiley had been in the seminary class one year ahead of Dad. In Alabama he had a reputation as a moderate, interested in human rights.

On Saturday night, Dad and Mom followed their usual rituals. Dad told each of us to bring our Sunday shoes. Then he lined them up, took out his shoe-polish tins and brushes, and buffed each shoe until it gleamed brightly. White for the girls, black or brown for the boys. We all took turns in the bathtub. When Ann and Susie were ready, Mom "put up" their damp hair in bobby-pinned ringlets, while we watched TV.

The next morning, after the usual last-minute frenzy, we clambered into the '55 Ford Country Sedan. Vestavia Hills was the next community south of Homewood.

Vestavia Hills Baptist Church was the strangest looking church I had ever seen. It was a round three-story sandstone building, surrounded by twenty tall red-stone columns. Built as his home by former Birmingham mayor George Ward in 1929, the building had been modeled on the Roman Temple of the Vestal Virgins. After Mayor Ward died in 1940, a flat-roofed addition had been built as a restaurant. This now housed the Baptist sanctuary.

After the worship service, Reverend Wiley welcomed us warmly. He talked with Dad about seminary professors they both knew at Andover Newton. Members of the congregation surrounded us and shook hands, saying they were delighted to have a new family joining them. With four young children, we represented potential new church members—important numbers for any church.

We returned that evening for another church service and training union. On the drive home, Dad told Mom he had talked with Reverend Wiley in his office during training union.

Dad said: "He was very friendly. I told him about my work with the Alabama Council. Said he was all in favor of human rights. He's been trying to find ways to integrate Birmingham. He says it will probably take twenty years to integrate his church, or maybe two generations, but—."

Mom asked, "Do you think he's sincere?"

Dad clicked his tongue, a sign he was thinking. "Seems to be. Some of it might just be southern hospitality. Talking to a fellow minister." He looked in the rearview mirror. "But I got the feeling that Wiley knows just how far he can go—what's safe. I don't think he'll be leading the charge."

Reverend Wiley had invited Dad to fill the pulpit for him, two weeks later. He would put Dad's job information in the church bulletin, so nobody would find out later and say, "Why didn't you tell us?" But he did ask Dad not to talk about segregation in his Sunday morning and evening sermons. Dad agreed that a guest preacher, new in town, should not raise a controversy in his first sermon.

As we drove up Shades Mountain on Sunday morning, August 20, Dad was quieter than usual. Mom fidgeted in the passenger seat. It was as noisy as always in the back, as we drew imaginary dividing lines between "my side" and "your side."

When we arrived, just before 10:00 a.m., Dad went to the minister's room to put on his black robe and prepare for the service. Mom led the rest of us into the sanctuary, where a smiling usher took us to seats near the front.

The church bulletin cover depicted the tall nave of a cathedral, with bright stained glass windows. Inside we saw this message: "Guest Minister: We welcome to our pulpit today the Rev. Norman Jimerson. Mr. Jimerson is a graduate of Andover Newton Theological School and has recently come to Birmingham to direct the Alabama Council on Human Relations. We are grateful to Mr. Jimerson for filling the pulpit in the absence of Mr. Wiley, who is in Florida with our young people. We anticipate a blessing from Mr. Jimerson's messages today."

As Dad began his sermon, he cited several Bible verses in which the children of Israel and, later, the early Christians, were called "a peculiar people." He explained that this meant distinctive or unusual, but that the colloquial meaning could also apply: "A real Christian will be regarded by others as peculiar in the sense that he is queer or eccentric."

He went on to discuss what he thought it means to be a Christian. "To accept Christ as Lord is a radical step," he stated. "A follower of Christ must renounce the goals, the customs, the traditions, the aspirations, and the gratifications of the society he lives in."

Then he quoted Jesus's charge to his disciples: "Behold, I send you forth as sheep in the midst of wolves: be ye therefore wise as serpents, and harmless as doves." This from Matthew 10:16, followed by verse 22: "And ye shall be hated of all men for my name's sake: but he that endureth to the end shall be saved." In reading these verses, Dad must have been thinking about the challenges facing him in Alabama.

Despite Reverend Wiley's hope of avoiding controversy, a storm of protest erupted when church members found out what the Alabama Council on Human Relations was up to. Dad's sermon about rejecting society's customs in order to follow Christ's teachings must have raised warning flags. But the presence of a civil rights worker, in this replica of the vestal virgins temple, sent seismic waves through the Vestavia Baptist congregation.

Both Dad and Mom applied to transfer their church membership from Hopewell First Baptist to Vestavia. Normally this would be a routine matter requiring only a pro forma approval by the board of deacons. But as we were discovering, there was no routine answer when race relations entered the scene. The deacons would take several weeks to discuss this request.

Despite these rumblings of controversy, Dad wrote in the October 1961 ACHR newsletter about his warm welcome to Alabama: "The entire family is enjoying the southern hospitality of the neighbors. It is easy to make friends in Birmingham." He added: "Shortly after arriving in Birmingham, the Director and his family joined a local Southern Baptist Church. The people in the church have been very friendly and both Mr. and Mrs. Jimerson are working in the Training Union Department."

By the end of October, however, the tensions at Vestavia Baptist erupted in fierce controversy. On October 29, while Dad was out of town, the Sunday school class spent an hour discussing him and the Alabama Council. Two men from the church visited Dad in his office the next Friday. They told him that his presence was causing tension and controversy in the church. They hinted that everyone would be happier if he withdrew his membership request.

On the same day, Wednesday, November 8, the president of the Sunday school class asked Dad to visit him in his downtown office. He asked if he could take Dad's name off the Sunday school roster. As they discussed concerns about Dad's work, he stated that Dad was like Hitler—but he never explained what he meant by that. He also said that he believed Hitler had many good ideas, and completely agreed with Hitler's philosophy of the pure race. This strange conversation ended with a request that Dad withdraw his request for membership at Vestavia Baptist. "This isn't the place you really belong," the Hitler admirer said.

Dad reported to Paul Rilling that this situation raised concerns about his work for the Alabama Council. "At the present moment I do not know whether I will continue attending the church, but recognizing the possibility of harmful repercussions on my effectiveness, I would not let a vote be taken if there was a possibility that there would be anything other than a vast margin of the people voting that I not leave the church. I sincerely doubt that it will ever come to a vote."

The tensions arising from Vestavia Hills Baptist Church deeply upset Mom. As she did on only a few occasions, when under great stress, she began keeping a diary, handwritten in pencil on lined punch-holed paper:

Sunday, Nov. 12, 1961: Went to Sunday school and church at Vestavia Baptist. I acted as a secretary of the class. Jim was spoken to by about three men. His presence "shook up" the class pres. as only the week before he had asked to take Jim's name off the roll. Jim wouldn't give him the satisfaction. As we walked down the aisle to our seats (all of us) a woman said aloud, "There they go!" I'm almost certain it was meant for us. The one man who had come to Jim's office to ask us to leave the church because we are splitting it, was overly nice in speaking. I ignored him. Only a few weeks before he had told me how nice it was to see me in the choir. The other one (mayor of Vestavia) taught the lesson—did not speak. I feel very frustrated because I know I will not be asked to teach and neither will Jim. He was asked once, but because of remarks made, refused. There is no point in teaching if we cannot express ourselves. Stayed home that night. Called pres. of S.S. class to resign as secy. She was astounded to hear of Jim's being asked to leave the class. Couldn't talk. Would call me, she said.

Monday, Nov. 13: Margaret Northrup from church asked me to go to meeting at school with her. Nothing said.

Tues. Nov. 14: Appointment with Dr. Dick (orthodontist) for Ann. Last week he had said he'd never heard of ACHR—said that if we were Presbyterian he'd invite us to his church. (Ha!) Jim drove to Tuscaloosa. Back late. Dad & Mother called.

Wed. Nov. 15th: Dad's birthday. Rainy—dental appointment for Randy. Came home—worked a little. Roberta called—told me she was deeply sorry for what the few church people were doing and how they must be hurting our family. Apologized over and over—said she was sorry to be part of a group who would do such a thing. Went for a walk in rain—too frustrated to concentrate. Called Faye to tell Doug to count me out of choir. She, too, said it saddened her—that she guessed they weren't as Christian as they thought. Made reservation for Randy to go to youth dinner—church secretary asked me back to choir. Faye assured me it was nothing personal. Everyone is afraid to really speak out for fear of what others will say or think.

Later, remembering the woman who said, "There they go!" during the Sunday service, Mom said: "I cried during the whole service—that people in our church would treat you like that! But that's when we quit. I said I didn't want to go back there."

As a matter of principle—and, no doubt, simply from curiosity about how people in the church would react to this unfolding drama—Dad wouldn't give up. The board of deacons still hadn't voted on their request for membership. When the deacons finally did meet, in early December, they discussed the situation at great length. The result was that, instead of allowing Mom and Dad to become members of Vestavia Baptist, they were asked not to attend the church. A minister turned away from attending worship services.

While the Baptists of Vestavia Hills were debating whether to admit an ordained minister and his family as church members, we had already begun searching for a more welcoming church home. Mom and Dad had grown up in American Baptist churches in the North, but in Virginia had joined a local Southern Baptist congregation. After being ostracized by Vestavia Baptist, they looked for another local Baptist church.

The neighbors who had welcomed us to Homewood when they saw our Virginia license plates, Dale Long and his mother, invited us to visit their church. Mrs. Long tried to assure Mom that the Baptist church in Homewood would welcome us.

If Vestavia Hills Baptist Church was the strangest church I had ever seen, Dawson Memorial Baptist Church was the largest. The Georgian colonial sanctuary building soared upwards, with enormous white columns in front and a tall white steeple.

"It's gi-normous!" Paul exclaimed.

We climbed a wide staircase to the front door, where enthusiastic members of the welcoming committee greeted us. The women wore white gloves and fluttered around us. "How nice to *see* you?" "Glad y'all can join us?" A male usher showed us to a middle pew, with a flourish of southern hospitality: "Thank you for comin'?"

The church service felt stiff and formal, despite efforts to appear warm and inviting. After Sunday school, six-year-old Susie got lost trying to find us. She was crying when someone finally brought her to Mom. Paul looked bewildered. Dad smiled to hide his anger about the minister's emphasis on the size of the church. "Typical edifice complex," he grumbled.

On the ride home, I pouted and said, "I don't like it!"

Ann added: "It's too big and confusing."

Mom looked at all of us, and said, "I don't think this is right for us. We won't be coming back!"

That was it. Mrs. Long and Dale stopped by the house later, to ask us to return next Sunday. For several weeks they tried to convince Mom and Dad to give Dawson Memorial another chance. But Mom kept her promise. We never returned.

After these two church experiences, Mom and Dad gave up on the Baptists. Mary Dougherty, a friend and neighbor of the Longs who lived down the hill on Windsor Boulevard, had asked our family to visit her Presbyterian church. She thought we would be accepted there.

Shades Valley Presbyterian Church practically straddled the line between Homewood and our more affluent neighbor, Mountain Brook. It looked like a smaller version of Dawson Memorial: Georgian colonial style, brick, with tall white columns in front.

Dad had heard that Reverend Tom Duncan was considered "moderate" on racial issues. In Birmingham, that meant that he would not speak in favor of integration, but he would also not support the extreme segregationists. Moderates would simply remain silent on the most pressing moral issue of the day.

Before long Mom joined the choir, and offered to teach Sunday school if needed. She said she felt comfortable with Mary and the other people in the church. Dad held his peace, despite Reverend Duncan's careful avoidance of saying anything that might be construed as a reference to civil rights, segregation, or racial violence. They decided to apply for membership, even though this meant leaving behind their Baptist affiliations.

One evening after supper, Mom told us to stay in our bedrooms for a while. She said, "Do your homework!" She would be in the kitchen, if we needed anything.

Mom said, "Don't go in the living room. Some men from the church are here to talk to Jim about membership." She kept wiping her hands on her apron and glancing over her shoulder. "I don't want them to see me. Your father will take care of it."

We could hear men talking, and the low rumble of Dad's voice, but couldn't make out what they were saying. When they left, Dad looked for Mom. By standing very still, almost holding my breath, I could hear them talking in the kitchen.

Dad chuckled and said: "Jeez, Mel, that was bizarre!" He laughed nervously. "They said that stories are going through the church that we are communists!"

I heard Mom's voice: "How did they ever get *that* idea!"

Dad's voice said: "They think someone who works in the bank found out we deposited a check for three thousand dollars. They know we don't have that kind of money, so they figured it was from the Communist Party!" Dad's laugh was loud.

"Jim, this isn't funny! How could they *think* such a thing?"

"Well, that's just a smear word for anyone they don't like. Call 'em commies."

They stopped talking for a minute or two. Then Mom said: "The check! That's how much Dad sent from his business, to help us out." She paused, then added: "But why would they assume it was from the communists?"

"People usually find what they expect to see. They know I'm in civil rights, so I must be a communist. Here's their 'proof'!"

"Oh, Jim! That must be why they wouldn't accept me to teach Sunday school. They just wouldn't. . . . Here they are begging for teachers, and when I offered—." I could hear her sobbing.

Meanwhile, news of our changing church attendance had spread through Shades Cahaba School. My seventh-grade English teacher took me aside one day after class and said, "What's this I hear that you're leaving the Baptist church and going to a Presbyterian church?" She made it sound like an irrational thing, or some sort of betrayal. Every Monday she asked all of us whether we had been to church, and where. So much for separation of church and state!

Susie, in first grade, had the same experience. Her teacher knew that her father was a Baptist minister. Just as my teacher did, on Monday morning she would ask the first graders, "How many of you were in Sunday school? How many of you went to church? Which church did you go to?" When Susie said that she had gone to a Presbyterian church, her teacher scolded her for not going to a Southern Baptist church.

A bit later, someone told Mom and Dad that a school teacher was overheard asking, "Who is that communist kid?" She meant Paul. The teachers were talking about the Jimerson children—but not about how well we were doing in school. They had labeled us as outsiders, undesirables.

As news of our exclusion from one church after another reached distant friends, several responded with encouragement and support. Benjamin Muse of the Southern Regional Council wrote to Dad: "It is disheartening, and it seems fantastic for a man to be censured by a Christian church for his devotion to Christian principles. But I know it is an old story in the Deep

South. I believe the Master said, 'Rejoice and be exceeding glad'—but here I'm getting into your field!"

A friend from Hopewell, Bill Blair, wrote on the day after Christmas: "Dear Melva and Norman, I imagined you would run into deep and hostile feelings in connection with your new work, but I am surprised that it came in the House of God. Perhaps I should not be since Christ was delivered to the Romans by the religious leaders of his day and human nature has not changed too much."

The next stop on our religious odyssey, seeking a church to call home, was Second Presbyterian Church, on the south side of Birmingham near downtown. At an interracial meeting of the ministers, in January 1962, Reverend Alva B. Gregg asked Dad about the Alabama Council, and then invited him to join his church. Dad told him about our difficulties with Vestavia Baptist and Shades Valley Presbyterian, but Gregg said that he thought the vast majority of his church members would welcome us as members. Second Presbyterian was quite conservative, but they allowed him freedom to deal with the race issue.

A week or two later, we got into the station wagon, drove over Red Mountain past Vulcan, and visited Second Presbyterian. That afternoon Reverend Gregg came to our house to speak with Dad and Mom about joining the church. He was especially interested in having new Sunday school teachers. Reverend Gregg followed this up with several phone calls, encouraging them to join. Adding to the membership rolls was an important responsibility for any pastor, and an ordained minister could be a valuable asset in the congregation.

Within a week or two, however, news of Dad's affiliation with the Alabama Council spread through the church. One Sunday, on our second or third visit to Second Presbyterian, hardly any adults showed up for Sunday school. When Reverend Gregg came to the house the next week, he spent an hour and a half talking about the church, Christianity, and other things, before coming to the point. He said that a woman in the church had called people to tell them not to come as long as "those communists" were attending.

A week later Reverend Gregg visited Dad's office, with a Howard College student who said that a "reliable source" had identified the Alabama Council as a communist organization. Charles Carney, a local real estate operator, had given Reverend Gregg a seven-page report containing specific charges against SRC and ACHR. Among its allegations were claims that the Alabama Council "is a clandestine organization," whose "meetings are held in secret and membership lists are not available to anyone." It linked SRC and ACHR to Martin Luther King Jr., Fred Shuttlesworth, and various alleged communists. It denounced Bob Hughes, Leslie Dunbar, and "Reverend Norman C. Jimerson, Baptist Minister, who resides at 1905 Saulter Road, Homewood, Alabama." Providing home addresses, in this manner, had long been a tactic used by the Klan to target people for harassment.

Although the report carried a disclaimer that not every member of these organizations was "a Communist" or "a deliberate subversive," it charged that "every such person is either knowingly or unknowingly lending aid to the subversive thrust of the Communist Party." The final sentence of this smear sheet—underlined for emphasis—stated: *"There seems to be little excuse for any reasonably well-informed citizen to continue association with these organizations."*

Reverend Gregg and the college student then asked Dad to explain or refute these charges. Dad gave them several documents that SRC had prepared for this type of unfounded attack, including a November 1961 telegram from President Kennedy to the Southern Regional Council president, which stated in part:

> In promoting good will and better understanding among people of all races, colors and creeds, the Council is serving not only the South but the whole country. In supporting efforts to secure the full constitutional rights of all our people, including above all the primary right to vote, you are helping to fulfill the promise of America.
>
> Cordially, John F. Kennedy

One final confrontation remained with Second Presbyterian Church. Since Dad and Mom had applied for membership, the elders had to make the decision. They invited Dad to speak at a meeting to consider his application to become a member of the church. Mom refused to attend.

Before the meeting began, one church member said he would not go along with the effort to exclude the Jimersons from his church.

"I won't vote," he told Dad. "I'll abstain."

This statement reflected the essential moral problem facing Birmingham, Chuck Morgan told Dad: "Not the 'extremists' who *attack* you, but the 'moderates' who *abstain*."

Discussion focused on Dad's work with the Alabama Council, the council's alleged communist associations, Dad's views about race relations, and his support for integration. They didn't talk much about church activities or matters of Christian faith.

During the meeting, one man who sang in the choir said he knew Dad and Mom weren't communists because he "watched how they worshipped."

Despite this show of support, the elders told Dad that his mere presence would create problems for an already splintered congregation. They asked him not to return.

Rejected by both Southern Baptists and Presbyterians, Mom and Dad next decided to try the Lutherans. Reverend James Pape, pastor of the Lutheran Church of Vestavia Hills, belonged to the Alabama Council board. Dad felt hopeful that we would be welcomed there.

After speaking with the pastor in March 1962, Dad told us: "He said that if his church asked us to leave, *he* would leave!"

We attended this Lutheran church from March to August 1962. Ann especially enjoyed the arts-and-crafts curriculum for Sunday school. Having been accustomed to informal Baptist services, I found the church liturgy formal and confusing.

On the drive home one Sunday, Mom told Dad: "I don't like all this emphasis on Original Sin. I think it scares the children." She was right. As with Dawson Memorial, we decided to leave this church on our own, without being asked.

During this long process of trying out new churches, we also visited several black churches. Dad knew most of their ministers through the Alabama Council. He thought joining a black church would be a good symbol of our commitment to integration.

When we arrived at the various black churches, the experience followed a similar pattern. Typically, a white-dressed and white-gloved woman would greet us at the door, and lead us to a pew. Ann whispered, the first time: "I've never seen a *woman* usher!"

The church choirs wore brightly colored robes. They swayed from side to side, almost dancing, while singing loudly and joyously. There were none of the strained and pinched voices of white church choirs. ("No offense, Mom!" we apologized.) During hymns, the entire congregation swayed back and forth, dancing in the aisles, with a louder sound than I had ever heard.

Offering plates circled through the pews two or three times during the service. Dad always contributed something.

The minister delivered his sermon without notes, in dramatic fashion. His voice would start slow and quiet, then build to a rapid delivery of shouted phrasings and appeals to the congregation. People kept interrupting him, shouting: "Amen!" "Tell it, brother!" "Hallelujah!" "Yes, Jesus!"

The services were exciting, arousing, but also confusing and a bit frightening. I didn't know when to stand up, or sit back down. Were white visitors expected to shout "Amen!" or keep a respectful silence? Should I try to clap along with everyone? What if I couldn't keep the beat?

For some time, our parents thought we might be able to join a black church. But the cultural differences—the unfamiliar aspects of the church services, at least—seemed daunting. In the end, it was too great a stretch. We seemed out of place wherever we turned: shunned by white churches, uncomfortable in black congregations.

Mary Dougherty finally coaxed Mom to come back to the Presbyterian church in Mountain Brook. She said they wouldn't shun us that way again. After nearly a year of wandering from one church to another, we did return to Shades Valley Presbyterian. Mom sang in the choir. She had found a real church home this time. Dad clenched his teeth during the sermons.

Meanwhile, Reverend Tom Duncan had started speaking against the tactics of the growing desegregation movement in Birmingham. Dad finally heard enough. He began attending Pilgrim Congregational Church in Mountain Brook. The minister, Reverend Al Henry, was strongly in favor of integration, and he preached it in his church.

Pilgrim Congregational Church members divided evenly on race issues, Dad told us. Some members began to resist Reverend Henry's efforts to accept integration. When he proposed hosting an integrated meeting of the

Congregationalists' association, the church members demanded a vote. It was 49 percent in favor of allowing a meeting that would include black Congregational ministers, and 51 percent opposed.

Dad said, "Al Henry has put up with a lot of hassles. The pest-control people showed up at his house one time and said, 'Somebody told us to come to this address to get rid of the pests.' Ambulances show up, just to disrupt things. One time a hearse arrived and said they were told to come to his house and pick up somebody for the funeral parlor."

We visited Pilgrim a few times. But Mom resisted Dad's entreaties to switch to the Congregational church. Reverend Henry and his wife visited our house and tried to convince her to come to their church. But Mom felt comfortable now at Shades Valley. She sang in the choir, and was active in Sunday school. She didn't want another relocation. The other kids and I also preferred to stay at the Presbyterian church.

This was the end of our religious odyssey. On most Sundays, Dad would drop us off at Shades Valley Presbyterian, and head off by himself to Pilgrim Congregational.

6

Welcome to Klan Country

Our problems in finding a church congregation that would welcome a civil rights minister and his family began a long, painful experience of ostracism and exclusion. In Birmingham even talking about race could lead to social rejection. Suspicious glares. Whispered conversations. Backs turned. Anonymous threats. Potential violence.

We heard stories of black people beaten by police, lynched by the Klan, attacked for seemingly innocuous offenses against the laws of segregation. Reverend Fred Shuttlesworth had been blown out of his bed by a bomb. Such violence and intimidation also targeted whites who spoke out on race issues. We knew about the cross burned on Reverend Bob Hughes's lawn. His own Methodist church had expelled him from Alabama. What could happen to Dad's predecessor, we knew, could happen to him.

At Shades Cahaba School ostracism assumed more subtle forms. We couldn't talk freely about our opinions on race relations or even about our father's job. We had to live, in part, in silence. To learn how to avoid topics that might reveal our true identity as "outside agitators."

Everyone knew we were Yankees. Even while learning to say "Yes, ma'am" to my teachers in Virginia, I had deliberately refused to adopt a southern accent. It bothered me a bit that Susie, having been a toddler when we first moved to Virginia, spoke with a lilting southern drawl. But it may have enabled her to fit in more easily.

The tension between our inner feelings and our public personas did not prevent us from experiencing a normal childhood in other respects. We made friends with other kids in the neighborhood, played games, rode bicycles around town, shopped at V. J. Elmore five-and-ten, ate hamburgers at Jack's, swam at the public pool. There were times when we could forget that we were "different."

Susie thought going to a new school was exciting. As a first grader, she felt proud to join her older sister and brothers in our school adventures.

Her best friend, Cheryl, lived a few houses up the street. They enjoyed the warm fall days, exploring in the woods and playing at a nearby creek. Travis and Tracy, twin boys in her class, also joined them in roaming through the neighborhood. Wherever Susie went, Spitzy usually followed.

Mom would say, "Keep Spitzy with you. She'll protect you." She didn't say from what. A dachshund did not pose much threat to larger animals or to people.

Ann always loved school, even old-fashioned Shades Cahaba. Outside of school, she joined a garden club, because in the South young ladies had to learn to make flower arrangements. She taught herself to sew, and made Barbie doll clothes. She finally got to start making money as a babysitter, especially for the young couple next door.

As Halloween approached, Ann and Susie began elaborate plans for their costumes. They would be a witch and her black cat. And they decided to enter the Homewood Halloween costume contest.

Mom usually gave Ann a free rein on her artsy projects. After all, as an architect, she had studied art and she placed a high value on creativity. With so many kids at home, Mom was relieved to have us entertain ourselves, if we caused little fuss.

Ann and Susie spent hours in the dank basement, making masks for their Halloween costumes. One of Ann's favorite afternoon TV shows, on the local educational channel, showed how to make papier mâché masks. They blew up balloons, tore newspaper strips, and mixed flour-and-water paste, adding layer upon layer as the paper dried, covering the balloons.

By the third day, Ann and Susie added a craggy nose for the witch and ears for the cat. Once the papier mâché dried, they popped the balloons. Ann used an X-acto knife to cut eyeholes. Then they painted the cat and witch faces. An old lampshade became the base for the witch's hat, and the cone-shaped top came from a paper grocery bag.

The clothes were secondary: just black robes for Ann as the witch and black sweatshirt and pants for Susie, the cat. At the last minute, they decided to borrow my belt to make a leash to connect the witch and cat during the costume parade in a supermarket parking lot.

Susie and Ann won the Homewood Halloween contest for their age group. The *Birmingham News* listed their names among the winners: "a witch and cat team, Susan and Ann Jimerson." The prize was a twenty-five-dollar gift certificate to V. J. Elmore's—a real windfall for 1961.

Only one thing disappointed Ann. "It didn't even matter that we made the masks ourselves," she complained. "Some of the other winners had *store-bought* costumes!"

Mom made it clear that Ann and Susie had done the work and would share the prize. "But this should be for the whole family," Ann said. "Each of us should get something from Elmore's."

Susie and Paul shared a red wagon. Ann enjoyed a few trips to Elmore's to buy craft supplies. Then she bought fabric and patterns to sew Barbie outfits, which she peddled in the neighborhood for thirty-five cents an outfit. I used my "share" of the prize money to get a light and generator for my bike.

When *To Kill a Mockingbird* came out, Ann told us that this 1961 Halloween contest showed that she and Scout were kindred spirits. Scout, too, had shopped at Elmore's. And of course, for the book's climactic scene, she was dressed as a ham—made of papier mâché.

As Dad's circle of contacts through the Alabama Council widened, we began to have growing numbers of interesting people visit our home. Dad quickly became the local contact person for white civil rights activists, northern journalists, ministers, and other visitors from distant places, seeking to witness what was happening on the civil rights front lines, or to be part of the action. They would meet Dad through meetings, or correspondence, or a recommendation as someone with access to both white and black community leaders. If someone needed a place to stay, Dad would offer our sofa or the roll-away bed in the small den. Our home offered these visitors a safe and quiet place to talk and a home-cooked meal.

Among the first such visitors, in November 1961, were two young men who quickly became favorites with the Jimerson children. Bob Zellner, the first white field representative of the student Non-violent Coordinating Committee (SNCC, pronounced "Snick"), was a native of southern Alabama. Bob was on his way to Mississippi to be arraigned for participating in a student protest, representing SNCC.

Traveling with him was Per Worsoe Laursen, a Danish journalist about twenty-four years old, who was touring the South to experience the civil rights struggle firsthand. He planned to write a book about the burgeoning movement.

Per Laursen seemed exotic to us children: his square face framed by bright yellow hair and a red beard—something almost unknown in the

United States at the time. He got down on the floor to play games with us. He enjoyed teasing Susie, who developed a big crush on him. Per let her wear his hat while he chased her around the house. After this first visit, Susie always got excited when Per was coming to visit. We never missed a chance to tease her about her "boyfriend."

Bob was quieter, more serious. His south Alabama accent made it hard to understand some of what he said. He was twenty-two—exactly ten years older than me—when he first stayed at our house. Bob's father was a Methodist minister, and his mother was a school teacher. Tall and sandy-haired, with a crooked smile, almost shy, Bob Zellner didn't look like someone who would put his life on the line, as he had done several times.

On their first visit together, Bob and Per stayed at our house for several nights. On Thursday, November 9, they accompanied Dad when he visited the Greyhound bus station to assure the manager that he had moral support in the community for serving black customers.

That evening after supper, while Per entertained Susie and Ann in the living room, Bob and Dad sat at the dining table, drinking coffee and talking. I sat quietly at the other side of the table, "all ears." Bob talked about being banned from returning to the campus of his alma mater, Huntingdon College in Montgomery, because of his involvement in civil rights meetings.

When Bob said that his father and grandfather had been Klan members, I felt my eyes bugging out in astonishment. After graduating from Bob Jones College in the 1930s, Bob's father had joined the conservative evangelist Dr. Bob Jones Sr. on a trip to Europe, seeking to convert Jews to Christianity. During a cold winter in Russia, Bob's father met a group of black gospel singers. They talked about home and food, sharing meals and lodging far from their native South. Bob's father later told him: "Things were never the same after living with my friends and not thinking about what color we were. It certainly ruined me as a Klansman, that's for sure."

The next day Dad asked me, "How about going to a football game tomorrow?" When we lived in Waltham, Dad and one of his friends from graduate school had taken me to my first football game. Boston University played Boston College. All I could remember was that, whenever a big play occurred, everyone stood up and cheered, and I couldn't see anything, even standing on the bench.

I said: "Sure. But will I be able to *see* the game this time?"

Not until we were in the Ford station wagon, on Saturday, November 11, did I realize that this trip would be connected to Dad's work. A month before, Paul Rilling had sent Dad a request for information about the location of Ku Klux Klan signs that "welcomed" visitors in a number of Alabama communities. Dad included a notice in the *Alabama Council Newsletter,* asking about Klan signs. One council member wrote back: "Each day I pass one in Tuscaloosa. It is on Route 11, the Birmingham highway."

Dad wanted to see this sign for himself, and decided to add the football game as an entertainment extra. Per Laursen and Bob Zellner eagerly agreed to join him, and Dad also invited our neighbor Dale Long to the game.

On the way to Tuscaloosa I heard more about Bob and Per's adventures. Bob had just started working for SNCC in September, in a new Atlanta office he shared with Jim Forman, the new executive secretary. SNCC hired Bob to recruit civil rights volunteers at white colleges around the South. Bob said: "I found out that you really only become a SNCC person by putting your body on the line. SNCC is determined to end segregation or die trying. You can't fear death if you join 'direct action' campaigns."

Per talked about observing the civil rights movement as an outsider. Dad had been called an "outside agitator" because he was from the North, but Per was *really* an outsider, from Denmark. He had been sending stories back to European magazines while planning a full-length book to explain the civil rights movement.

Bob had just gotten out of jail for participating in demonstrations. With his thick southern accent, I thought he was talking about Macon, a small city in Georgia. After a while, I learned he had actually been arrested in McComb, Mississippi.

Black high school students in McComb, located in the piney woods of south-central Mississippi, planned a march to protest the murder of Herbert Lee, a black man working on voter registration. SNCC went wherever there was a hot spot of civil rights activity, so Bob and others drove to McComb. There Bob joined a protest march. On the steps of city hall a large mob began punching and beating the activists. As they tried to drag Bob away, he grabbed the railing as lead-filled pipes and baseball bats smashed his hands. One man tried to gouge out his eyeball. The police looked on, making no effort to stop the attacks. A heavy boot crashed into Bob's head until he passed out.

When he came to in the police station, Bob heard the police chief saying, "I shoulda let them kill you! I shoulda let them take you." Bob told us he thought he *was* about to die.

Dad said: "Boy, I don't think I could do that. I'm not brave enough!"

Bob said: "Well, Jim, I don't have anything to lose. No wife, no children, no mortgage, no job—except with SNCC, where I'm paid to do this—so I'm not afraid to die, if it comes to that. In a way, your job is even harder. You have to walk a tightrope between the white community and the movement."

Per said: "I think Bob needs to have physical courage, Jim, and you need mental courage. Emotional courage. Bob has stepped outside the white community, but you still need to live within it. Even when they reject you."

As we approached Tuscaloosa on Route 11, all eyes focused on looking for the Klan sign. Just outside the grounds of Partlow School for the mentally retarded, on the north side of the highway, we spotted it, grouped among signs for Rotary, Kiwanis, Civitan, and other civic organizations. Dad pulled onto the right shoulder. Per took photos, while Dad started writing in his notebook.

Painted on a large industrial saw blade, the Klan sign showed a picture of a robed and hooded man on a horse and the brief message: "The Ku Klux Klan welcomes you to Tuscaloosa."

The football game—*my* favorite part of the trip—seemed anticlimactic. The Crimson Tide, on their way to an eventual national championship in 1961, beat the University of Richmond 66–0. Always rooting for the underdog—especially one from our former home state—I found this rout almost as dispiriting as watching the Pirates lose 16–3 to the Yankees a year before in the World Series—my one chance to see a World Series game, with Granddad.

The loudest cheering of the day came late in the game, just as Alabama was breaking the huddle and coming to the scrimmage line. "What happened?" Per asked. We looked around, trying to see why the fans were cheering so loud. None of us knew.

In the row behind us, a man holding a transistor radio to his ear said, "Auburn lost!" For diehard Alabama fans, the most exciting news was that their arch-rival had been defeated.

After the game, Bob gave directions as Dad drove through town to a gas station on the outskirts of Tuscaloosa. I thought he needed gas, but he just pulled over on the side of the road across from the station. "That's where Bobby Shelton works," Bob told us. We scrutinized the run-down station and its old-fashioned pumps.

I looked around, confused, then asked: "Who's that?"

Bob said, "He's the grand wizard of the Ku Klux Klan. One of the leading redneck segregationists in the state."

We stopped at a phone booth while Per, trying to use his credentials as a journalist, called Shelton's home phone. He hoped for an interview. Instead he talked with Shelton's wife, but couldn't meet the grand wizard.

Bob said, "This is the neighborhood where some of my relatives—a cousin and her husband—live. Don't know what they'd think about me working for SNCC. But I can't call them or they might be in danger from the Klan." He thought for a moment, his mouth turning down. "Some of these older Klansmen might have known my Daddy when he was in the Klan in Birmingham. The Tuscaloosa and Birmingham Klans have always been close."

So we saw the Klan on the way into Tuscaloosa and on the way out. "The Klan welcomes you." That could have been the slogan for all of Alabama, I thought.

After the trip to Tuscaloosa, Bob Zellner and Per Laursen continued on to Mississippi. Bob had to return to McComb for a trial on charges of disorderly conduct, breach of peace, and resisting arrest. He had been unable to find a white lawyer to defend him. One attorney he approached wrote to him: "Mr. Zellner you are a disgrace to your race. If you want to be a Negro why don't you just turn black? I wouldn't represent you under any circumstances, and I doubt that any white lawyer in the great state of Mississippi would either." Bob and his father contacted more than a hundred lawyers without success.

We would see Bob and Per again several more times. In January 1962, Per wrote to Dad from New York City:

> I regret that I haven't yet had a chance to wish you and yours a happy new year, and to thank you for the marvelous hospitality you extended towards me during my trips to Birmingham.
>
> What I had half-way expected would happen at one point or another in the course of my wanderings, did in fact happen; so when I found myself in the city jail in Albany, Ga., I was both surprised that it had happened at all, and amazed that it hadn't happened until now. That kind of feeling, you know.

Traveling with a SNCC field representative could lead to jail time, as Per had discovered. In December 1961 Jim Forman asked Bob to join him and other

SNCC activists—including Tom Hayden and Joan Browning—on a freedom ride by train from Atlanta to Albany, Georgia. Reverend Wyatt T. Walker, having left Petersburg to join Martin Luther King's Southern Christian Leadership Conference, provided SCLC money for the train tickets. They planned to integrate both the train and Albany's white waiting room.

Being arrested could pose delicate questions regarding Per's visa status. "But," he wrote to Dad, "it was well worth it. . . . 750 Negroes, including Martin Luther King, were arrested as a result of the arrest of us 11 'Freedom Riders,' so it provided an adequate climax to my travels, and, of course, a lot of excitement."

"Viking Press was naturally thrilled, and I expect them to buy the book within a week or two," Per added. "Bob Zellner, who was in jail with me in Albany, asked me to send his regards and thanks."

Meanwhile, several days after the University of Alabama football game, Dad and Mom received a last-minute invitation to the B'nai B'rith annual humanitarian award dinner, as guests of Ted Roth and his wife. Roth was manager of the shoe department at Parisian, one of Birmingham's largest department stores.

James "Jabo" Waggoner, one of Birmingham's three commissioners, sat at Mom and Dad's table. Mom reported that he "made some disgusting remarks about trouble at Negro football games and said they were just like African natives." Dad must have struggled to bite his tongue and not respond.

What should have been a nice celebration of humanitarian service thus became an occasion to rub shoulders with the city commissioner and to hear his racist vitriol. Where in Birmingham could people of good conscience avoid such hate-filled comments, one had to wonder.

At Shades Cahaba School we were beginning to wonder the same thing. Susie and I had both been confronted by teachers criticizing us for not going to the "right" church. Paul overheard another teacher whispering, "Who is that communist kid?" One could only imagine what they said about us in the teachers' lounge.

One day on my way to literature class, I heard rumors that the teacher had a bad hangover. When we entered the classroom, she had cradled her head in arms folded on her desk. When the bell rang to start the period, she roused up, bleary-eyed, and said, "Y'all take out your books and read quietly to y'selfs." For the rest of the hour, we traded smirks, made gestures commenting on her condition, and tried not to laugh aloud.

Another peculiar aspect of the school year came as a response to the Cold War nuclear threat. All students were told to bring an empty Clorox bottle to school, with a teaspoonful or so of Clorox left in the bottle. Then we filled them with water and stored them in the cloak room–closet at the back of the classroom. The Clorox was supposed to purify the water, so we could drink it after the atomic bomb detonated.

We ordered dog tags, like those issued to soldiers in World War II to identify bodies. But the teachers just said it was in case we got separated from our families during an attack. With our name, address, and phone number they would be able to match us up. We had to bring a quarter to school, to pay for the pair of dog tags. We wore them around our necks.

Some boys and girls would swap them—it was like going steady. The teacher scolded one boy, "What would happen if they find you with your girlfriend's name and address instead of your own?"

He answered: "I'd rather be taken to her house anyway."

The threat of nuclear attack led to Civil Defense procedures at schools around the country. Film strips and brochures showed us how to "duck and cover" by hiding under our school desks. Even as young children, we knew how foolish and ineffective this would be. At best, such drills seemed designed to give a false sense of security to prevent panic.

The administrators at Shades Cahaba had an even better idea: air-raid drills. The principal came on the loudspeaker to explain what we should do. The drill began with a loud blast from an eerie siren. Each class lined up in an orderly double row and walked calmly out the front door to the underpass below Route 31. This was the main highway linking Birmingham and Montgomery—a far more likely target than an elementary school, if such accuracy would even be possible for Soviet missiles.

One of the seasonal chores in October and November was raking leaves and pine straw from the steep front and back yards. Working with Dad was never easy. He set a fast pace for raking leaves and needles onto an old sheet, constantly giving instructions about how to handle the rake and commands to move faster. "Hay to the barn!" he called out. "Always rake towards where the leaves have to go." Since the front yard was too steep to rake up to the street, we raked downhill towards the back alley. A longer distance, but "gravity is on our side!" Dad said.

Dad always had to be on the go. He could only relax when he exhausted himself, at the end of the day. Then he sat by the TV, with a bowl of ice cream. His natural restlessness seemed to increase as the stresses of his job intensified. He would come home from work, jaw clenched tightly, and change from his ten-year-old suit and white shirt into even older dress pants, a sweater with holes at the elbows, and worn-out dress shoes. Then he looked for something to do: washing the car with a chamois cloth, oiling a squeaky screen door, or scrubbing pots and pans that had piled up in the sink. We knew not to pester him when he was in a scowling mood.

When Dad was able to be home for supper, he would often report the problems he encountered during the day. As a communications link between black civil rights activists and moderate white leaders, he heard firsthand news and unverified rumors from both sides. Sometimes he just couldn't wait until after supper to tell Mom what he had heard or seen. He hardly seemed to notice the puzzled or worried young faces staring at him from around the oval-shaped maple dining table. At other times he spoke directly to us, when he wanted us to know something important.

"There are some mean nasty things going on around town," he said. "I just want you to understand what's happening—what I'm doing all day." Often he looked worried, or angry. Sometimes he just shook his head. "I can't believe how crazy some people are. How can they carry so much hate? Or fear?"

It soon became clear that we were in the midst of significant events— things that could change people's lives, for better or for worse. Dad's daily immersion in civil rights investigations, meetings, entertaining visitors, and other exciting activities provided us a sense of adventure. Each of us felt, to some degree at least, that we also had become part of something important. The concerns that Dad talked about began to show up in the *Birmingham News,* and I sometimes even read the front page before turning to the comics and sports.

One week before Halloween, the paper reported that Judge Grooms declared unconstitutional the city ordinance maintaining segregated parks. Even in this conservative paper, editorials began stating that people in Birmingham must face the hard fact that the city had already suffered economically because of racial troubles. After Public Safety Commissioner Bull Connor said that he was in favor of closing all public facilities in Birmingham to prevent integration, a *News* editorial argued that parks should remain open.

At supper Dad gave almost daily updates on what he had heard about the parks issue. "Most of the people who talk to me don't want to be quoted," he said. "This one guy I talked to today said he'd have to hand in his resignation from his job the moment he suspected anyone knew he had talked to me!" He shook his head in astonishment. "And he's a public school superintendent!" He forced a laugh, then lowered his voice. "He's just completely discouraged that this state can't cope with racial tensions."

After Bob Zellner's visit in November, a second SNCC field representative spent two or three weeks in Birmingham. He set up meetings of students from Birmingham Southern College, a white Methodist school, and all-black Miles College. Dad told us, "Some people say they plan to organize sit-ins or boycotts for next spring."

Also during November, a field secretary for the Congress of Racial Equality came to Birmingham and organized a local chapter of CORE. He set up an office—CORE's first effort to have a presence in "the magic city." Dad reported: "He is thinking about starting direct action as soon as he can get a group organized to carry out sit-ins or boycotts of stores."

With this increased civil rights activity in Birmingham, reports began to circulate that the Klan was becoming more active in the community than at any time since the Freedom Riders attacks in May 1961. As Dad reported to SRC in Atlanta: "In Birmingham the climate is very tense. People in Birmingham and across the state think of this as the last stronghold of massive resistance."

Meanwhile, Dad had begun sending frequent updates on the situation in Birmingham, and Alabama generally, to Burke Marshall, a key figure in the Civil Rights Division of the U.S. Department of Justice. Marshall had expressed a strong concern about developments in Birmingham and asked the Alabama Council director to keep him regularly posted during these mounting tensions. Over the next three years, Dad would develop a close working relationship and friendship with Burke Marshall. With behind-the-scenes access to most of the key leaders of both the white business community and the black civil rights activists, Dad began to play an increasingly important role as mediator, communications conduit, and peacemaker.

Throughout December 1961 newspaper headlines gave daily updates about the controversy over integrating city parks. The city commissioners reduced the public parks budget and laid off 140 park employees. Birmingham would close all parks as of January 1, before the court's January 15 deadline to desegregate them. Mayor Art Hanes vowed that integration would come only at gunpoint. People who spoke in favor of keeping the parks open received threatening phone calls during the night.

On December 18, black leaders presented a public statement offering to meet with public officials to work out a constructive approach to the park situation. The city commissioners bluntly refused. They vowed to maintain complete segregation between the races.

Dad reported that in the black community there was a mounting unrest and vague but persistent feeling that large-scale riots could easily break out at any time. The possibility of violence loomed over Birmingham. Dad heard that some people in the black community warned that, if the Klan caused any trouble, "we will get a few Klansmen next time."

In the white community, segregationists threatened people who supported open parks. One woman making such threats stated ominously that Klan members had taken their robes out of the closet. Now they carried the robes in their cars at all times, ready for action on a moment's notice.

Welcome to Klan country.

7

Threats and Intimidation

The ominous presence of the Ku Klux Klan soon became personal and inescapable for our family. As late as December 27, 1961, Dad wrote to Alabama Council Vice-President Nat Welch of Auburn: "I have not had any crank phone calls. I had expected that it would only be a matter of weeks when I came in August that I would be under very heavy fire so I can say that I am rather surprised that I have not come under attack other than through the Baptist Church that I joined." That was about to change.

At first the threats came through surveillance, intimidation, and slander against the Alabama Council. On the same day that Dad wrote to Nat Welch, he informed Paul Rilling of the Southern Regional Council that two men from the Better Business Bureau had visited his office asking for the names of the ACHR board of directors. This was the same type of request that Bob Hughes had denied fifteen months before. Dad gave them the names of officers, but refused to divulge other names. The Better Business men said they had recently received dozens of calls about the Alabama Council, "and I don't have to tell you the nature of these calls." Dad told Rilling: "I'm guessing the heat will be on us this spring."

On Tuesday, January 9, 1962, we woke up to several inches of snow on the ground. No school! Dad was on a business trip, so we didn't have the hot cereal he usually prepared—oatmeal, Ralston, cream of wheat, or a mixture, if there wasn't enough of one for all of us. We ate corn flakes and Wheaties quickly, then ran out to enjoy the rare snowfall. This was one day we could put our Yankee background to good use, showing the Alabama kids how to make snowballs, snowmen, and snow angels. But we had to hurry, since the snow was already beginning to melt.

Dad came home that evening, after a long bus ride delayed by the snow. He had been in the Tri-Cities in northwestern Alabama to attend a local ACHR council meeting.

During supper we regaled Dad with stories about our "snow day."

"We made a snowman!" Susie said. "Mommy gave us a carrot for his nose, and we had rocks for his eyes and mouth."

Paul added: "And we got sticks for his arms! And your old hat!"

"I showed Susie and Paul how to make snow angels," Ann said.

"Mike and I had a snowball fight with the kids across the street," I said.

Susie added: "The best part was sliding down the hill in a box!"

Dad said: "I wondered why the front yard was so muddy! What did you do with the grass?" He laughed, so we did too.

While we were eating ice cream, Dad told Mom about his trip.

At the local chapter's monthly meeting, everyone was talking about the TV show sponsored by the Golden Flake Potato Chip Company being cancelled. In October a black mother had called up to see if her daughter could be on the early morning children's program. She was told on the phone that her child would be admitted, but when the girl arrived at the station she was told she could not be in the program. The black community became upset. Representatives from the local council of ACHR had talked with the TV station and the advertising firm representing the sponsors, but each side blamed the other.

Dad said, "Things rocked along for a while, but now this show has been cancelled, and local Negroes have started a campaign to educate Negroes and whites not to buy Golden Flake Potato Chips."

I dropped my spoon. "Does this mean no more potato chips?" I asked.

Dad frowned, and said: "Well, we want to send a message to the company about not discriminating."

"But you need Golden Flake bags for the free movies!" I said. "Besides, Coach Bryant is on the ads for Coke and Golden Flake: 'A great pair, says the Bear.'"

"If you're going to stand up for your principles," Dad said, "you have to make some sacrifices." The corners of his mouth curled up, but he bit his lip to keep from smiling.

"Yeah, well, I can just pick up empty Golden Flake bags along the road," I said. "Is that OK?"

On the way back from the Tri-Cities, Dad saw evidence of integration laws being violated. His bus connection in Cullman, about an hour north of Birmingham, was two hours late because of snow. He decided to get some coffee at the bus station restaurant. The door from the waiting room to the restaurant was completely covered by a large sheet of plywood. He had to go outside and then enter the restaurant from the parking area.

As Dad sat drinking a cup of coffee he noticed a crudely printed sign on the boarded-up door between the restaurant and the bus station. It said "To keep from serving Negroes we had to close this door." When he took out a small notebook and started writing, an elderly waitress said, "Are you writing down my sign?"

He responded, "Yes, I think it is a very interesting sign."

She said, "You're a reporter—that sign's not for publicity. It's just for local folks."

A few minutes later she returned and said, "If you cause me any trouble I'll shoot you!" She was smiling as she said this, but Dad felt like saying, "Your smile doesn't cover up your hostility towards me for disagreeing with you and your sign."

It had been eight months since mobs attacked the Freedom Riders in Birmingham and Montgomery, and burned their bus in Anniston. The Freedom Riders had sought to force compliance with a U.S. Supreme Court decision regarding desegregation of interstate transportation. Following the attacks, the Interstate Commerce Commission issued an order compelling all stations to comply with the Supreme Court decision. This boarded door marked Cullman's attempt to evade the ICC order and preserve segregated facilities. By forcing bus passengers to leave the station before entering the restaurant, they thought they could avoid integration.

One Saturday night at the beginning of February, Dad didn't come home for supper. He called to tell Mom he would be late. It was his first annual meeting of the Alabama Council, and he had a lot to do. I was already in bed when I heard the front door open. Soon I could hear Dad talking to Mom. I sneaked into the back hallway so I could hear without getting in trouble.

"How was the meeting, Jim?" Mom asked.

"Les Dunbar did a real good job for us. He gave an analysis of the South today and in the past," Dad said. "We've got a good man as head of Southern Regional Council."

"It's late. Are you hungry?" Mom asked.

"I'm *always* hungry," Dad said, laughing. "How 'bout some coffee? I'll get some shredded wheat." I heard dishes rattle and the refrigerator open, so I ducked behind my bedroom door. "Sorry to be late, but this libel sheet business is a mess."

"*Now* what?"

"It looks like these attacks against the council and SRC were written by lawyers, state legislators, and other government officials. They're trying to show the need for an Alabama Un-American Activities Committee. The main motivation is to attack the Alabama Council. We're just lucky it didn't pass in the last session."

"That sounds like Joe McCarthy all over again!" Mom sounded worried.

"The board voted to hire Morgan to investigate these libel sheets. We're looking into the possibility of a lawsuit."

Mom said: "Who can you sue? The legislature?"

"There's this guy Carney—Charles Carney—a local real estate guy. He's the one who gave Gregg at Second Presbyterian that report claiming the Southern Regional Council is full of communists and that the Alabama Council is subversive."

"Oh, Jim!" Mom said quietly. She sounded worried—and discouraged. I could hear water starting to boil in the tea kettle.

"Well, I'm not at all surprised by libel and slander," Dad said. "If anything it's a wonder there hasn't been more of it. Anyhow, Morgan thinks we have a good case against Carney."

I heard Dad's voice, now from the dining room. "Then there's the radio station stuff. Two or three people said that an editorial on WSFM slandered SRC. It said on the air that there were two communists in SRC. That there would be more editorials about this." I could hear a spoon clinking in a cup, and smelled coffee. Probably Sanka, since it was late.

Then Dad spoke again. "It's like the Klan is running this state. The radio station is playing their song. So is the *Birmingham News*." He paused. "I met with Red Holland, editor of the paper, and he was very hostile. He pulled out all the stops. *I'm* the big obstacle here, he told me. No progress because of *me*. He thinks the council's motives are all wrong. They proved this by hiring me—an out of state man—as their director. . . ." His voice trailed off.

"That's crazy!" Mom said. Now she sounded angry. "You can't let him talk like that."

Dad chuckled. "Sheesh! How dumb can he be? I'm the one trying to calm things down. Get people to talk to each other." He paused. "Whatta'ya gonna do?"

Mom said, "We'd better pray for guidance . . . and strength."

In the next few weeks, Dad collaborated with Miles College President Lucius Pitts to organize small interracial groups to discuss the continuing problems in Birmingham: resistance to integration, violence against blacks, employment discrimination, and closing of the city parks. Dr. Lucius Pitts assumed the presidency of Miles College at about the same time that Dad started with the Alabama Council. They soon became close friends and trusted allies. Dr. Pitts called Dad "my black-hearted brother." He said, "You're a great mixer. You're black or white, but you're neither. You're caught in the middle."

At the end of February, Dad met again with Red Holland at the *Birmingham News*. This time Holland was cordial and calm. He acknowledged that the interracial meetings had been helpful, and agreed with Dad that demonstrations would make it more difficult for whites to sit down and talk with Negroes. As Dad reported to SRC: "Among other things Holland felt there would very definitely be violence in Birmingham if there was a demonstration of any kind." Two weeks after calling Dad an obstacle to progress, Holland had changed from belligerent to polite and friendly.

From the time my father arrived in Birmingham, colleagues in the Alabama Council warned that the police had tapped his office phone. After a few months, they said they were certain that our home phone was also bugged.

People engaged in human rights activities regularly speculated about whose phones were being bugged. They used some discretion in speaking on the phones, but continued to conduct business more or less as usual. But Dad always had to remember that whatever he said or heard might be recorded. To ensure privacy he sometimes left the office to call from a nearby pay phone.

When calling his attorney, Chuck Morgan, Dad used a set of code words that they had come up with to avoid saying things that would arouse suspicion or using names of other civil rights sympathizers. "Just like the spy movies!" Dad said. It became a game, a form of amusement that helped break the tension of certain situations.

One time Dr. Pitts designed a test to see if his own office phone was tapped. He called a friend of his and said, "Now, tonight when I call you at nine o'clock, just respond normally, and whatever response seems appropriate, do that. Or just say, 'yes, yes, yes.'"

That night Pitts called and said, "You know, the students are planning to march downtown tomorrow at eleven o'clock, and go to certain stores. I was in a long meeting with them, and I couldn't talk them out of it." He didn't repeat this false report to anyone else. The next morning several students went downtown separately to see what would happen. Shortly before eleven o'clock, five or six police cars began to cruise the area. The police must have heard the information from Pitts's phone call.

One evening during supper, Dad said he wanted to tell us a funny story.

"Stanford, the FBI agent, came to my office today. I wanted him to see that my phone is tapped. He came over and noticed a clumsy, amateurish wiring of the phones between the small secretary's office and my small office. Wires had been taped up above the doorway in my office. You could see them. He got up on a filing cabinet and looked at the wiring."

Dad grinned and started to laugh.

"Then the FBI man said, 'This place must be tapped.' He looked around nervously, and said, 'I'm never coming *here* again.'" Dad guffawed and shook his head.

"I thought, 'You stupid jerk. What are you going to say, as an FBI agent, that you would worry about?'" Dad held his hands out, palms up—the sign for what-can-you-do? "But old Stanford is really just stupid. You know, he probably would come in out of the rain, but wait until he got real soaked before he did it." He shook with laughter. Watching him, we laughed too.

"You mean, he'd say, 'I wonder why I'm getting so wet'?" I asked.

Dad said: "Yeah. That's about right. Just couldn't figure out a simple thing like that." He laughed again. "These are the guys who're supposed to be investigating civil rights attacks. No wonder nothing ever gets done."

Civil rights activists throughout the South had long recognized that the FBI frequently cooperated with local police in suppressing demonstrations and thwarting their efforts to achieve progress in race relations. Under J. Edgar Hoover's leadership, the FBI displayed strong racial prejudices.

Despite such known collusion, in August 1963 Dad asked the FBI to check whether the local police had been tapping telephones in Dr. Pitt's home, the Alabama Council office, and our home. They never reported back to him. However, while we were on vacation, friends said the newspaper carried an article stating that three unidentified telephone lines had been tapped. That seemed to confirm Dad's suspicions.

As the tensions mounted in Birmingham, Dad's role as executive director of the Alabama Council on Human Relations attracted attention from the

Klan and other radical segregationists. Threats against council members increased. One faction of the governing board of a local church vowed to have an assistant minister expelled from his job if he did not resign from the Alabama Council. Another member reported that his employer called him into the office and asked if he was a communist, after hearing the slander directed against the council.

Under Bull Connor's orders, the Birmingham police sent spies to every meeting of the local Birmingham Council. Patrol cars circled the parking lots outside and wrote down license numbers. Information about meeting participants and issues discussed quickly circulated through the city. The Klan and other segregationist groups obtained names, addresses, and phone numbers of council members. Even financial details about my grandfather's business in Pennsylvania showed up in reports attacking the council and alleging its connections to communist organizations and individuals.

By early 1962, Dad's office in the Comer Building received a barrage of harassing phone calls. From the time he got to the office, people would call up to harangue him and his secretary. Only a handful of callers actually threatened to kill him. But several times a day, belligerent voices, threatening in tone, called them names and cussed them out. Nasty, derogatory remarks. Calling them communists, nigger lovers, whatever insults they could think up.

The office secretary, Mrs. Annette Cox, came from a poor-white background. "She's a plain, ordinary person, from a redneck family," Dad told us. "She gets so frustrated because she can't respond to them. She tries to answer, but they hang up after making some nasty remarks. It just drives her crazy."

When John Brewbaker, the Southern Regional Council consultant on school desegregation, visited Dad's office, he noticed that Dad always locked the door when he went out. Mrs. Cox reported that someone had just called and said, in a deep voice, "I'm coming up there and kill you all." Then he hung up. In his report to SRC, Brewbaker stated: "Jimerson said they had been receiving quite a few calls of this kind, and I could see that he was tense and jittery."

As the frequency of harassing phone calls increased, Dad asked David Vann for advice about how to respond. Vann told him the best thing he could do would be to "laugh it off." He said that, with the Chamber of Commerce and other business leaders being attacked as communists, the radical segregationists were going to "take enough rope to hang themselves."

"I don't know about that," Dad told us. "But I sure hope he's right."

"Rrriiiinng . . . rrriing . . . rrriiinnngg."

The telephone was in the small hallway at the top of the basement stairs, on a stand next to the bathroom door. Mom and Dad had gone to a meeting. I was babysitting.

"Rrriiiinng . . . rrriing . . . rrriiinnngg."

I walked to the back hallway, and picked up the receiver. "Hello?"

No one answered. "Hello?" I repeated. Nothing but silence.

"Who are you calling?" I asked. I could hear someone breathing heavily. A man, I thought.

"What do you want?" Nothing.

"I can't hear you." Still, he didn't speak. Finally, I hung up the phone. Not good manners, I knew, but what else could I do?

Before long, these anonymous telephone calls became frequent. Almost daily at times. Usually in the evening, sometimes late at night. Especially, it seemed, when Dad was out of town. Mom would answer the phone usually, or if she was busy I would. It was something the oldest child should do.

When people called our house and didn't say anything, I felt nervous. Only silence or heavy breathing. Sometimes I would just hold onto the receiver to see just how long they would stay on. And sometimes they'd wait, and I'd get tired and just hang up on them. Or I would try to talk to them. I'd say, "Stop bothering us. Leave us alone!" Or: "This isn't right! It's not how you should treat people." Then I would hear a click or a loud crash of the receiver being slammed down, and the electric buzz of the empty phone line.

"Another dud," I said after such silent phone calls. Mom said her friends called them "hate calls."

The silent harassment of these voiceless calls annoyed us—as intended. But threatening calls, when people cursed us or said they would kill us, produced shivers up the spine and a sense of dread.

One night when I answered the phone, a gravelly voice drawled, "Your daddy's gonna be six feet under if he don't stop."

I slammed down the receiver, went to the bedroom, and buried my face in the pillow.

When the telephone harassment that Dad received at his office reached our home, he knew he had to help us cope with the fear and frustration. He resumed the "family devotions" that had started in Hopewell when he was trying to decide whether to take the Alabama Council job. After dinner, he would round us all up in the living room. Often one or more of us would resist, or complain about being interrupted in watching TV or something else. Sometimes it took a threat of spanking or a slap on the bottom for one of us to obey. Not a good way to start a serious discussion.

As in Hopewell, Dad began with a Bible verse or prayer. Then he would tell us about what was going on—usually regarding the civil rights struggles in Alabama, or his own work. He tried to explain why people made threatening phone calls. About the long history of slavery and racial prejudice. About the Klan and White Citizens' Councils. About social classes—the Big Mules who ran the state, the poor whites, the factory workers, the black victims of oppression, violence, lynchings, and police brutality. He didn't read much, but he was learning from W. J. Cash's *The Mind of the South,* C. Vann Woodward's *The Strange Career of Jim Crow,* and Southern Regional Council reports.

Mom often tried to help him interpret these things in ways that we could understand. They discussed issues they thought we needed to know about. It was a chance for us to ask questions. We couldn't always articulate the worries or fears that crept up on us, or clouded our minds with anxiety or doubt. But talking together as a family helped. It created a bond, a sense of solidarity that we would help protect each other. We would face these difficult situations together.

Ann and I were old enough to feel engaged, to understand what was happening around us, to feel part of the movement. The harassing phone calls began just before Ann turned eleven and I turned thirteen. It seemed much harder for the younger kids, Paul and Susie. By March 1962 Paul had just celebrated his eighth birthday and Susie was six and a half.

Dad told us we were not alone. "These phone calls are common for anyone who takes even some moderate position on race," he said. "We get together with friends and compare notes on what kind of phone calls we've had lately." He grinned, thinking about this. "It's almost a competition, to see who got the worst call—or the craziest one."

"When calls come to the office," he said, "people find out I'm a minister, and then quote scriptures to me, supporting segregation."

"But what can you do to stop them?" Ann asked.

"You just don't give up," Dad answered. "You know you're doing the right thing. What Jesus preached. If you follow him, the world will revile you. . . . But you can feel good about yourself."

Threatening phone calls continued as long as we lived in Birmingham. One day in 1963, after my father had hired a black secretary, Mom and Dad had company, a northern minister visiting to learn about the civil rights efforts in Birmingham.

When the phone rang, I answered so they wouldn't have to interrupt their conversation.

"Hello?"

"We're gonna git you and your nigger secretary!" a harsh voice rasped. "Y'hear me? I got some rope and I'm gonna git you both!"

I banged down the receiver. I stood there looking at the ugly black telephone.

Mom's voice called: "Randy? Who was it?" Then she was standing next to me. "Are you OK?"

I told her what I had heard.

"Oh, no!" she exclaimed. She hugged me. "It's OK," she said. "They're too cowardly to do that. . . . We won't let anyone hurt you."

I went back to my room, as Mom returned to the living room. After a few minutes, I heard a knock on the door. Dad said that the minister wanted to speak to me.

We stood in the hallway outside my bedroom, next to the telephone.

"Son," he said. "I just want you to know: there are two kinds of men, good men and bad men." He looked into my eyes. "Your father is a good man. He's doing what God wants us to do."

He smiled at me. "Your father is one of the bravest men I've met. You need to be brave, too." He leaned over, so our faces were at the same level. "This is going to be all right. You're going to be OK." He paused and put his hands on my shoulders. "You should be very proud of your father. And your mother. And they can be proud of you."

One night when Dad was out of town, Mom heard a loud "Boom!" out front. Quickly she rolled out of bed onto the floor, away from the front bedroom window. She thought it was a bomb. But she soon realized it had been a car backfiring.

In the morning she told us what had happened. "The worst part is that I tried to save myself instead of protecting you children," she confessed. "I felt guilty all night about not being a good mother."

"You're the best mother anyone could have," we told her.

During ninth grade I had a paper route in the neighborhood. On Sundays, when he was in town, Dad sometimes drove me around, because the papers would not all fit in my bicycle baskets. Paul, a fourth grader, sometimes helped. One of the women on the route was Paul's Cub Scout leader, who lived down the street. She also attended Pilgrim Congregational, the church where Reverend Al Henry had been threatened for speaking out on civil rights issues.

In July 1964, while Dad was out of town for several days, a barrage of harassing phone calls began. Mom answered the phone for the first call.

A woman's voice said: "I don't want you or your children coming to my church and Sunday school." She said we were communists and "nigger lovers."

Mom said: "Those are all lies! Who is this?"

"Never mind," the woman answered. "Are you going on vacation with the Henrys? I just thought maybe we should fumigate the church while you're gone. It's smelling of niggers these days. We thought maybe we'd better fumigate to get rid of the rat smell."

Mom replied: "I think it would be an excellent idea—and get rid of *yourself*." She hung up.

A short while later the phone rang again. Paul answered this time: "Hello?"

A woman said: "You tell your father I'm sick and tired of seeing him deliver papers, and I'm going to place a complaint to the *Birmingham News*." Then she banged down the receiver.

Mom had picked up the other phone, in her bedroom, just in time to recognize that it was the same woman. She began crying.

Paul asked: "What's the matter, Mommy?" She told him what the woman had said earlier.

"Why would she *do* that?" he blurted out. "She's my den mother!"

Paul had recognized her voice. He admired his Cub Scout leader. When he heard the hatred in her voice, he became very upset. It was a real shock that an adult he liked and trusted would be so mean to his mother.

Mom placed a pencil near the telephone and began taking notes about the phone calls that came in while Dad was out of town. The next threat came the following day. She wrote:

Sat. July 18.
To Paul: "Is your mother going to sing a spiritual at church?" (No answer.)
      "Well, is she going to sing a spiritual?"
Melva: "Don't you speak to my child! Don't speak to my child!"

Voice: "Are you going to sing a nigger spiritual?"

Melva (sweetly): "No, but I will if you want."

Voice: "No, we don't want that."

Melva: "I'll be glad to sing one."

Voice: "I understand your husband has the countenance of a dog." (Some more degrading words.)

Melva: "Do you know my husband?"

Voice: "No—but I understand he looks like a dog."

Melva: "If you don't know my husband then you have no right to say anything about him—he's a fine Christian man."

Voice: "He's sold out to the niggers."

Melva: "If you don't like Negroes, you'd better check your Christianity."

Voice interrupts: "You've sold out to the niggers too."

"You're supposed to love everyone. That's all I have to say." I hang up.

Monday July 19th.

Caller (voice disguised as Negro): "Your husband and Mr. E——, that Commie, make a good pair."

Melva: "Go ahead."

Caller: "You have a lot of nerve, don't you?"

Melva: "Uh huh. Go ahead."

Caller: "Well, that's not all you're going to have—we're not done with you (or words to that effect)."

A few minutes later. Again, voice disguised as Negro.

Caller: "I hear your husband and that nigger secretary of his sho' are havin' a time down there. You'd better check into it."

Melva: "You're being very adolescent doing all this calling, you know. Who are you?"

Caller: "I'm askin' the questions."

Melva: "You're being very immature with your telephoning."

Caller: "Well, you'd better see what that nigger and your husband are doing."

Melva: "I'm not worried about my husband. You can't scare me that way. GOOD BYE."

Mom's last note read: "She's talking away as I hang up."

The tension created by threatening phone calls and other forms of intimidation began to take a toll on each of us. Especially Paul. The vicious attacks from his Cub Scout den mother undermined his sense of security and his trust in human kindness. It didn't help that Dad frequently came home and reported his own observations of bigotry, violence, and hatred on the civil rights front. As Mom said, he brought home all the grief he carried around during the day, and unloaded it at the supper table. Finally, our pediatrician told Mom that Dad had to stop placing this psychological burden on his family. It had begun to affect our health and mental outlook.

One incident stands out. Members of the American Baptist Convention's Evangelism Committee traveled to Alabama to present a check to Dr. Martin Luther King Jr. They contacted Dad, who had retained his American Baptist ministerial credentials. Dad invited them to visit our house. They talked about the racial tensions in Birmingham and other concerns. Paul must have overheard enough of the conversation to recognize that their support for integration could arouse hostility among white supremacists. When they left, Paul said, "Do you think they'll bomb the house tonight?" Until then, Mom and Dad didn't know that he was carrying that much fear.

Mom later said: "I shall never know the stigma of being black, but after three years of being ostracized by most whites around us in Alabama, I could sense just a small taste of the feeling of being shunned by fellow human beings."

8

A Good Samaritan

"Hey, Randy, did'ja hear? Mike got shot?"

Monday morning. I was walking to school. One of the younger boys in the neighborhood ran to catch up to me. He said my best friend had been shot.

"Yeah . . ." I mumbled. I was confused. Who would shoot Mike? Why? Would he die? I didn't want to let on that I didn't know something this important about my best friend. Why didn't I know?

Hushed but excited whispers quickly spread the news through Shades Cahaba School. Mike Ham's father was manager at The Club, an exclusive members-only gathering place atop Red Mountain, overlooking Birmingham. The city's wealthiest—businessmen, lawyers, doctors—belonged. On Sunday morning, Mike accompanied his father while a security guard inspected a door that didn't swing properly. As the guard bent over to inspect, his revolver fell from its holster to the floor. The gun discharged, sending a bullet through Mike's chest. It collapsed a lung, but did not kill him.

An ambulance crew had rushed Mike to the University of Alabama Medical Center, at the foot of Red Mountain. By the time I heard the news he was recovering from surgery and in stable condition. Still too soon for visitors.

By Wednesday, Mom said it would be OK to see Mike. After school I took a bus to the medical center, found Mike's room, and tentatively knocked on the door.

My best friend, looking pale, lay propped up on a high bed, with tubes attached to his arm. He wore a hospital gown. He looked like a patient on *Dr. Kildare.* He smiled when he saw me.

"How'ya doin'?" I asked.

Mike said: "OK. Gettin' better, I guess."

"Some people will do *any*thing for extra attention!" I said. "Everybody's talkin' about you at school."

Mike tried to laugh. "Well, I don't recommend it."

I remembered the box of chocolates I had brought, and held it out. "Here," I said. "Best medicine for someone who's been shot."

As I waited for the bus to go home, I thought about Mike's accident. I had never known anyone who had been shot. Mom always warned us about playing with BB guns. Her grandfather had lost an eye, as a boy, trying to shoot an arrow through a keyhole at his family's sheep farm in England. A neighbor at the Reformatory in Virginia had lost his right eye from a BB gunshot. But this was a real gun. Mike came a few inches from being killed.

Mike's accidental shooting made the stories I heard of black people being shot, beaten, and lynched seem more real. Fortunately, he was not killed or permanently injured. But the possibility of being shot now seemed closer. More personal.

As the early Alabama spring arrived, with songbirds and flowering dogwoods, Dad's cross-state travels increased. Delays inherent in relying on bus transportation—such as the January layover in Cullman due to snowy roads—irritated an impatient man with work to do. At the February 1962 board of directors meeting, he proposed purchasing an automobile for his travels. Instead, the board approved increasing his mileage allowance.

With this modest financial support, Dad decided to buy a second car. Otherwise, he would either have to rely on an inconvenient bus system or leave Mom without a car during his frequent trips. The car he settled on was a used 1958 Volkswagen beetle, an inexpensive but cantankerous vehicle.

The rust-colored "bug" featured a rear-mounted engine, a small front luggage compartment with a spare tire, and narrow running boards. The engine roared loudly, so it was difficult to hold a conversation, and it chugged slowly up hills. Someone had already popped the colorful front medallion. It was hard to find a VW with an original company medallion, since teenaged boys prized them as souvenirs.

When I had a day off from school, Dad sometimes took me with him on a business day trip. On one trip, along a lonely concrete road between Birmingham and Montgomery, the car ran out of gas.

"Watch this!" Dad said. "This VW doesn't need a gas gauge. It's got an emergency tank."

He reached below the dashboard and turned a L-shaped metal handle. "This opens the spare tank. It's got just enough gas to get us to the next filling station."

Dad turned the key, but the ignition only sputtered and did not crank over. "Hmmm," Dad said. He tried again. Nothing. He opened the hood and looked in the gas tank.

Dad slid back in behind the steering wheel. He looked at me sheepishly. "Well, I guess it works better if you remember to close the emergency tank *before* it uses up all the gas."

I waited in the car while Dad hitched a ride to a gas station.

On another trip, the VW chugged along a narrow county road, with hot wind whipping through the open windows. Suddenly the front hood popped open and flew up in front of the windshield. I thought we were about to die in a fiery crash.

Dad bent low to peek through a small gap at the bottom of the window, while he braked to a stop on the weed-choked shoulder.

"Forgot to tie that down last time I got gas!" he explained.

I began to understand why Mom was always on alert when Dad drove. "Jim, watch the road! Not the scenery!" she would say. When Dad's eyelids started to sag shut, or his chin drooped towards his chest, she would cry out: "Wake up, Jim!" Then: "If you're tired, pull over!"

Mom and I both thought Dad would more likely die in a car wreck than a Klan ambush. Although both seemed possible.

"Where's Susie?" Mom asked. "Has anyone seen her?"

Ann said: "She was playing with Cheryl a while ago. I saw them going down to the creek."

Six-year-old Susie always had a lot of energy, running freely around the neighborhood. Some people called her a "wild child" or a tomboy. But she never got into trouble. And she had never stayed out after dark like this.

Mom sent Ann, Paul, and me in different directions. "Find her!" Mom cried out. "Look everywhere!"

"Susie! Where are you!" we yelled. We searched the woods near the creek, all through the neighbors' yards, behind bushes and fences.

Mom called Cheryl's mother, and then the parents of Travis and Tracy, the twins Susie often played with. When Dad came home from work, he knocked on the other neighbors' doors.

Paul and I searched through the house, every room, behind the shower curtain, inside the kitchen and bathroom cupboards. I could smell the pungent odor of ammonia. Mom was soaking all our combs and brushes in the bathroom sink. Then we scoured the basement, including the crawlspace.

Grandma Jim was visiting, from Corning, New York. As Mom frantically ran through the living room, where she was calmly rocking, Grandma Jim said: "I never lost any of *my* children. If you look after them properly. . . ."

Mom gritted her teeth, but didn't say anything.

The longer Susie remained missing, the darker our imaginations grew. We feared the worst. An hour seemed like a week.

Finally, Susie walked into the living room. I heard Ann yell: "Here she is! She's OK!"

Through sobs—mixed with fear and embarrassment—Susie began to tell what happened. She had stayed out as late as she could with Cheryl. When she did come in, she said, "I wondered how long it would take you to notice if I was back."

She decided to hide in the hall closet. When she realized the commotion she had created, she crawled under our parents' bed. Susie thought it was funny at first. Then she realized she would get in trouble when she came out from hiding. The longer she waited, the more frightened she grew.

Everyone felt relieved that she was safe. But then Mom and Dad got angry, because of the fright she had given them. For punishment Susie got a real scolding, but not a beating. Worst of all, she said later, it was embarrassing, especially since Grandma Jim was there.

"At least it wasn't the Klan," I thought.

"We'll have to eat without your father," Mom said. "I don't know why he's not here yet."

As we sat around the oval dining table, ready for fish sticks and mashed potatoes, the phone rang.

"Hello?" Mom answered.

"Jim, where are you?" A long pause.

"Oh, no!" Mom said. "Yes . . . yes. . . . Let me know when you can. I'll save supper for you."

When she came back to the table, Mom looked upset. "There's been a terrible accident. Three young people in a convertible. . . ." She wiped her eyes with a napkin. "One of them is dead. Your father saw the accident, and stayed to help. He's going to the hospital with the other two."

An hour or two later, after I finished washing the dishes and started my homework, the phone rang again. This time I answered.

Dad's voice: "Randy? Tell your mother I'll be back late. I'm at the hospital."

"What happened?" I asked.

I could only pick up phrases: "Three Howard College students . . . speeding . . . convertible hit a tree . . . one died at the scene . . . one will survive."

Mom had picked up the phone in her bedroom. "Oh, Jim! How awful!"

Dad said: "I've been with the young woman. The doctors don't think she'll make it. A metal bar went right through her throat. . . . All I can do is hold her hand and pray for her."

It was after midnight before Dad's VW chugged to a stop in front of the house. I was supposed to be asleep.

I could hear Dad tell Mom: "I held her hand until she died." I thought about the parable of the Good Samaritan. The man who stopped to help a stranger along the road. That's what Dad would do. Whenever he saw someone in trouble, he stopped to help. A good neighbor should help anyone in need. That's how Dad saw himself. But he also simply wanted to be part of the action.

The Alabama Council on Human Relations provided a perfect opportunity for someone who wanted to be part of the action in the volatile field of civil rights. A Good Samaritan found plenty of people in trouble, needing assistance.

During the spring of 1962, Birmingham's racial climate grew increasingly tense, with threats of violence a constant undercurrent. Students at Miles College launched a "selective buying campaign" to encourage blacks to patronize only stores that did not discriminate against them. Since boycotts were illegal, they passed out mimeographed sheets urging people to spend their money "wisely." By the end of March, black leaders estimated that this campaign was 80 to 85 percent effective. White store owners admitted it hurt their business.

Through his friendship with Dr. Lucius Pitts, Dad served as liaison between the black leaders and moderate white business owners and clergymen. He and Dr. Pitts arranged meetings for a small group of students and businessmen to discuss the students' demands. The white community leaders engaged in these meetings included Sid Smyer, president of Birmingham Realty, Episcopal Assistant Bishop George Murray, and downtown ministers such as Reverend Ed Ramage of First Presbyterian Church. Dad thought these meetings were very productive. White leaders acknowledged that racial policies needed to change, and blacks recognized the whites' willingness to make progress. Both sides got acquainted and learned to discuss their concerns openly. This would be especially significant a year later, when Birmingham's racial problems boiled over.

Because he had quickly established a reputation for honesty and fairness, my father gained access to some of Birmingham's most powerful business leaders. Most southerners would trust a white Baptist preacher, even a Yankee. They could tell an outsider things they would never entrust to anyone in their own social circles. On March 7, for example, Dad met with Arthur Weibel, president of the Tennessee Coal and Iron Division of U.S. Steel Corporation, one of the most influential business leaders in Birmingham.

Weibel asked for suggestions for how he might help to promote peaceful solutions of racial tensions. After the meeting, Dad sent him a detailed letter outlining steps that the company could take. The first step should be to establish a corporate policy to endorse "preservation of public school and recreational systems as essential to the economic stability of the area," and to support "peaceful compliance with decisions of the courts, State or Federal," to maintain law and order.

After other recommendations, Dad concluded the letter to Art Weibel: "I am confident such action by you, as indicated above, would have an enormously beneficial effect upon the whole situation in Birmingham. I appreciate the courtesy which you have shown me in discussing at length the situation in Birmingham and assure you of my interest in and understanding of your situation. Please feel free to call upon me at any time that I may be of any assistance to you."

At the same time that he developed good working relationships with the white business community, Dad also strengthened his ties to the black leadership in Birmingham and throughout Alabama. He also made important connections with national leaders, including federal government officials, journalists, and religious leaders.

Reverend Herbert Oliver, a black minister who had been investigating police brutality, asked Dad to help him in planning and leading a human relations workshop, held March 21–23, 1962, at Miles College. The main speakers included Dr. James McBride Dabbs, president of the Southern Regional

Council; Reverend Andrew Young, one of Dr. Martin Luther King's lieutenants in the Southern Christian Leadership Conference; Dr. Charles Gomillion, president of the Tuskegee Civic Association (and a long-term member of the Alabama Council); and Mrs. Frances Pauley, executive director of the Georgia Council on Human Relations. Dad served as one of the discussion leaders. In a bow to ecumenism, Rabbi Harold Gelfman of Macon, Georgia, spoke at a concluding chapel meeting, on "Judaism's Position on Contemporary Problems."

Following the Miles College workshop, Dad traveled to Washington, D.C., in late March. The extent of his contacts there—with federal officials, journalists, and other prominent figures—would be impressive for anyone, let alone an obscure staff member of a Deep South civil rights organization. Key Kennedy administration figures he met included: Burke Marshall, assistant attorney general for civil rights issues, and two of his staff members; Berl Bernhard, staff director of the U.S. Commission on Civil Rights, and several of his staff; and John Field of the President's Committee on Equal Employment Opportunities.

On Capitol Hill, Dad met with Alabama Senators Lister Hill and John Sparkman, Senator Phil Hart of Michigan, New York Senator Kenneth Keating, and the administrative assistant to Senator Jacob Javits of New York. When Dad went to meet with Senator Hart, he was in the midst of a critical debate on the Senate floor. He left the debate to talk with Dad for ten minutes. Senator Hart told him, "The only reason I came off the floor was because I wanted to see what someone who would take the job you have would look like."

Developing his connections with journalists, Dad met with Bob Baker and Jim Clayton of the *Washington Post* and Herb Kaplow of NBC-TV. He talked with influential columnist Drew Pearson by phone, and one of Pearson's writers interviewed him at greater length. During this trip, Dad also spoke to a women's group and an "informed couples" group at an Episcopal church in Mt. Rainier, Maryland, and attended the Annual Clearing House of the American Civil Liberties Union. He also contacted Harold Fleming, of the Taconic Foundation, as a possible funding source for the Alabama Council.

These connections helped bring the racial problems in Birmingham to national attention. Dad soon gained a reputation as the person to contact when journalists and others interested in learning more about civil rights visited Birmingham. Dad suggested whom they should meet, and helped facilitate introductions. Among the many people that Dad helped, in addition to those he met on the March trip to Washington, the names he often mentioned included Richard Valeriani of NBC News and Robert Coles, prominent Harvard professor and child psychologist, who had gained national recognition for his articles concerning children desegregating New Orleans schools. Coles's visits—Dad drove him around the city to meet key people in the civil rights controversies—made Dad especially proud.

Throughout his years with the Alabama Council, Dad maintained communications with influential contacts in the federal government, the national media, and non-profit organizations. In particular, he provided frequent reports and updates to Burke Marshall, John Field, and John Doar, an attorney with the Justice Department's Civil Rights Division.

Returning to Birmingham after his March 1962 trip to the nation's capital, Dad found progress on racial problems slowing down. Despite the advances being made, behind the scenes, in the interracial meetings that Dad helped set up, City Hall continued its adamant opposition to reducing segregation barriers. On April 3, the city commissioners eliminated Birmingham's contribution to the surplus food program. When Bull Connor moved to cut off the food program in retaliation for the selective buying campaign, it carried unanimously. A *Birmingham Post-Herald* editorial argued that blacks boycotting stores "are being shortsighted indeed," since this cut-off of food distribution would hurt the needy. The editorial stated that, "carried out to the ultimate, it could result in the building of another Berlin Wall between the races and strident demands for tough reprisals including the loss of jobs."

In a confidential report to the Southern Regional Council on April 5, Dad discussed the food program and other issues. "The political pot is boiling in Alabama," he wrote. Among other improvements, several blacks had been accepted as candidates for the Democratic Committee of Jefferson County, which included Birmingham. But they would be running under the state party emblem, a white rooster with the slogan "white supremacy for the right."

Another state political issue could affect racial policies and the interests of black people. David Vann, who largely kept secret his affiliation with the Alabama Council, led a committee seeking to reapportion the Alabama legislature. The local papers quoted him saying that "the Black Belt counties have an unfair advantage. They now dominate the entire state." Since the nineteenth century the humus-rich Black Belt, forming the agricultural heart of central Alabama, had retained the political power first established by cotton-growing plantation owners. Birmingham and other urban industrial cities complained of under-representation in the political system.

In his quarterly report for March–May 1962, Dad reported to the Southern Regional Council some signs of progress in Birmingham and Alabama: "There are indications that gradually more businessmen are recognizing that racial problems must be solved if the state is to develop economically. The local chapters of the Council do little more than meet regularly, but in Alabama this is still an accomplishment and provides a very important benchmark of good will and decency to give members some sense of stability."

By early 1962, Paul Rilling began to recognize the important achievements of the Alabama Council director. After a visit to Birmingham on February 23, Rilling reported: "One of the most depressing factors of the Birmingham situation is the apathy and divisiveness of the Negro community. The Ware group, the Shuttlesworth group, the Gaston circle, are working at cross-purposes and constantly at loggerheads." He concluded that Dad's close friend Lucius Pitts could "play an extremely strategic role." As president of Miles College, he had "an automatic status position," and as a newcomer to the city he remained free from "any of the cliques or factions in the community." During the primary campaign for governor, attorney Charles Morgan Jr. "expects that Connor will make a major issue of the Alabama Council in the later stages of his campaign, attempting to use it as a whipping boy." This growing attention gained by the council thus brought the danger of further attacks.

Rilling concluded: "It seems to me that Jimerson is moving with great skill and responsibility in this situation. He has spoken personally to most of the leading persons involved, including the white businessmen, and has established excellent rapport with several. He already has better contacts with the white leadership than did Bob Hughes. This may be a sign of the changing times."

During the first week of March, Rilling again came to Alabama. His "Travel Memo" to SRC Director Leslie Dunbar reported that the white leadership seeking to reduce tensions fell into two camps: those who urged moderate action, but refused to meet with black leaders under any circumstances, and a second group of businessmen willing to consult with black leaders. Prominent in the latter group were James Head, chairman of the Committee of 100 and a liberal businessman, and Sidney Smyer, president of the Chamber of Commerce. Rilling commented: "Smyer is a Dixiecrat politically, but seems sincerely desirous of working out a mutually satisfactory arrangement which would involve some changes." These were two of the men with whom Dad had worked closely in setting up biracial discussions about the selective buying campaign.

Again, Rilling concluded with praise for the Alabama Council director:

> I am quite impressed with the vigor and skill with which Jimerson seems to be operating. In Birmingham he seems to have complete access to the Negro leadership and is generally trusted. At the same time, he has access to business leadership reaching high into the power structure, and is trusted by these men with attitudes varying from appreciation to skepticism to patronizing. Head speaks of him with warm appreciation. . . . I was impressed during the conference Friday at the number of people who pass messages through him, back and forth across the racial lines and across factional lines within the Negro community. I doubt if in any other state, with the possible exception of Virginia and Tennessee, does our director have as open access to as many elements in both communities.

In the openly hostile environment of Birmingham, being able to bridge the racial divide required skill, patience, and tact. Few people could win the trust and confidence of both sides. In just over half a year since arriving in Alabama, Dad had achieved recognition for his peacemaking efforts.

At Shades Cahaba School, however, I began to feel more and more antagonism. Criticism for not attending the "approved" Baptist church first alerted me to my teachers' disapproval. It seemed bad enough to be a "damn Yankee"— but being called a "nigger lover" and a "communist" made me begin to feel like a social outcast.

My seventh-grade math teacher was a small thin woman with dark hair. I remember three things about her, but not her name:

First: After each test, she seated us by our test score, front to back from right to left. Usually I earned a seat in the first row, along the right wall. But one time I scored only 40 percent on a test, and had to move all the way to the left row, near the windows. It was Dr. Dick's fault. My orthodontist had to pull my four "eye" teeth, because I had fangs. New teeth had grown over my existing teeth and protruded through the gums. I had to leave school at lunch time for a painful extraction of the two right-side eye teeth. Instead of going home, in pain and numbness, I returned to school to take a math test. I had to wait until the next test to return to my usual "neighbors" on the right side of the classroom. By then I wore the uncomfortable metal rings, wires, and rubber bands of new braces.

Second: Fortunately for me, my math teacher was a baseball fan. When I saw an ad in the paper that Jimmy Piersall, one of my favorite major league players, would be demonstrating a new batting-tee device at Newberry's Department Store, she gave me a permission slip to leave school. I took a bus downtown to meet one of my heroes. Not Roberto Clemente, unfortunately, but Piersall would do.

I asked for his autograph, and he handed me a promotional card with his photo and a printed signature. "Here, kid," he said.

"But that's just a copy; I want a *real* autograph," I said. He sighed, but reluctantly signed the newspaper ad, which I had brought with me. I still have it.

Third: My most vivid memory of math class occurred one day when I was sitting in the front seat of the first row. I had scored the highest grade on the previous test. In the midst of class—with no lead-up or transition that I could remember—the teacher said: "These communists are trying to ruin our way of life. All these organizations that are called 'human rights' or 'human relations' in their names are just *full* of communists."

I froze in my seat. I couldn't understand why she had said this. "Doesn't she know my father works for the Alabama Council on *Human Relations*?" I wondered. "She must be talking about *me!*"

I wanted to say, "That's not true!" but I couldn't speak. We were supposed to respect adults, especially teachers. We weren't supposed to question their authority. I didn't know what to do. Later, I felt embarrassed that I had not said anything. I didn't have Dad's courage.

My best friend moved away. Mike Ham's older brother, Lamar, had recently gotten his driver's license. One chilly day, he drove down Saulter Road in his parents' huge black Buick, with wide flat tail fins. After going only a block, he leaned over to adjust the heater. The car swerved right, off the road. A boy in Ann's fifth-grade class was sweeping his driveway. He died instantly.

After the funeral, the boy's parents asked the Hams not to park the Buick on the street, where they had to see it almost every time they left their house.

The Hams had to park in back, in their driveway that, like ours, came up steeply from the narrow back alley.

The Hams decided it would be best to leave. They moved to a house across town, closer to The Club, where Mr. Ham worked. After they moved, I only saw Mike occasionally at school. Our friendship lasted only as long as we lived next door.

Soon our neighbors on the other side also put up a "For Sale" sign and moved away. They had a young son. Ann had been their regular babysitter. So she lost her best customers.

They left without saying good-bye. Later, another neighbor confided to Mom that the young woman had said they found out that Dad worked in civil rights. They didn't want to live next door to communists. They thought we would sell our house to "nigras." Mom cried when she told us this.

What Mom didn't tell us, until much later, was that the constant accusations that the Alabama Council was a communist organization—and that Dad must be a communist—had begun to shake her up. She had started reading parts of *Masters of Deceit,* by J. Edgar Hoover. If the FBI director thought that all civil rights organizations had been infiltrated by communists, perhaps some of these charges were true. Maybe the neighbors were right.

Mom had only known Dad for a few weeks when they married. Could he have been a communist before that? Was becoming a minister merely a cover? What about the Austrian couple active in the Alabama Council, Frederick and Anny Kraus? She began to imagine what they might be doing as subversives.

Hoover's book, and the allegations being made about the Alabama Council, almost convinced her that her husband might be in the wrong place, doing the wrong thing. "Maybe Jim got mixed up with dangerous people—without realizing it," she worried. These doubts came and went. But her uncertainty deeply troubled her sometimes. Social ostracism and hatred caused enough heartache. Thinking that the accusers might be right felt unbearable.

Occasionally when Dad grew bored or wanted some added excitement—or just somebody to talk to—he would look up Chuck Morgan, the attorney on retainer with the Alabama Council. One night in late April 1962, while talking in a motel lobby near the Birmingham airport, they bumped into Buster Hogan, Jim Folsom's campaign manager. It was the final weeks before the

Democratic primary for governor. "Big Jim" Folsom, seeking to revive his political career with a third non-consecutive term as governor, faced stiff competition from his former protégé George C. Wallace, Bull Connor, Attorney General MacDonald Gallion, and Ryan De Graffenried, a young state senator from Tuscaloosa. Wallace had promised to "stand in the door" to prevent school integration. He, Connor, and Gallion competed for the votes of die-hard segregationists. All three attacked Folsom for his lack of vigor in shoring up segregation.

On April 6, during a campaign speech at the courthouse square in Talladega, fifty miles east of Birmingham, Folsom had encountered a demonstration by black students from Talladega College. An increasingly militant student protest demanded desegregation of public accommodations.

After talking with Morgan and David Vann, Dad had decided to go to Talladega as a mediator to get conversation started between the demonstrators, who were being arrested by the police during lunch-counter sit-ins, and the segregationists, who supported the police. On April 11, Dad drove to Talladega. First he visited the three drugstores where black students had been arrested for sitting down at lunch counters, and talked with the store owners about setting up negotiations with the demonstrators.

Then he visited Talladega College, which had been started by Congregationalists during Reconstruction. Reverend Everett MacNair, a retired white Congregational minister serving as college chaplain, invited Dad for lunch at his home. They had corn-on-the-cob and a pleasant conversation.

After lunch, they went to the college and met with Dorothy Vails, a young student who had organized the demonstrations, and several other students. The students expressed no interest in negotiations. Dad said: "They were really angry about segregation. They were angry with the police. They were angry about everything. And they were not the least bit interested in talking with me about negotiations. They weren't really angry *at* me, but totally uninterested in anything I had to say."

At Talladega College, Dad also met with Dr. Arthur Gray, president of the college. Dad said: "He is a typical hat-in-hand Negro, bowing and scraping, trying to avoid trouble."

The demonstrations continued for more than two weeks. Now, on April 25 at the Birmingham airport motel, Folsom's campaign manager told Morgan that the demonstrations damaged Big Jim's campaign. People viewed the demonstrators as making an appeal to a sympathetic candidate for help. After learning about Dad's position with the Alabama Council, Buster Hogan began begging Morgan to send Dad back to Talladega to try to quiet things down.

The next day, April 26, Dad returned to Talladega. This time he talked to the chief of police, offering to assist in arranging negotiations to end the confrontation. The chief said, "You live in Talladega?"

Dad said, "No."

He said, "Where you from?"

Dad said, "Birmingham."

The police chief said, "Get your ass back to Birmingham."

It was a short conversation.

Later, Dad said: "I thought that was really ironic." He laughed. "I was a *Yankee* from New York State, and all he wanted was for me to get back to *Birmingham*. Sheesh! If he knew where I'm really from—." His voice trailed off.

Before heading home, Dad attended a meeting of the white ministers group of Talladega, as the guest of Reverend MacNair, a member of the group. Dad introduced himself as a Baptist minister from Birmingham, working with the Alabama Council on Human Relations. He said he came to Talladega to try setting up negotiations. Then they debated for forty-five minutes, whether to let him attend the meeting.

After about a half-hour, one minister looked at Dad and said, "I know one thing. I'm smart enough to know when I'm not wanted."

Dad thought, "Well, I may not be smart enough, but this is so *curious,* I wouldn't want to leave." Finally they decided he could stay. Dad speculated that the ministers feared someone dealing in race relations might contaminate the group. But they definitely were not interested at all in getting involved to set up negotiations, which was his purpose in going to Talladega.

That was Thursday. On Sunday, April 29, after attending church and having lunch, Mom and Dad sat on aluminum and plastic mesh lawn chairs on our small front porch, reading the newspaper. We children played in the yard, enjoying a warm sunny afternoon. A lazy day in Alabama.

"Jim, look at this!" Mom exclaimed. A front-page article in the *Birmingham News* stated "200 Demonstrators Arrested in Talladega." She told Dad: "Your name is here!"

Dad read the long article about demonstrations, and how long they'd been going on. At the very end it said that Attorney General MacDonald Gallion had petitioned the court to issue an injunction against black students and other demonstrators. It named Carl Braden, a radical and alleged communist connected to the Highlander Folk School in Tennessee, which taught nonviolence and how to organize people to support the poor. The injunction also named President Arthur Gray, Reverend Everett MacNair, SNCC activist Robert Zellner, and—the last name in the *News* article—"Norman Jimerson of Birmingham, Alabama."

On the way home from church, Dad had just bought some small plastic pots of flowers to plant. They were on the porch steps. As soon as Dad read his name, he dropped the paper. He said: "Ann, it's time to plant the flowers." He picked up a trowel, and said, "Ann, let's go get our work done." They planted the flowers in front of the living-room window.

That evening Dad called Chuck Morgan to find out what an injunction meant. Morgan said, "Well, since they have enjoined you without any logical or reasonable cause, they could arrest you for breaking the injunction, or even saying anything. It's illogical, unreasonable, and irrelevant. But your normal line of work across the state—anything you do—you can be arrested for breaking the injunction." Dad could not be involved in demonstrations in Talladega, or perhaps elsewhere in the state. Even though he had *not* been involved. In Talladega, he had simply talked with black demonstrators, and with white businessmen, trying to set up some negotiations. Serving as a peacemaker.

The Jimerson family at the First Baptist Church in Hopewell, Virginia, during the time Dad was thinking about taking a job as director of the Alabama Council on Human Relations. Left to right: Melva, Randy, Paul, Jim, Ann, and Susie.

Randy Jimerson, seventh grade school picture,
fall 1961.

After the bombing of Sixteenth Street Baptist Church on September 15, 1963, one stained glass window remained largely intact, except for the face of Jesus. Courtesy Birmingham, Ala. Public Library Archives.

The bomb detonated at the rear side of the church, filling the street with rubble, shattered glass, and wrecked cars. Courtesy Birmingham, Ala. Public Library Archives.

Re-dedication service for Sixteenth Street Baptist Church following its renovation, August 30, 1964. Left to right: Reverend Oley Kidd, Reverend Norman C. Jimerson, Reverend Allix B. James, Reverend Ed Stanfield, and church pastor, Reverend John Cross. Reverend Joseph Lowery is out of the picture frame on left side. Mrs. Maxine McNair, mother of one of the four girls killed in the bombing, is in the choir, upper right. Photo courtesy Chris McNair Studio.

Melva Jimerson holding the stained glass before its donation to the Birmingham Civil Rights Institute, in 2002. Photo by Ann Jimerson.

The only known photograph of Dad with Martin Luther King, Jr. With Coretta Scott King and Senator Hubert Humphrey at the May 1964 American Baptist Convention in Atlantic City. *Crusader* magazine, 1968. Courtesy of the American Baptist Historical Society, Atlanta, Georgia.

The Jimerson children in February 1963. Left to right: Randy, Ann (holding Mark), Paul, and Susie.

9

Brother Mark

As the constant tension of threatening phone calls, social ostracism, and potential danger created intense stress, Mom found comfort in two things: an informal network of white women supporting integration and civil rights, and anticipation of a new baby, due in late July 1962, approximately one year after our family's arrival in Alabama.

In Birmingham and its suburbs the Alabama Council and its local chapter, the Birmingham Council on Human Relations, consisted mainly of male members. A small nucleus formed among doctors and faculty at the University of Alabama Medical Center. Council members included white clergymen, lawyers, and a variety of other concerned citizens. However, some women, especially spouses of male members, participated in meetings and assumed active roles in the Birmingham Council.

A small group of these women began meeting informally for coffee and discussions at each other's homes. This support group shared stories of exclusion, hostility, and estrangement. Knowing that other people in Birmingham held similar beliefs helped to ease the sense of isolation and despair that might have otherwise engulfed them. Besides, southern ladies have long enjoyed a tradition of tea-and-coffee socializing. Rather than talk about society gossip while being served by black maids, however, this civil rights group discussed sensitive matters such as integration, racial equality, women's rights, and resisting peer pressure to conform to the South's racial exclusion.

In the midst of our problems with Vestavia Hills Baptist Church in 1961, Mom recorded this diary entry concerning one such meeting: "Thurs. Nov. 16th: Went to Jackie Mazzara's with interest group. Had interesting discussion on race. Eileen Walbert has very compassionate feelings. Ann Thorpe, Atlantan, but very much opposed to racial situation, felt that not enough of us speak out—not willing to be unpopular. Helen Knox finds it difficult to talk with people on opposite side—it upsets her emotionally."

Mom had her hands full with four children, and soon a fifth on the way. Since Dad traveled frequently, she faced continual challenges keeping up with housework and childcare. She had little time to get to know people, except this group of women associated with the Birmingham Council on Human Relations. Eileen Walbert and her husband Jim, a music teacher and performer, had moved to Birmingham in 1946 from New York City, where Eileen had been a model. She became involved with the Alabama Council around 1958, through her friend Anny Kraus. Refusing to participate in segregated organizations, Eileen stopped going to the Episcopal Church, which had some members active in the White Citizens Council. Eileen said that she felt shunned sometimes at public events, such as concerts at Birmingham Southern College, because people didn't want to be associated with "communists."

Originally from Austria, Anny and Frederick Kraus had been active in civil rights concerns almost from their arrival in Birmingham in the early 1950s, when Frederick was recruited to develop a school of dentistry at the University of Alabama Medical Center. Frederick and Anny had helped to form the Birmingham Council as an integrated organization dedicated to keeping lines of communication open between blacks and whites in the deeply segregated city. They were members of the Unitarian Universalist Church. Anny mentored Eileen and others interested in the civil rights movement.

Another woman active in this support group, Peggy Fuller, was married to well-known architect John Fuller. Peggy started a group called Friendship in Action, to bring together blacks and whites for social events and parties. At times it seemed to Peggy that John's firm lost potential contracts because of their involvement in civil rights.

Mom had also gotten to know Bette Lee Hanson, who had her own afternoon talk show on WAPI, a local television station situated on Red Mountain. Because of her professional work Bette was not part of this circle of women who met during the daytime. Using her maiden name to avoid social repercussions, she had invited black guests, such as Dr. Lucius Pitts, on her program to discuss issues. But she had to steer clear of direct conversations about racial issues. Bette was pretty, fashionable, and a great conversationalist. Her husband, Roger Hanson, played an active role as head of the Birmingham Council. As a research scientist at the medical center, he remained safe from reprisals or threats to his career. He had helped David Vann convince Chuck Morgan to represent Bob Hughes in the Harrison Salisbury incident.

For the women who were involved in the informal support group, the meetings provided reassurance that they were not alone in opposing racial discrimination and segregation. The group also discussed other issues, such as women's role in society. They exposed Mom to Betty Friedan's pioneering book, *The Feminine Mystique,* and to other ideas considered daring for the time.

During one social gathering with this group of socially committed women, Mom realized, for the first time, her symptoms of pregnancy. She didn't mention this realization to her friends. But soon after, the doctor confirmed her suspicions.

At first, news of her pregnancy worried Mom. She had not anticipated having a fifth child, and dreaded Monty and Granddad's reactions. They would not think it was a good idea, especially under such difficult circumstances as we faced in Alabama. However, gradually Mom welcomed it. She now had something positive and delightful to occupy her thoughts. By concentrating on the imminent new arrival, she could suppress many of the fears and anxieties that otherwise might overwhelm her.

As children, now ranging from thirteen to six (almost seven) years old, we became fascinated with the prospect of a new baby brother or sister. As her belly grew, Mom felt for the baby kicking. She let us place our hands on her tummy to feel the movement. I gingerly laid my hand on her swollen stomach. Soon I felt a distinct pushing from within. "I feel it!" I cried out.

Susie said, "Mommy, let me feel!" Each of us took a turn.

Before the baby arrived, Mom and Dad asked me to babysit one evening. "We're going to a Planned Parenthood meeting," Mom said. I didn't ask questions, but I thought, "They don't need to *plan* for this. It keeps happening anyway." Only much later did I realize my parents had needed information about birth control.

In late spring the 1962 Democratic primary race for governor left telephone poles, storefronts, and almost any vertical surface covered in campaign posters. Photos and slogans of the candidates competed for attention and votes. Eugene "Bull" Connor, George C. Wallace, Albert Boutwell, and Attorney General MacDonald Gallion courted the segregationists' votes. Jim Folsom, the folksy former governor, began as a moderate on race before making a last-ditch effort to claim a share of the large anti-integration vote. The one promising new face was Ryan De Graffenried, a handsome thirty-six-year-old lawyer from Tuscaloosa, the most moderate candidate.

Far too young to vote, I could still express my political opinions. One of Bull Connor's posters, on a telephone pole near High-Kel Drugs on the Montgomery Highway, insulted my sense of right and wrong every day as I walked home from school. One afternoon I picked up a small rock. I looked around to make sure no one was watching. Then I went into my windup and pitched a strike from twenty feet away. Bull's-eye! Literally. A small hole, right between Bull Connor's bigoted hateful eyes.

In the May 1 primary election, Wallace and De Graffenried qualified for a run-off campaign. One month later, Wallace easily defeated his more moderate challenger. Without a competitive second party, everyone knew that Wallace would beat the Republican challenger in November, and be inaugurated governor of Alabama in January 1963.

Following the primary and run-off, in addition to the political aftermath, there remained a practical challenge. How could local authorities remove the thousands of campaign posters? A local radio station had the solution. It offered to give S&H Green Stamps to anyone bringing in a campaign poster for disposal. Mom got S&H stamps at Hills Grocery, as an incentive to shop there. After pasting the stamps in small booklets, we could redeem them for small gifts.

I got busy. For delivering more than 120 posters to the radio station office on Red Mountain, I got enough Green Stamps to fill several booklets. Combined with the Green Stamps that Mom had brought home from the grocery store, I had enough booklets to redeem for a portable hi-fi record player.

By the start of summer, the crisis atmosphere in Birmingham became less intense. Dad kept busy with meetings, speaking engagements, and other Alabama Council business, but he seemed less highly stressed. Maybe it was the warm weather, or more likely, a decline in confrontations and direct action. Ebb and flow. Summer brought a lower tide of tensions.

In late spring the Alabama Council printed a new brochure to distribute in seeking new members and contributions. The front of the brochure featured the slogan "Let's work together," with a list of three concerns: "Keep our schools open and accredited; Keep our industries expanding; Create more and better jobs for our people." The green-and-red color scheme in-

cluded illustrations of two white youths walking in front of a school building, and a white man in work uniform carrying a lunch pail in front of a
smoke-spewing factory. Mom drew these illustrations, using her architec-
tural and artistic expertise.

Before the brochure could be printed, Dad had to ask permission from
officers to include their names. ACHR President Powers McLeod asked to
delay printing until after the Methodist Annual Conference. Otherwise, like
Bob Hughes, he might be forced to leave his church.

From May 23 to 27, Dad attended the American Baptist Convention in
Philadelphia, both to keep his "ecclesiastical standing in good order," and to
establish contacts for future fundraising. He spoke at four breakfast meetings of various Baptist departments and distributed about a thousand of the
new Alabama Council brochures. Following the convention, he traveled to
meet representatives of the New World Foundation, the Field Foundation,
the National Council of Churches, and the United Church of Christ. At the
NCC he attended a meeting to plan "the first interfaith conference on race
relations," bringing together Protestants, Catholics, and Jews.

Anticipating the upcoming trial in Talladega, in early June 1962 the
ACHR Board authorized its executive director to identify the Council Board
members if required to do so in court. Recognizing the possible repercussions of being publicly associated with the Alabama Council, President
McLeod sent letters to each board member. He stated that membership records would not be given to the court, but officers and directors would be
identified if demanded by the court. The only option to prevent such disclo-
sure would be to resign from the board.

As Dad wrote to the other Southern Regional Council state directors:
"Each Board member was notified and we only had four resign from the
Board." The four included David Vann, who had chaired the committee that
hired Dad as executive director. He resigned to protect his reputation as an
aspiring political leader seeking to change Birmingham's form of government. The climate of fear in Alabama made the resignation of "only" four
board members seem a sign of progress.

During the summer of 1962, at thirteen years of age, I realized that I would
never achieve my most passionate lifetime goal. Despite my modest farm-
league success in Hopewell, winning two league championships and being

the best player on my team as a twelve-year-old, I now knew I would never play for the Pittsburgh Pirates. Nor any other team, junior high or above.

I began baseball season optimistically. Too old for Little League, I tried out for the Shades Valley Pony League. I made the Indians team, and received my first real flannel uniform, white with green trim and a large "7" on the back. The bright green ball cap featured a white "I." David Walbert, whose mother had become a close friend of my mother's, was one of my older, more experienced, teammates.

We played on a real baseball diamond, with metal bleachers, covered dugouts, and tall banks of floodlights for night games. For the Indians, those were the only highlights. I played second base—sometimes as a starter, other times as a sub. The only game we won took place one evening when I missed the entire game because I had to attend a church youth dinner.

Neither did I enjoy any personal highlights. A few memories linger. Racing back for a high pop-up, which I lost in the bright lights. Swinging at pitch after pitch, only to see many of them drop away at the last second, so that I swished awkwardly. The fourteen- and fifteen-year-old pitchers had learned to throw a curveball.

By the end of the brief Pony League season, I knew I wouldn't be back the next year. My dream had died. I would need to find a new career plan.

I already knew I would never be a mechanic or handyman. Neither would Dad. But necessity pushed him to make one successful attempt. Our old push lawnmower could not compete with the steep front yard on Saulter Road. We couldn't afford to buy a new gas-powered mower. What to do?

Poking around at the Homewood hardware store, Dad found an old mower with a good engine but a broken chassis. "Too bad," he said to the store manager. "I could sure use a cheap mower."

The store manager said he might be able to help. He knew someone in town who had the same model mower, but with a blown engine. He thought the chassis was in good condition. So Dad ended up paying five dollars for the mower with a good engine, and five dollars for the one with a good wheel base.

Dad brought home the two mowers, and put them side by side in the garage. I helped him loosen the bolts and switch the good engine onto the good chassis. Mostly, I watched and handed him wrenches.

Dad poured gas into the tank. "The moment of truth!" he said. "Cross your fingers." After several yanks on the starter rope—with some scary grunts and cries of "Doggone!" and "Dagnabbit!"—Dad got the engine to sputter to life.

He grinned as if he had just invented the two-stroke internal combustion engine. "How's that for a ten-dollar power mower?" he crowed.

The next day I took the broken engine to the basement workshop—the open space next to the garage—and tried my hand at mechanics. I took out the bolts and screws, looked at the valves, piston, springs, and other parts I couldn't name. I found a crack in the piston housing, and broken piston rings.

A few days later, after leaving the parts on a cardboard sheet, I put the engine back together. There were only a few leftover parts when I finished. "If it wasn't broken before," I thought, "it sure is now."

Every time I mowed the yard, I thought about the insides of the engine. I was glad not to have to push the hand mower up the steep front yard.

Not long after Mike Ham moved away, I found a new best friend. Tony moved in with his sister and her husband, who lived halfway towards Montgomery Highway, on the "high" side of Saulter Road. Their house had a steep driveway up from the street, and a flight of steps up to a small porch. Neighborhood rumors said Tony had just gotten out of reform school, and his parents wouldn't let him back. His sister agreed to take him in while he was on probation. I never asked if any of this was true, and he never talked about his past.

Tony did talk about cars. He always pointed out car models, especially ones he liked. He taught me about engines, horsepower, wheel bases, drag racing, and how to identify almost any model of the past five or six years.

To me Tony seemed loud, energetic, adventurous, unafraid. I felt quiet, hesitant, and cautious. I didn't know exactly how old Tony was, probably two or three years older than me. He was tall, thin, and jumpy. Always on the go. We made an odd pair. But we felt comfortable together.

Tony's sister liked Johnny Mathis records, which always seemed to be playing in their house. I wondered if she realized that Mathis was black. Would it matter to her?

"Wonderful Wonderful." "The Twelfth of Never." "It's Not for Me to Say." "Chances Are." "When I Fall in Love." I loved his velvety voice, the soft romance he promised. Girls had begun to seem interesting to me. But I didn't let anyone know, not even Tony. Especially not my parents.

But I couldn't understand one of Johnny Mathis's songs, "Stars Fell on Alabama": "Moonlight and magnolia / Starlight in your hair / All the world's a dream come true. . . ." This was not the Alabama I knew. Not the Alabama of the Ku Klux Klan, of Bull Connor, of George Wallace. How could a black singer croon dreamily about "moonlight and magnolia"?

The Alabama Council on Human Relations engaged in two key developments in June 1962. A looming legal struggle threatened to overshadow one of the most positive initiatives taken in months.

On June 8 and 9 the Alabama Council sponsored a workshop on Equal Employment Opportunities, held at Miles College. Dr. Vivian Henderson of Fisk University developed the program and conducted it with assistance from Charles Clark of the President's Committee on Equal Employment Opportunities in Washington, D.C. As a result of the workshop, committees and individuals began working on employment needs in Birmingham, Montgomery, and Huntsville. For the Alabama Council, this represented a significant accomplishment, particularly since it featured two prominent national figures.

In a letter thanking Charles Clark for his excellent presentation, Dad added a revealing comment: "At times the racial situation looks almost hopeless, but then we are reminded that there are very competent and dedicated people like you who are laboring incessantly and making important contributions to race relations."

Following this successful workshop, Dad had to contend with legal proceedings arising from the April injunction against planning, organizing, or participating in illegal demonstrations, sit-ins, and related activities in Talladega. For a small organization teetering on the edge of financial distress, the prospect of high legal fees seemed daunting. But without challenging the injunction in court, the Alabama Council would be forced to curtail its activities.

A representative from the State Attorney General's Office indicated they had three weeks of evidence to present. As Dad commented: "At $250 a day for legal fees this seems like an awful lot of evidence, especially when almost all of it will be irrelevant to the Alabama Council." It would be an expensive trial. Vice-President Nat Welch sent a letter to all council members, asking them to contribute to a special defense fund.

On June 18, Dad went to the State Circuit Court in Talladega with his attorney, Chuck Morgan. The state Attorney General's Office asked that the temporary injunction remain in force until October, when they requested a hearing as to whether the injunction would be made permanent. The court approved this request. Dad's "day in court" would not begin until October 8.

During the months between the preliminary injunction in April and the trial in October, Dad continued to follow his standard work procedures. Morgan told him he could be arrested, but he said, "Well, Morgan, I'll do what I need to do and take my chances." He continued going to meetings of the local chapters of the Alabama Council.

In Mobile, at the southern end of the state, he visited Father Foley, a Jesuit priest at Spring Hill College, who was a former president of the Alabama Council. "He's a very daring activist," Dad told us. "Foley is the kind of guy that goes to Klan cross-burnings, and writes down license numbers of the Klansmen. I don't know exactly what he plans to do, but he must be trying to identify prominent people in town who are in the Klan."

Surviving in the pressure cooker of Alabama race relations required a good sense of humor. Dad especially enjoyed one story he heard about the beginning of integration in Mobile. Whites were picketing a restaurant because they began serving blacks. The pickets carried signs that said "Don't eat here—they serve niggers" and similar slogans. When it came to be lunchtime, they leaned their picket signs up against the windows and went in the restaurant they were picketing to have lunch. Dad laughed every time he repeated this story. "Well, you have to take a break for lunch, I guess," he would say.

With few crises to manage, Dad spent much of the summer attending meetings, presenting speeches, and dealing with day-to-day problems. In June he met twice with Birmingham Mayor Art Hanes to discuss concerns about discrimination. After one meeting, Dad said: "He told me that, if equalities are ever accepted in our country, democracy will be completely destroyed. He feels personally that democracy is best operated when there are six or seven classes of people."

During the summer of his injunction Dad also spoke to the Kiwanis Club of Mobile, made a brief presentation at the State Conference of Christian Churches of Alabama in Birmingham, and attended some sessions of the statewide Workshop of Principals and Supervisors at all-black Alabama State College in Montgomery. He also addressed a Methodist College Youth Group at Auburn University on "The Church and Race." In August, when John Brewbaker contacted school officials in several Alabama cities facing desegregation, Dad introduced him to three persons in Birmingham concerned with keeping the schools open. The threat of integration had led extreme segregationists to demand closing public schools rather than face racial mixing.

❖

"I'm *bored*," I whined. "There's nothing to do!"

"Go outside and play," Mom said. She was resting on the sectional sofa in the living room. "Go find Tony, or one of your friends from school."

"Tony's not home," I complained. "I don't *have* any other friends."

"Then just go outside!" Mom said. Being pregnant made her impatient.

"It's too hot!" I pleaded. "I'll melt!" I just wanted to lie on the hall floor, under the ceiling fan. And complain.

There were only two ways to escape the overwhelming heat of an Alabama summer. Go swimming, or find some place with air conditioning. Two miles to the public swimming pool. Even on a bike you would get even hotter riding there, and heat up again on the way home.

If we were lucky we could go to Walberts' pool. Mom would drive all of us over there for a delicious break from the heat. We followed the maze of streets between Saulter Road and Oxmoor Road to find the Walberts' ranch-style house. We parked on the street, since Mr. Walbert (Jim, like my Dad) taught piano lessons, and the students' mothers parked in the driveway. Mrs. Walbert (Mom called her Eileen—the same as Mom's sister, Aunt Eileen) welcomed us with southern hospitality, fussing over us, showing real interest in our activities, and serving up icy cold lemonade. During piano lessons we didn't enter the house but walked around to the backyard.

The swimming pool occupied most of their backyard, surrounded by a high wooden fence. A concrete area surrounded the pool, just big enough for a table and chairs on one end and room to lie on a towel on the sides. The cool water felt like heaven. It had less chlorine than the Homewood pool. We splashed around for an hour or two. Ann and I dove in at the deeper end, and Paul and Susie made cannonball jumps where the water wouldn't be too deep. They each tried to make the biggest splash.

Mom didn't want to impose on the Walberts, so we only went to their pool a few times during the summer. At the end of August, though, we held Susie's seventh birthday party there, just for our family and the Walberts.

Most times we went to the Homewood pool, usually with Dad. Ann dove from the diving board. I jumped. Dad counted while all of us tried to hold our breath under water. Always at the shallow end, so Susie and Paul could join the contest. Dad organized splashing fights, which usually ended with a loud whistle from the lifeguard. "No horseplay in the pool!" he yelled.

One time Dad forgot to take off his watch. "Consarn-it!" he said. He had to get a plastic cup from the concession stand and keep the watch in water until he could take it to a repair shop. "Otherwise, it will rust," he told us "and then it'll be ruined."

Susie and Ann were water nuts, like Dad. Mom spent most of her time on a lounge chair. When she got in, she squinted and twisted her face to keep as dry as she could.

Susie joined a swimming team, even though she had to be at the pool five days a week at 6:30 a.m. for practice. One time when we all drove to a meet at the Homewood pool, Susie finished second in freestyle. She might have won, but she kept bumping into the ropes. We all cheered for her.

When we couldn't escape the heat by swimming, air conditioning offered a second option. We couldn't afford it for our house. The only heat relief came from an industrial-size fan built into the hallway ceiling. Its wide louvers opened as it sucked some of the steamy air up into the attic, and drew cooler air up from the basement. We never pulled down the attic stairway in summer. Too much heat up there.

Even shopping seemed bearable in stores with air conditioning. But Homewood Theater offered the best choice. We could enjoy even the silliest movie when it offered a cool respite.

Being strict Baptists in their upbringing, neither Mom nor Dad would let us go to the movies on Sunday. They discouraged heavy labor—except homework, unfortunately—on Sundays, as well as movies, baseball games, card playing, and other intrusions on God's day of rest.

But several times, on Sundays when Dad's friend Reverend Lou Mitchell took his family out of town, the Mitchells let us spend the afternoon in their air-conditioned home. After church—and a cafeteria lunch—we drove to the Mitchell house. In the air-cooled living room, we read books, watched TV, or just rested.

The heat affected Mom even more than the rest of us. Entering her final months of pregnancy, the added weight made it harder to move around, clean house, and take care of four children. Despite such discomforts, she glowed with excitement as she focused her attention on the imminent arrival of a new baby. It helped take her mind off the threats and tensions.

After school ended, Monty and Granddad drove down from Pennsylvania for a visit. When they left, they took Ann and Susie back to Beaver Falls, until the baby arrived. This would reduce Mom's responsibilities—and give the girls some relief from summer heat.

In early July, Dad took a week's vacation. He spent his time doing odd jobs around the house and trying to help Mom cope with being pregnant amid the oppressive heat of an Alabama summer. Dad also tried to keep Paul and me out of Mom's way.

On July 30—exactly one year, to the day, after we first arrived in Birmingham—Mom gave birth to a baby boy. They named him Mark Douglas. The middle name came from Granddad, James Douglas Brooks, always known as "Doug" or "J. Douglas."

Monty and Granddad drove down from Beaver Falls with Ann and Susie. They arrived on the very day the baby was born. Monty wanted to help Mom when she returned from the hospital.

Children couldn't visit the maternity ward, so Dad drove to the hospital one evening with all of us kids in the station wagon. He parked on a street behind the hospital and showed us a window on an upper floor to watch. He went in, and ten minutes later we saw him and Mom waving from the window.

Granddad's job was to get the boys out from underfoot. So, even before Mom and baby Mark came home, Granddad took Paul and me to Florida for a vacation. We drove through the small southeastern Alabama town of Enterprise, which featured a statue honoring the boll weevil.

"Why would they do that?" I asked. I knew the song about the boll weevils eating all the cotton plants and ruining the crops.

Granddad said: "That forced the farmers to plant other crops—diversify —and that kept them from complete failure during the bad years."

Granddad had been to Florida many times. It was our first visit. He took us to all of his favorite tourist attractions: Cypress Gardens, where women strolled the grounds in "Gone With the Wind"–style long dresses and wide frilly hats, holding pastel-colored parasols. A water-skiing extravaganza climaxed with a pyramid of female water-skiers standing on each other's shoulders, with the woman on top waving an American flag. Silver Springs featured a ride in a glass-bottomed boat, watching fish and plants under water. At Weeki-Wachee Springs we entered a small auditorium to see an underwater show featuring brightly costumed mermaids swimming in formations. They took turns going to an air hose. A man's voice on the loudspeaker told the stories they performed.

In St. Petersburg, we stayed at a motel with a shuffleboard court. Paul and I begged Granddad to keep playing even after bedtime. The next day we picked up Cousin Ron, who had flown down from Beaver Falls. We drove to the house where he and his family had lived for a few years after Uncle Paul died. "My old stomping grounds!" Ron said proudly.

Granddad wanted to see the space complex at Cape Canaveral, so we drove all the way across Florida. There were a few old rockets on display outside, but not much else to do. I was getting hungry, so I thought Granddad would be taking us to supper soon.

Instead, we got on the coastal highway heading north. Granddad kept driving. I thought I would starve. Next to me on the back seat, Paul started whimpering. Ron turned around, from the shotgun seat, and whispered, "Don't say anything! He'll just get mad." It seemed like the trip would never end.

It was long past dark, nine o'clock at least, when Granddad finally stopped at a motel near Daytona Beach. Their restaurant was closed already, so we had to drive around to find a place to eat.

The next day we stopped at St. Augustine, the oldest permanent European settlement in North America. Founded in 1565, it beat Jamestown by forty-two years. We visited the Spanish fort, Castillo de San Marcos, overlooking the Atlantic Ocean. I enjoyed climbing on the walls and squeezing into the corner lookout posts, narrow round turrets with holes for firing hand weapons.

The route back to Homewood took us past Waycross, Georgia, and Phenix City, Alabama. Located near Fort Benning, Georgia, Phenix City developed a reputation in the 1940s for gambling, prostitution, organized crime, and all sorts of things the Bible—and Granddad—frowned upon. He said it had earned its reputation as "Sin City." We didn't stop, or even look over our shoulders like Lot's wife in the Old Testament when leaving Sodom.

By the time we arrived home, Mom had mostly recovered from childbirth. Monty had set up a household routine for the new baby, and Ann and Susie acted like assistant mothers. "Look at our baby brother!" they boasted. "Isn't he beautiful?"

While Dad kept busy with his work, the rest of us focused attention on taking care of baby Mark. Ann became a second mother to the baby, and I felt like his second father. We helped with feeding, rocking, changing diapers (I agreed to change wet diapers, but not smelly ones), and playing with Mark. Paul and Susie also enjoyed holding the baby, playing with him, and watching him develop.

Through a Birmingham Council friend, Dad and Mom received a white-painted crib for the baby. It had a famous pedigree. It had once been the crib of Supreme Court Justice Hugo Black's grandson.

One afternoon, I sat in our large black wooden rocking chair, rocking the baby to sleep. As a thirteen-year-old boy, I went for speed. I rocked harder and faster. Suddenly I realized I had passed the tipping point. The rocker began falling backwards toward the floor. In a brief moment, I considered my options: (1) hug the baby tightly against my chest (2) put out an arm to try to cushion the fall; or (3) hold the baby at arm's length and use my arms as shock absorbers. I didn't have time to think of a fourth possibility. I chose option three, holding baby Mark at arm's length as the rocker crashed backwards on the floor. I bumped my head, but the rocker didn't break. And Mark cried with surprise, but suffered no injuries.

As the new school year loomed ever nearer, our baby brother provided the best entertainment of late summer. We saw him quickly change from a newborn to a beautiful, developing baby boy. Brother Mark.

10

Eye of the Storm

Mark's birth had marked the end of our first full year in Alabama. As a family, we had grown accustomed to experiences almost unimaginable twelve months before. Telephone hate calls. Death threats. Church ministers and congregations asking us not to worship with them. Epithets of "commie" and "nigger-lover" added to the familiar "damn Yankee." Teachers criticizing us for leaving the Baptist church. Neighbors moving away rather than risk associating with us.

Yet there had also been wonderful new discoveries. Meeting exotic visitors: northern journalists and ministers, young SNCC activists such as Bob Zellner, the glamorous Danish journalist Per Laursen. Feeling a sense of solidarity with the local white people willing to risk danger by speaking up against hatred and oppression. Sharing Dad's adventure stories and his excitement at being near the epicenter of momentous historical events. By now I had become aware, as never before, that we lived in the midst of important political and social changes. It felt both exhilarating and frightening.

Most of all, the birth of a baby brother had brought us a positive sense of joy in the miracle of new life. Taking care of Mark, watching him develop and grow, took our minds off the tensions and dangers surrounding us. If it often seemed that we lived on a small island in the midst of swirling seas of chaos and hostility, at least we had security in our family sanctuary. Our home became a "safe house" not only for visiting civil rights activists but also for ourselves—the eye of the storm.

Sometimes, however, the turbulence surrounding us made even home feel threatening. Dad's volatile temperament often created instability and uncertainty. The anger he sometimes displayed may have arisen in childhood, perhaps from his father's untimely death—which he later described as a devastating experience—or his mother's failure even to tell the ten-year-old that his father had died. He told us he had to read about it in the newspaper.

From what we saw and heard of Grandma Jim, we could easily imagine how difficult she might have made our father's adolescent years.

Mom said that Dad had a hard time in the Army. He didn't talk about it. Only after marriage did she find out he had had a nervous breakdown after the war. In the South Pacific he contracted infectious hepatitis after weeks of dysentery. "His officer called him a 'goldbrick'—a lazy guy faking sickness— and ordered him back to work," Mom said. "So that put him under a lot of stress. Your Uncle Ced told me one time Jim just snapped."

At the end of the war my father went to the Philippines and then Japan, with the occupation forces. From November 1945 until January 1947 he was hospitalized for depression, much of that time at an Army hospital on Long Island. He had electric shock therapy, before they used anything to lessen the pain. After difficult months, while medical student Ced worried about his brother's health, the psychiatrists released him from treatment. His medical record showed no restrictions on his suitability for any type of employment. However, he suffered most of his life with depression and anger.

Dad never talked about this. But one time he gave me a leather wallet with a picture of a horse's head. He said he made it when he was in the hospital.

When we did learn about some of these problems, it helped explain the anger Dad always seemed to bottle up inside. He would lash out at times, unpredictably, particularly towards his sons. Paul took the worst of it. I learned to stay out of trouble by keeping quiet. Paul pushed back.

Paul and I both had a complicated relationship with our father. We both recognized him as a principled man, taking bold risks to follow his conscience. On the other hand, we also saw another side of him—angry, confused, sad—that made it difficult to relax with him. His energy level always seemed ramped up, and he expected us to keep up with him. Stormin' Norman.

At the end of August 1962, on behalf of the Alabama Council on Human Relations, Dad sent a memo to the U.S. Commission on Civil Rights, concerning the situation in Birmingham. He reported that the "selective buying campaign" organized by students at Miles College in the spring had become less effective. But, although large numbers of black people now shopped in downtown, enough refused to concern the merchants. Miles students had sent a letter to businessmen stating their hope that discrimination issues could be negotiated, but warning they would redouble the selective buying campaign during the Christmas shopping season.

Noting that Martin Luther King's Southern Christian Leadership Conference would hold its annual national convention in Birmingham at the end of September, Dad reported hearing rumors that the conference would mark the beginning of major demonstrations in Birmingham.

Another concern focused on civil rights violations by Birmingham policemen. On August 29 a federal grand jury indicted two police officers charged with assaulting two black men. Dad commented: "Perhaps there will be some long-sought relief from police brutality in Birmingham and other parts of the South."

On the same topic, Dad reported that two weeks earlier he arrived at a laundry in Birmingham shortly after three police officers beat up a black employee, who refused to leave the plant when asked to do so because he was drunk. Dad stated: "The foreman told me that he was sure that one of the police officers would have shot and killed the Negro, while he was lying down, if another employee had not thrown herself over him." One officer threatened to arrest the foreman for interfering with an officer, because he begged him not to shoot the black man.

As director of the Alabama Council, Dad regularly issued such reports to federal authorities. This provided valuable evidence for the U.S. Commission on Civil Rights as it investigated alleged violations. In addition to such formal reports, Dad also maintained regular communication with federal officials Burke Marshall and John Doar.

For me the start of a "new year" meant transition to a new school. Compared to Shades Cahaba Elementary, Homewood Junior High seemed modern, sprawling, and intimidating. Built into a hillside near the Edgewood neighborhood, the school consisted of several buildings connected by covered outdoor walkways and stairs. It took several days to learn the school's geography: separate classrooms for each period, gym for physical education class, band room, cafeteria, school office, athletic field.

Once again, as in Petersburg, I had to ride the bus to school. This required waking up early—not easy for me. Two miles seemed too far to walk in the morning, but I often walked home after school. I learned several different routes through the twisting side streets to reach Saulter Road.

When Dad was home, he often drove me to school on the way to his downtown office. I enjoyed having a few minutes with him. Some days he would be cheerful and tell jokes. Other times he would be quiet or worried, or tell me about the problems he had to face. The VW putt-putt-putted down Oxmoor Road, turning right on Dale Avenue—just before the vast Dawson Memorial Baptist Church—and then up the circular driveway to the Homewood Junior High entrance.

Eighth grade brought some surprises. I had expected classes to be more interesting than elementary school, but I found some of the teachers just as old-fashioned and poorly educated as at Shades Cahaba.

One day in English class, Mrs. Glodt discussed homonyms. "Homonyms are words that sound the same but are spelled different," she said. I winced at the word "different" instead of "differently."

"They mean different things, too," she said. She turned to write on the chalkboard.

"These are examples of homonyms," she said. She had written several pairs of words: blue/blew, red/read, aisle/isle, maid/made, him/hem.

I looked at the list, as she pronounced them carefully, reminding us what each word meant. With the last pair, she said: "Him (H-I-M) means 'that boy'; him (H-E-M) means the seam at the bottom of a skirt."

"What?" I thought. "That's not right!" But what should I do? Say something? Let everyone in eighth grade think this was correct? I didn't want to tell the teacher she was wrong. But she was. Her southern accent had betrayed her.

I raised my hand, hesitantly. "Excuse me? Miz Glodt?" ("Mrs." pronounced like a southerner. Ironically beating the feminists to "Ms.," Alabamians pronounced both Mrs. and Miss as "Miz.")

I paused, trying not to sound like a know-it-all. "Miz Glodt, I thought that 'him' and 'hem' are pronounced differently . . . ?"

I heard the class begin to buzz with surprise and curiosity. No one was supposed to question the teacher or her authority.

"Well, I never . . . !" Mrs. Glodt sputtered.

For the rest of the year, whenever I raised my hand in English class, Mrs. Glodt's face turned stormy. Her eyes narrowed and her forehead wrinkled. "What *now,* Randy?" she growled defensively.

My grade for the report card period dropped from B to C. It was enough to keep me out of the Junior High Honors Club.

Ann said she had had a similar experience the year before in fifth grade at Shades Cahaba. Her teacher, Mrs. Allen (Miz Allen), said there were two words, spelled the same but pronounced differently, that meant totally different things. Rebel: re-BELL and REB-el.

"Re-BELL means to fight against authority," she said. "That's something very bad to do." She looked around the room, making sure the students were paying attention.

Mrs. Allen continued: "REB-el is a southern patriot. From the War for Southern Independence. A REB-el is a hero!" She paused for dramatic effect.

Ann's hand shot up. She didn't worry about coming off as a know-it-all. "But those words have the same root! A REB-el is someone who Re-BELLed."

"Oh no," her teacher rebutted. "There is no connection between these two words. They are as different as night and day. Wrong and right. Black and white."

Spelling and grammar were my best subjects in school. Mom deserves most of the credit. Whenever one of us misspoke, she immediately corrected us.

"Mike and me are going—" I began.

"Mike and *I*," Mom quickly said. "If you aren't sure which form to use, try saying the sentence with only the pronoun. You wouldn't say 'Me is going,' so don't say 'Mike and *me*.'"

In Hopewell I had won the school spelling contest for sixth grade. The next year, at Shades Cahaba, I beat Gregg Beasley in the seventh-grade spelling bee. But I lost quickly in the next round of all seventh graders in the area, held at Homewood Junior High.

I felt confident going into the eighth-grade spelling bee. I studied the practice booklet a little but couldn't pay attention for long. Doing almost anything—even doing nothing—seemed more interesting than studying a spelling book.

This time Gregg and I again faced off, as the last two eighth-grade spellers. Gregg was tall and slightly pudgy. Not well coordinated, not athletic. His dark horn-rimmed glasses made him look like a bookworm. My nemesis.

In the final round, I choked. I spelled apostrophe "a-p-p-o-s-t-r-o-p-h-e." Gregg won. The competition had evened.

Later in the year, Mrs. Glodt assigned Gregg and me to prepare a joint book report on *David Copperfield*. I went to his house once or twice to plan what we would say. He turned out to be a pretty nice guy. We never became close friends, but I gained a grudging respect for him.

While I navigated eighth grade, Ann entered Mrs. Jones's sixth-grade class at Shades Cahaba.

"It's like a time warp," Ann said. "Just like Dick and Jane's school." Miz Jones's techniques seemed as old-fashioned and hard as the desks.

Ann told us about Mrs. Jones's rules. They had to conjugate verbs just as in the 1930s. Only black or blue-black ink. No ballpoint pens allowed, but in a concession to sixties technology, cartridge pens—fountain pens you could refill by popping in a cartridge of liquid ink instead of drawing it into the pen from an ink bottle—were permitted. Three tenses on the front of the sheet, three on the back. No crossing out and no erasing. If you slipped up, you had to start a new sheet.

Ann said: "Terry Sue showed me how to use Clorox to dab out a mistake. You have to be careful not to bleach out the blue rule lines or the double pink line at the left margin."

Mrs. Jones made the students fill a geography notebook with carefully colored maps. They had to draw freehand—no tracing or they wouldn't learn the shapes of states. They had to list principal exports and raw materials. They filled English notebooks with grammar rules copied from Mrs. Jones's curly cursive on the chalkboard.

Ann reported one day: "Kerrie Shwartz says Miz Jones dyes her hair red. And she lives with her mother."

They'd heard the other teachers call her "Beanie." When Mrs. Jones stepped out of the room for a moment, Kerrie would croon, "I dream of Beanie with the dyed re-e-d hair. . . ."

Mrs. Jones was harsh, strict, opinionated, and a bully to one or two kids she'd designated as the class dummies. Ann and her classmates claimed to suffer under her tyranny and perfectionism, but the other sixth graders admired them. They were a class apart. Judging from the excitable seventh-graders who flocked back to visit from junior high, if you survived Mrs. Jones, you apparently worshipped her afterwards.

We weren't the only white kids who wanted to talk back to authority figures. David Walbert, Eileen and Jim's son, spoke about his first act of civil disobedience. As a junior at Shades Valley High School in Homewood, he and a friend hatched a plan. They got a ladder and a can of paint.

About midnight they drove over to Red Mountain and parked on Cobb

Lane. They leaned the ladder against a large billboard that taunted: "What's wrong with being right? Join the John Birch Society." The John Birch Society at this time was one of the most popular of the neo-Nazi organizations, vehemently opposed to integration.

David and his friend painted over the word "right" and painted "Nazi" above it, so the sign read: "What's wrong with being Nazi? Join the John Birch Society." That made the front page of *The Birmingham Independent* newspaper, published by the John Birch Society. They showed a large photograph of the vandalized sign. The accompanying story said it was obviously the work of local communists. They even used red paint.

"That's the only color of paint we could find in my buddy's garage," David said, laughing. "But the *Independent* has to make everything a communist conspiracy!"

As we started the new school year in Homewood's still-segregated schools, Dad tried to mediate a dispute over integrating schools in Huntsville. A black Army sergeant stationed at Redstone Arsenal tried to enroll his daughter in an all-white school. Dad talked with the school superintendent and attended a hearing of the school board. The girl's mother asked him to come as her spiritual advisor, because he was a minister and because of his position with the Alabama Council.

When the Huntsville school board postponed a decision for twenty days, Dad wrote to Secretary of Defense Robert McNamara concerning the problem of desegregating the school. The Department of the Army's Special Assistant for Personnel, Roy K. Davenport, replied that pupil placement of military dependents remained the responsibility of local public school officials. He stated that the Department of the Army would not condone segregation in any situation affecting its personnel and had eliminated segregation in "on-post" schools. However, he declared that "the local command is prevented from interceding with the operation of local law."

Dad replied to Davenport, pointing out that the all-white school stood on land formerly owned by the U.S. government and bought with federal assistance. Army officials had told the sergeant that it would be an embarrassment to the Army—and that his child might be hurt—if he tried to enroll her in the white school. "As a former Army officer, I personally am grateful to know that the Department of the Army does not condone segregation in any situation affecting its personnel," Dad wrote. "But the official policy of non-discrimination also must be carried out at the lower echelons of command."

In addition to school desegregation, Dad continued to work on employment issues for black people. The success of a June 1962 workshop on equal employment led the Alabama Council to sponsor similar workshops around the state. In October, Dad wrote again to John Field of the President's Committee on Equal Employment Opportunity, asking whether Field could send someone to lead another workshop in November. Dad also tried to involve members of the Civil Rights Commission and the United Steelworkers of America in this workshop.

When she went downtown to register to vote, Mom ended up providing research information about voter registration problems. Since she had moved to Alabama from Virginia, Mom needed to apply to be added as a local voter. Several people, both white and black, waited in line to sign up as new voters.

The clerk told Mom she had to take a citizenship test. "Who was the first president of the United States?" he asked.

Mom answered, "George Washington."

"Congratulations," the clerk said. "You pass."

But as she left with her new voter card, Mom overheard the clerk asking a black woman to explain an obscure clause of the U.S. Constitution. When she couldn't do so, the clerk said she was unqualified to vote.

"I have a college degree and keep up on politics, and I could never have answered that question," Mom told us. "It's obvious they are trying to prevent Negroes from voting!"

"Thanks, Mel," Dad said. "I'll pass on this information."

During the fall of 1962, Dad faced two major crises. First, he would finally have his day in court. The State of Alabama sought to make permanent the temporary injunction against him and other civil rights activists, following sit-ins and kneel-ins the previous spring. Dad would have to testify in court, seeking to be removed from the injunction. The second crisis would be trying to mediate between the white and black leaders of Birmingham, in an effort to delay Martin Luther King Jr.'s plans for massive demonstrations in the city. Dad's reputation as the one person both sides trusted would be put to the test, as would his ability to convince King and his Southern Christian Leadership Conference to wait until a more propitious time for direct action in Birmingham.

11

State of Alabama v. *Norman C. Jimerson*

Few people outside the state of Alabama had heard of Talladega in 1962. It was a typical sleepy southern town, far from the big-city bustle of Birmingham, the political center of Montgomery, or the civil rights symbolism of nearby Anniston. The Talladega Superspeedway would not be built until 1968, and NASCAR would not hold its first "Talladega 500" race until a year after that.

Typical of rural Alabama county seats, Talladega huddled around its court-house square. A two-story brick courthouse, surrounded by narrow green lawns, dominated the town center. The four facing blocks of small shops and offices included hardware and farm stores, a five-and-ten, drugstores, small diners, and offices for lawyers, doctors, and businessmen.

The civil rights demonstrations that began in Talladega in April 1962 made few headlines outside Alabama. The confrontations did not lead to violence, as did similar demonstrations in McComb, Albany, Selma, and some other communities. Yet the very ordinariness of what happened in Talladega represents the majority of civil rights initiatives. Throughout the South local issues and concerns led black people to demand change in relations between the races. In Talladega and hundreds of other communities, such power struggles took place without notice by national media. These sit-ins and kneel-ins, led by local people willing to risk their personal safety to overturn centuries of discrimination and oppression, produced small gains. Yet they signified the power of ordinary people to change the political and social system through direct action.

In Talladega my father first found himself confronted by the traditional power and authority of the State of Alabama. Following the demonstrations in April 1962, the state attorney general threw him in with a group of civil rights activists barred by injunction from demonstrations and other activities threatening the racial status quo. Although Dad had sought to open communication and negotiations between the black and white communities, and did not engage in direct action protests, his tactics did also seek to overturn segregation in Talladega. In October the case known as *State of Alabama v. Norman C. Jimerson*–one of several parallel cases for various defendants– went to trial in Talladega's historic courthouse.

While waiting for the trial to begin, Dad's lawyer, Chuck Morgan, advised him to keep his distance from the other defendants. Since Dad's defense would be based on the fact that he had neither participated in nor assisted the demonstrations, it seemed prudent to avoid being seen speaking to anyone who had been involved. Radical activist Carl Braden, in particular, had been labeled a communist, partly because of his outspoken support for civil rights. Dad had talked with him several times in the past two years. Braden attended the 1962 Alabama Council annual meeting, in the auditorium of the Gaston Building in Birmingham, and Morgan warned Dad not to be seen with him.

Dad said: "My approach is a little different from his, and I don't talk in quite such angry terms as Braden does. So staying away from him is no problem."

Morgan also advised Dad not to communicate with Bob Zellner before the trial. Bob came to our house and asked for a ride down to the trial in Talladega. Dad called Chuck Morgan, who said, "No. Don't take him in your car. You shouldn't be seen with him." Dad reluctantly followed his attorney's advice.

The trial in Talladega courthouse began October 8, 1962. With so many defendants on trial at once, this would be a potentially very lengthy process. Each of the individually named defendants had the right to be represented by legal counsel, to testify and call witnesses, if desired. Dad reported that Circuit Judge William Sullivan stated he could not predict how long the trial would last.

For the first two days, the state called only one witness, Police Chief Victor Dyson. He testified that the demonstrations in April had brought on high tension, threats, and violence. Under cross-examination by Arthur Shores, a black attorney from Birmingham, the chief stated that there had been too many people to arrest during a march from Talladega College to downtown. "I'd still be arresting them if I'd started that," he declared.

Reporting on the trial, the *Birmingham Post-Herald* identified my father at greater length than any other defendant:

Jimerson is a white Baptist minister, executive secretary of the Alabama Council on Human Relations, and has sought to have himself removed from the injunction restrictions on grounds that he was in Talladega twice in the role of "peacemaker" rather than as a planner or participant in the demonstrations.

He maintains he was there to try to open lines of communication between the races to prevent such disorders as occurred.

After two days, Dad told us the trial was entertaining. "Morgan thinks it will last all week—and then some," he said. "Guess I don't mind. It's something different." He grinned—a mouthful of big teeth. "It's kind of like vacation time, going down to the court."

Dad told us: "After lunch today, Morgan gave me a slip of paper that said, 'Be sure to take real good notes. I've got to leave the court room.' When he got back, he said: 'I had to go over to the police station and get a license. I just found out you have to have a *pistol* permit for this town.'" Dad laughed at this, shaking his head. "That's Morgan! Always something bizarre."

The third day featured testimony from Bill Orr and Robert Slay, co-owners of City Pharmacy. Orr stated that during sit-ins at his drugstore—and two others in town—Talladega's courthouse square was not a safe place to be. Several men had requested acid or strong irritants. As one said, he wanted "something I can throw on somebody and burn them."

Under cross-examination, Orr stated that he and owners of two other drugstores agreed by telephone not to serve any blacks engaged in sit-ins, and not to meet with black leaders. Slay corroborated Orr's testimony.

The following day, Slay concluded his testimony, and L. M. Stone, owner of Stone Drug Company, took the stand for the remainder of the day. Stone testified that he did not serve blacks at his lunch counter because, as the *Post-Herald* reported, "to do so would mean the end of his business."

Stone also mentioned that Reverend Jimerson had spoken with him on two occasions. One time, he claimed, as the newspaper reported, "Jimerson mentioned that he ought to integrate his store." Stone stated "that Jimerson had talked to him briefly about setting up a bi-racial committee to air Talladega's racial problems." The *Post-Herald* added: "This is what Jimerson has maintained he was in Talladega for at the time." On cross-examination, Stone "changed his testimony to say Jimerson had not told him he ought to integrate the store."

After only four days of testimony, Judge Sullivan recessed the Circuit

Court hearing until October 22. Only four witnesses had been examined, with up to sixty on the state attorney's list. Dad wrote to Paul Rilling of the Southern Regional Council, providing a progress report on the court hearings: "So far in court the police chief stated that he saw me talking to state police officers after a parade had been broken up and one of the druggists testified that I did talk with him about a bi-racial committee. . . . He testified that I was sympathetic to his problem." Dad added: "Morgan says that we are doing as well as can be expected. This doesn't necessarily mean that we are doing very well. Alabama justice is an amusing thing to behold."

During the court recess, Dad also wrote to Burke Marshall, assistant attorney general in the Civil Right Division, who had asked Dad to keep him informed about the racial front in Alabama. He commended Marshall for his "excellent work in Mississippi"—where he helped protect James Meredith, who enrolled as the first black student at Ole Miss—and for his "continued concern about the situation in Alabama."

Then Dad reported the progress of his trial: "Hearings began October 8th, and after four days court was recessed until next Monday, October 22nd. The state says that it considers this an extremely important case and it is preparing to spend many weeks in court."

Eleven days later, when the trial resumed, the national news focused on a missile crisis in Cuba. American spy planes had discovered secret Soviet missile bases on Fidel Castro's island nation. Soon President Kennedy and Soviet leader Nikita Khrushchev engaged in high-stakes diplomacy, while people around the world watched fearfully. Newscasts raised the specter of atomic warfare and nuclear annihilation.

Meanwhile, in Talladega, Dad had his own day in court. On the witness stand, Dad summarized his activities in Talladega during the April demonstrations. The sit-ins began on April 8 and 9. He said: "I first learned about the demonstrations when my wife phoned my office to say she heard about them on the radio."

After thinking it over, he decided to go to Talladega on April 11. Before leaving home, he tried to phone Talladega Mayor James Hardwick to offer his assistance in establishing communications and starting negotiations between the white community leaders and the black students. His wife answered, and Dad left a message with her. Then he drove to Talladega, stopping first to talk with Dr. Arthur Gray, president of Talladega College and a member of the Alabama Council Board. Gray felt hopeless about setting up communications in Talladega. He opposed the demonstrations and said students should be studying. If they wanted to demonstrate they should drop out of college. Dr. Gray also said he thought it would take many years to end segregation in Talladega.

In an effort to mediate between the demonstrators and white businessmen, Dad talked with the owners of two of the three drugstores where there had been sit-ins, urging them to establish lines of communication with the Negro students. Jack Landrum of Landrum Drug Company seemed "very friendly and smiling, but he wasn't going to give an inch in talking with Negroes."

Dad told Landrum that in other communities tensions eased when businessmen and black leaders sat down to talk. As he testified: "My philosophy is that the fact that you listen to a person—whether you give an inch or not—makes it more difficult for him to maintain anger and continue demonstrations."

L. M. Stone, owner of Stone Drug Company, seemed more willing to negotiate with the demonstrators, but said he would be driven out of business if he served blacks while others did not.

Then Dad tried to mediate with the Negro demonstrators. In the afternoon, Dr. Gray invited Dad to attend a meeting of students at the college. For two hours the students debated what to do next. Should the arrested students come out on bail? Bob Zellner and another SNCC organizer—Dad didn't know his name—argued for a militant approach: refusing to post bail to put pressure on the jailers. Dad testified that he urged the students to encourage the mayor to set up a biracial committee to talk over problems and ease tensions. He said that they had no interest in his suggestions.

Demonstrations continued, and on April 26 my father returned to Talladega. Again he talked with the owners of the drugstores, discussed the situation with two or three white ministers, and attended a meeting of the Talladega Ministerial Association. After seeing the police stop students marching towards town by setting up a barricade and threatening to use fire hoses against them, he talked with the police chief about establishing communications with the protesters. He even commended the police for maintaining order during these tense times.

One of the local white ministers Dad spoke with, Reverend Woods, said that in his Presbyterian church he couldn't express his own belief that discrimination was wrong, or he would lose his pulpit.

Before leaving Talladega late that night, Dad reported, he had spent an hour and twenty minutes talking with another minister, Reverend McGahee. He said that the kneel-ins at his church had polarized the church members, making people less willing to tolerate black visitors. Although he opposed discrimination and talked about "the evils of segregation," McGahee did not seem willing to take initiative. Dad said he urged the minister to meet with black leaders to help them see that not every white person is a rabid segregationist.

Repeatedly, Dad emphasized in his testimony that he had tried to serve as a peacemaker, to open communications between the races. His goal had been to end the demonstrations and start negotiations. As Chuck Morgan stated, the director of the Alabama Council on Human Relations went to Talladega to seek common ground between the black demonstrators and white businessmen. That was his job, and the purpose of his organization.

After each day in court, Dad drove home from Talladega. Following his day on the witness stand, he called us into the living room for family devotions.

Dad asked: "Do you remember what Jesus said in the Sermon on the Mount? I was thinking about the Beatitudes today." He opened his Bible and handed it to Ann. "Please read Matthew 5, verses 9 to 12." Ann read:

> Blessed are the peacemakers: for they shall be called the children of God.
> Blessed are they which are persecuted for righteousness' sake, for theirs is the kingdom of heaven.
> Blessed are ye, when men shall revile you, and persecute you, and shall say all manner of evil against you falsely, for my sake.
> Rejoice, and be exceeding glad: for great is your reward in heaven: for so persecuted they the prophets which were before you.

Dad said, "I sure hope Jesus was right! Because that's how I feel right now." He glanced at Mom, who curled her lips and gave him a warning look.

Then Dad told us about his trial testimony. He described how he had tried to get the student demonstrators and white businessmen to talk to each other. He repeated most of what he had said in court. "But I didn't have time to tell everything about the ministers' meeting," he said. "That was one of the most fascinating meetings I've ever attended. They approved a statement condemning the students and all demonstrations. But before that they voted to force Dr. MacNair, the white chaplain at Talladega College, out of their group."

Ann asked: "Because he likes Negroes?"

Dad said: "Well, basically, yes. That's why." He startled chuckling. "It's just so crazy—." Then he shook his head. "This one Southern Baptist preacher said, 'The Klan is strong in our area. And in our churches. For the glory of the Kingdom of God we must be careful what we do.'"

I asked: "Why do they want the Klan in their churches?"

Dad said, "He meant: if we offend the Klan it will hurt church attendance. Imagine that! He's more worried about numbers than doing what's right."

Dad told us: "It fascinated me, listening to them talk at such a fevered pitch for over half an hour about whether I could speak. For once in my life I was so busy listening I didn't much care whether I spoke or not!"

Hard to believe: Dad not wanting to talk.

"It was so bizarre!" he said. Then he continued.

After about forty minutes, Dr. MacNair said he would leave the room so they could vote on whether *he* could continue as a member of the group. I decided to leave with him. I stood up and said, "I can't really say it was a pleasurable experience being with you, but I'm grateful for the opportunity to see this."

Then the president of the ministers' group said, "You may come back any time." I couldn't believe it! I said, "Do you really mean that?" And he nodded yes!

Talking about this seemed important to Dad. He needed to explain what he had experienced, both last spring during the demonstrations and now in court. He remembered something else that amused him: "After court today I asked Morgan how much time I'd get. He said, 'Gee, whiz. Are you worried about questions like that? My gosh, you don't need to worry.' I said, 'Morgan, I'm not all that worried. I'm just curious. I'm not the one that's carrying a *revolver* around in his briefcase.' Which *he* was doing!" Dad laughed, remembering this. "Here's this big tough lawyer, carrying a gun into court!"

The next night at supper, Dad could hardly wait to tell us about the trial. "One preacher was testifying about Easter Sunday services. He said they were worshipping, and the spirit of Jesus was with them. Then the demonstrators came. What they call a kneel-in. It caused great confusion and destroyed the spirit of worship. And he knew that this was not 'of God' because in the Bible it says, 'God is not the author of confusion.'"

That didn't sound right to Dad. "During a break I went to the court library and looked it up in the scriptures. Paul was saying, 'Do not speak in tongues unless there's an interpreter because it will cause confusion and God is not the author of confusion.' So I wrote a note to Morgan. He asked a couple of questions, then asked the minister if this Bible verse really refers to speaking in tongues." Dad stopped to chuckle at the scene. "That old red-neck preacher said, 'It's blasphemous for a lawyer to be asking questions about the Bible in court.' Imagine that!"

Odd incidents during the trial amused Dad every day. One time a witness said that somebody got real angry. The prosecutor said, "Are you a psychiatrist?"

Dad thought, "What has that got to do with anything?"

But the prosecutor said, "Judge, I request the testimony be deleted because it's an unqualified expert."

During cross-examination, the defense attorney said, "That's right. But in your best judgment was he angry?"

Dad explained: "He's not a psychiatrist, so he couldn't say that the person was angry—just that in his *best judgment* the guy was angry." This made Dad laugh. He shook his head. "All these little nuances—trying to block justice—are intriguing."

Orzell Billingsley, one of the black lawyers, said to a white preacher: "There's a water fountain out here. It had a sign on it for whites only. And another fountain said, 'Colored.' Now they've taken down the signs and they've turned off the water so that *nobody* can drink. Do you think that's good?"

The preacher said, "Well, I don't know because I'm not a plumber."

Dad told us: "All straight-faced. Here's this poor unlettered guy in court, and he doesn't know which end is up. He's not a *plumber,* so he doesn't know anything about *segregation*!"

Mom said she wanted to see for herself the strange events that Dad had been telling us about.

"Don't you think we can leave Mark with the MacNair's in Talladega?" she asked Dad. "They seemed so nice when I met them."

"I'll ask them," Dad said. "It would be good for you to be involved in this. Otherwise, you might not believe my stories."

Ann said, "Daddy, can I go too? I want to see it!"

Quickly, I said, "Me too!"

Dad looked our questions back to Mom. She nodded. "It would be a good learning experience," Mom said. "I don't like you kids to miss school. But this is something you'll remember when you're older."

So Mom wrote notes to our teachers, being careful to give enough details to justify our absence. But not so many as to raise concerns about our father's potential criminal record.

On the designated morning, Ann and I excitedly prepared for our big adventure. Paul and Susie were too young to understand the trial, Mom said, so they headed off to school. Mom had arranged for them to go to the McConnells after school, so there would be someone to take care of them. Then Mom loaded Mark's diaper bag and sleeping bassinet into the station wagon. She held him in her arms, in the front passenger seat.

During the drive to Talladega, Dad went over the "do's and don'ts" of visiting the courtroom. Pay attention. Look around. Absorb it all. Watch the judge, the jury members, the lawyers, the people in the audience. Be polite. Don't talk, don't eat, don't cuss. He laughed at his own joke when he said "don't cuss."

When they turned on the car radio, the news focused on the Cuban Missile Crisis. Only ninety miles off the coast of Florida, Cuba seemed dangerously close to us in Alabama.

I asked Mom and Dad: "Will the bombs hit us first?"

Mom said, "No, don't worry, Randy. We can only pray that President Kennedy can keep us from going to war."

Dad said, "Neither side wants to back down. Kennedy and Khrushchev are trying to make the other guy blink." He listened to the reporter describing the naval blockade of Cuba. "Besides, apart from a few military bases, there aren't any major targets in Alabama. The Russians would go for New York or Washington, if anything."

"Let's not worry about that today," Mom said. "Jim, please turn off the radio."

In the silence, I thought about the TV program about the atomic bomb I saw when I was six or seven. It showed horrible drawings of terrified horses and crying people. Mom had said they came from a painting by Pablo Picasso. Guernica. A city bombed during the Spanish Civil War. The images gave me nightmares for weeks after. Would it be like that if bombs fell on us now?

After a few minutes of tense silence, Dad asked Ann and me: "Do you remember Bob Zellner? The white student prevented from returning to his former college?"

Ann said: "Was he with Per? I remember *Per*!"

I proudly stated: "I do! They came to the football game with us. He got beaten up in Mississippi."

"That's right," Dad said. "He's one of the people in the injunction. But he probably won't be in court today. They're not talking about his involvement."

Mom said: "What a nice young man! It's a shame Chuck wouldn't let you give him a ride to the trial last time."

Dad said: "Well, I want you kids to understand something." He looked over his shoulder at us, to make sure we were listening.

"Jim, watch the road!" Mom said.

Dad continued: "During the demonstrations, Zellner and I disagreed on what to do. I attended a meeting with him and Negro students at the college. They spent about an hour arguing over whether the students arrested should accept bail. They argued everything would be lost if students accepted bail. I jumped in and suggested there might be a time when a demonstration is the only way to show dissatisfaction. But now they should start communications. Plan a *strategy* instead of just marching on the town."

"Slow down, Jim," Mom said. "You're speeding!"

Dad kept talking: "Zellner came up with the idea that they should not accept bail. He talked a long time. The students agreed with him. They made a lot of emotional statements. But they didn't know what they were aiming at other than *complete* elimination of discrimination. They couldn't agree what they should do or what they wanted to accomplish."

Dad glanced back at us, but quickly put his eyes on the road. Mom was watching him.

He said, "I argued with Zellner about this. I said they were making statements which they couldn't support by any evidence. They hadn't considered the economic cost of getting people arrested or the cost to their families for disrupting their education by being arrested."

I said: "But I thought you and Bob were on the same side?"

Dad responded: "We are. But we're trying different ways to get the same result." He paused, watching a large cotton truck heading toward us in the opposite lane. "Zellner and the students think the only way to end segregation is direct action—sit-ins, demonstrations, marches, making demands. It's what Martin Luther King and many other civil rights leaders think."

Ann said: "Do you think they're wrong?"

Dad thought for a minute, then spoke slowly. "No, Annie. I think they're trying to get people's attention. But once they get noticed, people have to talk together. Communicate. The demonstrators get white folks scared—or mad." He scratched his ear and looked at the speedometer. "So I talked to the whites and said, if you'll talk to the Negroes, you can reduce tensions and end the demonstrations."

Ann asked: "Did it work?"

Dad smiled. "Sometimes it does. We just keep trying."

I said: "So you're really on the same side? Working together?"

Dad replied: "That's right. I think we need both approaches. With demonstrations, the white people can't ignore the protesters. They might get mad, but they do notice them. And I try to get both sides to talk about what they want. What they need. Try to find common ground. Something that can satisfy everyone—or at least be equally *un*-satisfying!" He laughed. "You can solve a lot of problems if you talk to other people. You find out they are *people,* not some monsters."

"You want to hear something funny?" Dad said. "You've heard all the news about the missile crisis in Cuba?" He looked back at Ann and me. We nodded yes. "Well, yesterday one of the prosecutors talked about it with me before court started. He said, 'Boy, they really need somebody like you to negotiate, to get this thing resolved down there.'" He chuckled. "They need somebody to negotiate. Not me, but someone *like* me. And he was serious. The funny part, of course, is that then he took his normal role as a prosecutor. *Against* me."

After driving more than an hour, we arrived at the big white southern-style home of a genteel elderly couple. Reverend MacNair, the white minister at the Talladega College chapel, was another defendant in the injunction. Mom carried Mark while Dad got the diaper bag and bassinet from the car. Mrs. MacNair cooed and fussed over the baby while Mom gave her feeding instructions. "We'll come back at lunchtime, when court recesses," Mom said.

Dad steered into the center of town and parked in front of a large brick building in the center of courthouse square, occupying a full city block. On each side tall trees shaded a poorly tended lawn and park benches. Ann's eyes looked wide as saucers. Mine probably did, too. This was the Talladega

County Courthouse that Dad had told us so much about. As in many small southern towns, the courthouse formed the focal point of Talladega.

The town looked tranquil and pleasant. I wondered if I had been here before. Then I realized I was thinking of Mayberry from *The Andy Griffith Show*. I half expected to see Sheriff Andy Taylor and Deputy Barney Fife leaving the barber shop.

We walked solemnly into the courthouse, Dad in his usual faded dark suit, white shirt, and narrow dark tie. Mom wore one of her church dresses, with round white clip-on earrings, and bright red lipstick. Ann and I wore our nicest school clothes. The building interior was dark with worn wood paneling and heavy doors. We noticed the two drinking fountains, an old ceramic bowl with a small sign "Colored" and a newer metal water cooler marked "Whites only."

We climbed wide steps to the second floor. Dad led us into the courtroom. While he went to meet Chuck Morgan in the attorneys' room, we found seats on an old wooden pew in the whites-only section on the right. Each side of the central aisle held about fifteen pews. Mom pointed out the spittoons at the end of each row of seats. A sign said, "Don't spit on the floor." Ann and I glanced at the spittoons all morning, curious to see someone put them to use. But they seemed more traditional—symbolic of the folksy heritage of southern justice, perhaps—than functional. This didn't look like Perry Mason's courtroom. Later, we would recognize the 1930s courtroom in the movie *To Kill a Mockingbird* as a closer match.

The elevated jury box was empty, but there were some state prosecutors on the next level down. After a few minutes, Dad and Chuck Morgan entered from a door on the right front. They sat behind a big wooden table, facing the judge on the right-hand side with the other defense attorneys. On the left-hand side were the state prosecutors.

When the judge entered and perched behind a central desk on a raised platform, everyone slowly moved into action. People shuffled in and out, with little apparent order—much more casual than Perry Mason. A policeman kept guard, but with eyes closed most of the time. I kept peeking to see if he was asleep. The lawyers huddled in front of the judge, speaking in legalese whispers. Ann looked quizzically at me, and I looked to Mom. She just raised her eyebrows and shrugged.

When not required to speak with the attorneys, the judge sat with his feet up on his bench, and almost fell asleep. Another court official—I couldn't tell what his function was supposed to be—sat in front, smoking a cigar and reading a newspaper. There never seemed to be a moment when everyone got quiet and paid attention to the same thing at the same time.

Other than the defendants, sitting in the front row, most of the people in the courtroom looked like stereotypes of southern rednecks or hayseeds. I thought, "It's not right to think that . . . but it's true!"

During a break in the proceedings—"How can you tell the break from the hearing?" I wondered—we visited with Chuck Morgan and Dad in the lawyers' room, which had heavy dark wood paneling, shelves lined with old law books, and a long oak table. Mr. Morgan joked with us, asking how we liked watching Alabama justice in action. He fussed over Ann and me and made us feel part of something special. "You're old enough to remember this," he said. "What your Daddy is doing is important, going up against the State of Alabama. He's got a hell of a lot of guts—sorry, Melva, excuse my French."

When court recessed for lunch, we went to the MacNairs to get Mark. We wouldn't return for the afternoon session. After a refreshing lunch, with iced tea and lemonade, under towering live oaks and exotic conifers on the side lawn, Ann gathered a sackful of cones. "I never saw any like these!" she exclaimed.

Mrs. MacNair said, "Yes, these are lovely. When they open they look like a rose in full bloom. Or maybe more like a camellia blossom." Ann took the cones home and put them in a drawer of the dining-room hutch—reminders for the future of our day in court with Dad and Mom.

The Talladega court proceedings ended anticlimactically. On October 20, after two weeks of hearings, Judge Sullivan postponed the trial until February 8, 1963. Morgan had told Dad that the best they could have hoped for was such a postponement. He expected Richmond Flowers, his former classmate at the University of Alabama Law School, to win the November 6 election to succeed Attorney General MacDonald Gallion. Morgan thought he could convince his friend to drop Dad's name from the injunction.

After Flowers took office in January, Dad visited him in the State Capitol building. The new attorney general made no promises. Dad said: "But it was kind of like, 'Give us some time . . .' and then I will be dropped from the injunction." That is what happened. When the Talladega proceedings resumed, Dad's name was not on the list. That was the end of his trial, *State of Alabama v. Norman C. Jimerson.* As Chuck Morgan later wrote: "Evidence introduced during the trial was wholly insufficient to support the charge that the peacemaker had in fact been engaged in any activity other than trying to make peace."

After some additional legal maneuverings, the state's case against the other Talladega defendants fizzled out, and the judge lifted the injunction against them. Several months later—a year before the 1964 Civil Rights Act guaranteed equal access to public accommodations—white businessmen and black leaders worked out a local agreement to integrate the lunch counters in Talladega. This local solution characterized many of the South's steps of progress in civil rights.

Meanwhile, in early November 1962, Dad wrote to acknowledge a financial contribution from a new member of the Alabama Council on Human Relations. "Your moral and financial support inspire me to continue to do all that I can to serve the South amidst all of the frustrations and tensions that confront us in the Alabama Council," he wrote. "You are truly on a front line in the struggle for decency and human dignity." As our family would soon realize, the front lines didn't get any more dangerous than in Birmingham.

12

Behind the Scenes

By late 1962, racial tensions in Birmingham had built pressure that threatened to explode. People used different clichés: a powder keg waiting for a spark, a match near a short fuse, sitting on a case of dynamite. But for us, it felt like a pressure cooker, with steadily increasing intensity and no sign of a safety valve.

Ever since the 1954 Supreme Court decision overturning "separate-but-equal" schools, Birmingham's uneasy race relations had polarized the community. Violence against blacks led to beatings, lynchings, and dynamite attacks. Unlike Atlanta—"the city too busy to hate"—Birmingham tolerated malicious hatred toward its black citizens. The "Magic City" touted in Chamber of Commerce brochures became known as "Bombingham." So many blasts had occurred that one black residential neighborhood gained the nickname "Dynamite Hill."

The vicious beatings of black and white Freedom Riders at Birmingham's Trailways bus station on Mother's Day 1961 brought the city to worldwide attention. In Tokyo for an International Rotary Club convention, prominent Birmingham real estate attorney Sidney Smyer saw the front-page photograph of a white mob bludgeoning Freedom Riders in his hometown. "When you said you was from Birmingham," he later told Dad, "boy, they didn't have anything to do with you." This jolt to his local civic pride did not convert the long-time Dixiecrat into a champion of civil rights. But it did make him realize that bigotry and violence harmed Birmingham's reputation. This would not be good for business.

Shortly after my father arrived in Birmingham in August 1961, Sid Smyer met with him several times. They talked about changing the city's reputation by reducing racial violence and intimidation. Smyer declared his willingness "to take the bull by the horns." He and other prominent businessmen recognized the harmful effects of intransigent racism. They found they could confess their doubts to Jim Jimerson. As Diane McWhorter later observed in her 2001 book about Birmingham's civil rights revolution: "It was as if the natives had been waiting for years to unleash their pent-up moral confusion on a stranger—Jimerson was from New York State—who wouldn't tattle on them at the country club."

As the civil rights movement gained momentum throughout the Deep South in 1962, Birmingham remained the strongest bastion of segregation. Immoveable and uncompromising, the three city commissioners, led by Commissioner of Public Safety Eugene "Bull" Connor, refused to give an inch to demands for integration. Birmingham's moderate segregationists—such as Sid Smyer—and its few liberal civic leaders—such as the Alabama Council's David Vann—realized that the only way to avoid catastrophe would be to remove Bull Connor from power.

As president of the Birmingham Chamber of Commerce, in February 1961 Smyer had asked the Birmingham Bar Association to create a special committee to examine the feasibility of altering the city's form of government. Changing from the city commission, easily dominated by the autocratic Connor, to a mayor-council system might enable moderates to depose Connor by eliminating his office. By late 1961 the effort to change the form of city government had gained support from prominent white moderate businessmen and attorneys.

One of the leaders in mobilizing support for this effort was my father's friend David Vann, a former law clerk for Supreme Court Justice Hugo Black. Vann enlisted sympathetic members of the Young Men's Business Club to create a new group, Citizens for Progress, to spearhead the reform campaign. Following the August 1962 primary elections for Democratic and Republican candidates for local offices, Citizens for Progress circulated petitions for a referendum to create a new municipal government. They set up card tables around the city and gathered more than enough signatures to put the measure on the city ballot for November.

In a related effort, at the end of August, Smyer convinced the Chamber of Commerce to form a new group, called the Senior Citizens Committee. The Senior Citizens, in turn, created a subcommittee on race, which Smyer chaired. Its biracial membership included reform-minded black and white businessmen, among them prominent black moderates John Drew, A. G. Gaston, and Lucius Pitts. The Birmingham moderates at last seemed poised to respond to the city's polarized racial climate.

❖

As these developments unfolded, rumors that Birmingham would be the next civil rights battleground grew more persistent. As early as February 1962, Dad had informed Paul Rilling that major demonstrations in the city seemed likely. The first rumors that Martin Luther King Jr. planned to bring his nonviolent campaign to Birmingham surfaced in the spring. By summer, after King announced that his Southern Christian Leadership Conference would hold its annual convention in Birmingham in late September, many in the civil rights movement assumed demonstrations would begin then. But nobody knew. Then in August the SCLC announced plans for direct action during the convention.

During supper one evening, Dad told us: "Many Negroes say that King's plan to come here shows he thinks Birmingham has made some kind of progress, so it will be relatively safe to have demonstrations." He leaned back in his chair and shook his head. He almost whispered: "But I think it could be a bloody mess."

Mom said: "Why? Could it get any worse?"

Dad replied: "The Klan is just itching for an excuse. It could be a massacre."

"What do Chuck and Dave think?" Mom asked.

Dad answered: "It threw Vann into a tizzy. He says demonstrations will defeat his effort to change city government. Whites will think Connor is the man they want, to stop agitators."

He added: "But white leaders are really angry with old Bull. He promised to keep out *all* demonstrators awhile back—Negroes *and* whites. Then he allowed the Klan to demonstrate. The white power structure wants a strong segregationist, but not that strong. They want Birmingham to keep a good image."

Mom twisted the napkin in her hand. She said: "What will happen now?"

Dad replied: "Vann wants me to carry his message to King. He said, 'Jim, you've got to go to Atlanta and talk with King. Talk him out of having demonstrations before the election. We've decided that you're the only one that can do this. Try to change his mind.'"

He laid down his fork and shook his head. "I said, 'Dave, you know what that means? That's a *white* man telling King to go slow and wait. And King says *wait* means *never*.'" Dad grimaced and rolled his eyes. "King won't want to hear that!"

Mom said: "So? Will you go?"

"Yes. As soon as possible," Dad said.

A few days later, Dad returned from a one-day trip to Atlanta. After supper, he herded us all into the living room for family devotions. Before telling us about his trip, he said: "Susie-Q, do you know what time travel is?"

Susie said: "Is it when you go backwards, to horse and buggy days? They did that on TV!"

Dad said: "Yes. That's what happened to me!" He grinned, so we knew he wanted to tell a joke. "I left Atlanta today at 5:15, and got to Birmingham at 5:05. Ten minutes *before* I left!" He laughed, while we looked at each other.

Paul said: "How could you *do* that?"

Mom said: "He's just kidding you. Atlanta's in a different time zone. It's an hour later there. When it's five o'clock here it's already six o'clock in Atlanta."

Dad said, "Yeah. But Birmingham still *feels* fifty *years* behind Atlanta!"

Then he told us about his trip:

David Vann and some other guys wanted me to ask Martin Luther King to postpone demonstrations until after the election. So I called up King's office in Atlanta to try to get an appointment. They couldn't give me a specific time, but I went over there to see him when I could.

I went to his office and sat around about two or three hours—something like that. King was talking to reporters from *Newsweek* and *Time*. The reputation King has among us human rights workers is that he won't find time to talk to *white* people working in civil rights. He doesn't seem to think that's important for his strategy. That's okay with me. But some people, like the director of the Georgia Council, feel left out. Think they should have access to King. They assume it's because they're white.

He paused for a moment.

That's probably true. . . . So I kept trying to talk to King or anybody else in the office, and got no place. Finally, I said I was heading to the airport.

While I was waiting for my flight, I saw Wyatt T. Walker. Maybe he was coming in from a flight. I couldn't tell. But I talked with Walker. He's King's number one lieutenant now. Executive director of SCLC.

When we were in Virginia, he was pastor of a Negro church in Petersburg. I preached in his church and helped him serve communion. He never accepted my invitation to preach at the reformatory. But one time he did speak to a Hopewell First Baptist group. Probably the first Negro ever to speak there. So I knew him very well. I called him "Tee." He invited us to his home for dinner one time. Do you remember that?

We all shook our heads no, except Mom. She smiled and nodded yes.

So anyhow he knows who I am, and I know him. At the airport, I said, "I came here to explain the reasons why the demonstrations should be postponed."

His response was, "I don't want to hear it." For about forty-five minutes, I kept trying to figure out every possible way I could to get my foot in the door, to get him to listen to my message.

I said, "Well, Tee, you know, the next flight I'm on my way back to Birmingham. And it really doesn't make any difference to *my* plans whether you want to hear me or not." I'd say things like, "Just out of *curiosity,* you might want to listen. I'm not asking you to *act* on the information I have, but I'd like to give it to you." He'd shake his head side to side. Then I said, "You know, it's just *conceivable,* that maybe if you heard what the white liberals in Birmingham are doing, that it might be interesting for you as you make your plans." I probably didn't say anything like "Ignorance isn't going to be any better." But in every way I could think of, I said, "I'm not asking you to *do* anything. Just listen."

"Why wouldn't he?" Paul asked.

"That's not polite, is it, Mommy?" Susie said.

Dad said: "Well, Susie, it's like when you know what someone is going to say, and you don't want to hear it."

Paul said: "Like 'Clean up your room!'?"

We all laughed. Dad said, "That's just about right, I guess, Butch."

Then Dad continued his story:

I hung in there like a bulldog. I wasn't going to let go. Finally Walker said, "Well, now I'm not making any commitment to do anything, but I'll give you a couple of minutes." So in about ten minutes I told him what the plan is—Vann and his group are trying to get rid of Bull Connor through a referendum, and demonstrations will cause it to fail, and that will keep Connor in power.

So finally he listened to me. He didn't thank me. He didn't make any promises. He just said, "It's up to the folks in Birmingham." That means Shuttlesworth will decide. Then we said goodbye, and I came back home.

Mom said: "Now what? Will they postpone demonstrations?"
"Wish I knew," Dad said. "I wish I knew."

The weeks leading up to the Southern Christian Leadership Conference convention in Birmingham sizzled with tension. Civil rights activists, including Reverend Fred Shuttlesworth, anticipated the long-awaited start of direct action in the most-segregated city of the South. Moderate black leaders feared violent confrontations that could ignite the city's volatile racial antagonisms. White city leaders prepared for armed clashes. The Klan mobilized its forces to oppose expected demonstrations. As Paul Rilling, Dad's liaison with the Southern Regional Council, observed during a visit to Birmingham: "The mood in the city is ugly, the reactions of Bull Connor uncertain, and some elements in the Negro community no longer seem wedded to non-violence."

Seeking to maintain peace, Dad and the Alabama Council tried to establish lines of communication between the white and black leaders. Dad already enjoyed the trust of both black and white moderates in Birmingham. He needed to strengthen his connections with direct-action activists. Although Reverend Fred Shuttlesworth had moved to Cincinnati as pastor of Revelation Baptist Church, shortly before we arrived in Birmingham in August 1961, my father had met with him several times since then. For example, they had worked together to assist a young white woman whose parents forced her to leave home when she joined the civil rights movement in 1961. As King's SCLC convention neared, on September 10, 1962, Dad addressed a meeting of Shuttlesworth's Alabama Christian Movement for Human Rights. He hoped this would strengthen his credibility with the fiery activist and his followers.

Five days later, the executive committee of the Alabama Council met to develop a plan for keeping peace. Lucius Pitts had just returned from Washington, where he met off-the-record with Attorney General Robert Kennedy and his assistant for civil rights, Burke Marshall. They assured Pitts that the Justice Department would have an observer on hand during the week of the SCLC convention, and that marshals would be available nearby in case of severe trouble. They would not offer more than this. Pitts had also met with selected black leaders to gauge their feelings. He said that Shuttlesworth could call off demonstrations if he desired. As Paul Rilling observed, "Wyatt Walker gave the same impression to Jimerson several weeks ago."

The Alabama Council executive committee decided to approach Sid Smyer, one of two white business leaders most receptive to negotiating with black spokesmen. They agreed to tell him clearly and firmly that the only possibility of avoiding demonstrations would be for white leadership to make some specific and visible gesture of concession or good will. Pitts expressed confidence that black leaders would accept such an arrangement. The group arranged to meet with Smyer the following day.

At 9:00 a.m. on Sunday September 16, Smyer drove in from his country home on Shades Mountain for a meeting with Alabama Council leaders Dr. Lucius Pitts, Nat Welch, and my father. They told him that white businessmen must make meaningful and visible gestures, such as removing all segregation signs from water fountains and restrooms in downtown stores. White leaders also had to commit themselves publicly to forming a "status-backed" interracial committee. If Smyer and his fellow white business leaders achieved these steps, the Alabama Council delegates would recommend to black leaders deferring demonstrations for sixty days.

Smyer indicated that he felt these suggestions were possible and reasonable. He would do what he could to carry them through. He said that a group of top-level businessmen, fearing violence, had met at least three times to discuss how to forestall demonstrations. Smyer expressed confidence that the "whites only" signs would be down within forty-eight hours and that his group would publicly announce formation of an interracial committee. Pitts and Smyer each pledged to seek agreement from their respective leadership groups. In this crisis atmosphere the Alabama Council director would continue to act as go-between and negotiator.

Only a week before the Southern Christian Leadership convention, King and Shuttlesworth still planned demonstrations during the conference. Within days, however, the timing of King's Birmingham campaign changed. Dad said, "I found out from local Negroes. They're surprised that demonstrations are going to be postponed."

Acting as liaison between the white and black communities, my father had played a key role in securing this postponement. His meeting with Wyatt T. Walker at the Atlanta airport first alerted the SCLC to the concerns of Birmingham's moderate white leaders. As he later stated: "My report is probably the only direct information King had about the political situation in Birmingham. So my feeling is that my trip made the difference."

The second key factor that contributed to this decision, made by Shuttlesworth and King, came from the discussions Dad arranged with Sid Smyer to gain concessions from white businessmen. He therefore contributed in two vital ways to changing the timing of Birmingham's confrontation with its racial destiny. By the time King led demonstrations in the Magic City, in April 1963, the local situation had become more favorable for success.

By early October, Dr. Pitts told Dad that Sid Smyer's group, the Senior Citizens Committee, "are getting with it." Downtown stores in Birmingham had painted over segregated restroom and water fountain signs. Business leaders seemed more willing to negotiate with blacks. However, tensions remained high.

Alabama Council President Nat Welch reported: "The Birmingham racial situation is acute at this time. Our executive director, Reverend Norman Jimerson, has been in Alabama a little over a year. He has concentrated his major effort in the 'Johannesburg of North America.' On his own initiative he has done a terrific job this past year in establishing rapport with the leading businessmen in Birmingham. Jimerson has been particularly effective with the Chamber of Commerce group."

As Welch observed: "Reverend Jimerson is the only man in Birmingham who has the confidence of both Negro leaders, including Reverend Fred Shuttlesworth and Reverend Martin Luther King, and the white Senior Citizens Committee. When Martin Luther King's group was in Birmingham last week for their meeting the situation was explosive. Jimerson was able to work out a plan where the downtown merchants agreed to remove signs from drinking fountains and restrooms, and the Senior Citizens Committee agreed to form a bi-racial committee to deal positively with the racial situation in general and job classifications specifically."

Despite these temporary signs of racial progress, by late October, Dad wrote to Paul Rilling: "The situation in Birmingham is difficult to assess. It looks as if the Senior Citizens Committee is still meeting, but since Miles College students plan to resume a Selective Buyers Campaign, many of the Senior Citizens are taking the attitude that you can't trust or work with Negroes. Their decision to take further steps is no longer unanimous." He also stated that Chuck Morgan "has filed two historic cases in which he is charging that white man's justice Alabama style precludes the possibility of a Negro getting justice. He is enumerating a long list of law enforcement and court procedures that point up the discriminations a Negro faces, from the cradle to the grave." Morgan had told Dad, "The only thing that is not segregated is the electric chair, and that is because there is only one."

Nat Welch and Paul Rilling weren't the only people to recognize my father's success in promoting peaceful changes in Birmingham's racial tensions. Segregationists also took notice. On October 19, Dad wrote to Burke Marshall, his contact in the United States Department of Justice: "Wednesday noon Radio Station WAPI reported that Bull Connor admitted that he had an informer at the meeting held the night before by the Birmingham Council on Human Relations. He misquoted me and others. His purpose was to link the Council with those who are interested in changing the form of city government, which is to be voted on at the November 6th election. I had a premonition that this might be the occasion that he would use information about me and the Council that he has been so carefully preparing during the past year."

Bull Connor's informant also fed information to the strongly segregationist newspaper *The Jeffersonian,* published by the White Citizens Council. Its October 1962 issue carried several articles attacking the Alabama Council. Under the bold heading "RACE AGITATORS IN ACTION," it carried an "Exclusive" account of the Greater Birmingham Chapter of the Alabama Council on Human Relations meeting on October 16: "Rev. Norman C. Jimmerson [*sic*], white, . . . and a known integrationist, . . . is a bosom friend of Carl Braden and Anne Braden. Carl Braden is an identified Communist, who was recently released from the Federal pen for contempt of the House Un-American Activities Committee. Anne Braden is a reporter for the 'Southern Patriot,' official magazine of the Southern Conference Educational Fund. This publication is on the subversive list published by the Senate Internal Security Committee."

The article reported Dad's remarks about his Talladega trial, and stated that a black woman "got up and made a talk about the Negroes using the white rest rooms and restaurants in the stores and told them that the Birmingham Police Department could not put them all in jail, to go ahead and use them. Jimmerson made the statement that 'Bull Connor would put them all in jail.'" Dad's prediction turned out to be correct. Connor did fill the jails during the April–May 1963 confrontations in Birmingham.

The overall tone of *The Jeffersonian* articles was menacing and hostile. When Dad sent a copy to Paul Rilling, he responded by urging the Birmingham Council to follow a policy of closed meetings, except when a public meeting seemed necessary. "No one can avoid leaks from time to time," Rilling advised, "but I see no need to admit any persons to regular meetings not known to or vouched for by members."

Dad replied that "the local officers are all hepped up on maintaining a posture of open meetings with the public invited." But he said he agreed with Rilling and would seek to convince the local council to follow his recommendation for greater security.

In the absence of mass demonstrations in fall 1962, the November 6 referendum to change Birmingham's form of government passed. The powerful three-man city commission, dominated by Bull Connor, would give way to a mayor and city council in the spring. There would be a vote for city mayor and council members in April 1963.

After returning from the National Sharecroppers Fund Convention in mid-November, Dad wrote to Paul Rilling: "Birmingham is still in a state of flux. Most people assume that Birmingham will be able to make some significant changes under a Mayor-Council form of government, which was approved on November 6th by the electorate. I understand that there are a lot of behind the scenes discussions trying to encourage high caliber men to run for the office of mayor and the city council."

He added that efforts to launch an all-out selective buying campaign in Birmingham had started, but did not yet seem effective. "It seems difficult to understand what can be accomplished by squeezing the merchants at this time, because they have demonstrated good faith in trying to take down signs. I am told that Blach's Department Store refused to put the signs back up, even after the city officials were getting after store owners to replace signs that had been taken down." However, soon the good faith of white businessmen proved temporary. Without continued pressure, most stores quietly re-segregated their facilities.

In November, James D. Herndon, a white southerner, wrote a letter to the editor of *Newsweek* expressing his faith that his fellow citizens desired truth and justice. Dad took the opportunity to reach a national audience with his own message of hope for improvements in race relations. Published in the November 26, 1962, *Newsweek,* Dad's letter stated:

Mr. Herndon's statement is an excellent refutation of the thought that people do not change.

One important step in resolving our racial tensions across the country is the establishment of lines of communication between people of various races. More and more businessmen in Alabama are realizing that they must establish such lines of communication in order to develop a peaceful resolution to the problems connected with segregation and thus to protect their financial future. Mill hands, factory workers, and farmers can be expected to learn that mob rule and mass defiance will cause economic hardships.

This public statement stands out as a rare instance in which Dad stepped out of the background to seek a wider audience. Working behind the scenes, he continued to fulfill his role in promoting communication, negotiations, and reconciliation between the black and white communities in Alabama. He did not aspire to leadership or public recognition. Yet in some ways his work with the Alabama Council on Human Relations made possible the slow progress in race relations that occurred in the months leading up to Martin Luther King's Birmingham campaign of 1963. Direct action—or even the threat of mass demonstrations—made progressive white leaders willing to make concessions. But without a mediator to bring the two sides together for serious negotiations, the impasse would remain. My father played this role of go-between carefully and effectively, behind the scenes.

13

Family Time

Although Dad poured his energies into civil rights concerns with intense missionary zeal, he sometimes paused to catch his breath. His work and travel meant that for long stretches Mom by herself had to tend to five children, including a young infant, take care of the household needs of a growing family, and try to manage the stress and anxiety of being an outsider in a foreign land. As feelings of ostracism and exclusion clouded our individual minds, we grew to rely on each other for comfort and security. As children, although we each enjoyed time spent with friends, we often felt most comfortable with each other and with Mom. At home.

During the fall of 1962, as the tensions of Dad's work seemed to ease a bit, he began to spend more time with the family. On a few occasions during our time in Birmingham, the whole family joined Dad at Alabama Council meetings, where we met some of Dad's colleagues and experienced the black culture from which segregation laws sought to exclude us. The daily routines of school, homework, and household chores set a steady beat of normality to cushion the occasional staccato counterpoint of threatening phone calls and harassment, with less frequent cymbal clashes of jarring news of civil rights abuses, violence, and crisis.

My first experience with the power of music in the civil rights movement came during an Alabama Council meeting I attended with my parents. I had heard marvelous gospel singing by the choirs of black churches we had visited. At the time I thought of such singing as religious expression, not political. During a council meeting at Talladega College, before and after speeches that seemed boring to me as a thirteen-year-old teenager, the all-black student choir led rousing renditions of both religious and political songs. Old Negro spirituals from the days of slavery couched freedom to come with God's kingdom in a message that I now realized had been an appeal for the end of slavery. Folk tunes and newly composed civil rights anthems roused the audience to an emotional release that sent chills up my spine.

Hearing the choir sing "Oh Freedom" and "We're Marching On to Freedom Land," I began to understand why civil rights activists relied on singing to inspire people to support the movement. "We Shall Not Be Moved" showed the defiant spirit necessary to stand up to angry white mobs, police batons, and paddy wagons. The choir reached an emotional peak with a passionate rendition of "The Battle Hymn of the Republic," which connected the civil rights movement to the abolitionist campaigns of the Civil War era a century earlier.

Just when I thought the singing could not get any more powerful than this, the first notes of "We Shall Overcome" brought us all to our feet. Black and white members of the audience crossed arms and held hands with their neighbors in the pews. Hearing the words of resolve and hope—the optimistic vow that the movement would succeed despite oppression and suffering—tears ran down my cheeks.

> We shall overcome, We shall overcome
> We shall overcome, some day
> Oh, deep in my heart I do believe
> We shall overcome, some day
> We'll walk hand in hand . . .
> We are not afraid . . .
>
> Black and white together . . .
>
> Oh, deep in my heart I do believe
> We shall overcome, some day.

Shortly before Thanksgiving, one of Dad's friends offered to let us use his cottage near Mobile Bay for a holiday respite. Dad clearly needed a break from the tension, and we all looked forward to a few days apart from the routines of school and home. There would be no ringing telephones, no hate calls or threats.

We piled into the Ford station wagon, with our dachshund, Spitzy, and a bassinet for baby Mark. During the long drive, the radio played "Sugar

Shack" by Jimmy Gilmer and the Fireballs so often that we kids could all sing along word for word.

As we neared Mobile Bay, the narrow toehold that linked Alabama to the Gulf of Mexico, we saw strange gray clumps of something hanging from tree branches. It looked like long gray beards.

"What's that?" we asked.

Mom said: "That must be Spanish moss. It's not really moss, but some kind of plant that grows on trees this far south."

Closer to the coast, some trees were covered so thickly that you couldn't see anything but the exotic Spanish moss.

Leaving the Montgomery to Mobile highway, we headed down the eastern shore of Mobile Bay on narrow roads. Mom tried to follow the directions written on a small sheet of paper. But at Fairhope, Dad had to stop and ask for help. We finally found the small cottage, dwarfed by tall live oak and cypress trees draped in Spanish moss. The cottage itself was dark and musty. It was kind of creepy, really. Not the vacation home I'd envisioned.

We enjoyed a quiet Thanksgiving at the cottage, with no homework, no phone calls, or distractions. One day we took a side trip down the western side of Mobile Bay to Dauphin Island, a quiet haven of white sandy beaches and small cottages. Because of my interest in Civil War sites, Dad took us to visit Fort Gaines, a partially restored fort that guarded the entrance to the bay. It was windy and cold, but I enjoyed exploring the ramparts and gun emplacements, mostly World War II vintage but close enough that I could imagine Union Admiral David Farragut sailing past the cannons to capture Mobile in 1864.

On Sunday we loaded the station wagon for a drive into Mobile, a brief detour before heading home.

"Randy, put down that book and help me carry things to the car," Dad said.

Dad drove down the main street of Mobile while we gawked at the stores and advertising signs. Suddenly we heard a police siren behind us, and a cruiser pulled us over.

Dad asked Mom: "What's going on? I wasn't speeding or anything. . . ."

Mom said: "I hope this isn't some kind of harassment. They have your license number from the council meetings."

A policeman walked up to the driver's side and motioned for Dad to roll down the window.

"What's the matter, officer?" Dad asked.

The policeman said: "Sir, I saw this on your bumper. Thought you might not want to lose it." He handed Dad a book. My library book. I must have tucked it between the tailgate and bumper. So much for fears of police surveillance and harassment. At least for now.

As the University of Alabama 1962 football season began, Granddad asked Mom to get tickets for one of the games. The promising young sophomore quarterback for the Crimson Tide, Joe Willie Namath, had been a star athlete at Beaver Falls High School. He had been recruited by the University of Maryland, but poor SAT scores prevented his admission. Legendary Alabama coach Paul "Bear" Bryant offered him a full scholarship.

At Granddad's suggestion, Mom wrote a letter to Namath. As a fellow graduate of Beaver Falls High, she asked if he could get her tickets so her father could come down to Alabama to see him play. In reply, Namath sent a handwritten letter. He stated that he could not send complimentary tickets, but he offered to sell her good tickets. He apologized but said this was one way he was able to pay his college expenses.

Granddad bought tickets, but not from Joe Willie. He and Monty drove down for the final game of the season, December 1, 1962. 'Bama played its arch-rival Auburn at Birmingham's Legion Field. We parked in the large gravel lot on the west side of the city and walked into the open-girdered stadium. Chants of "Roll Tide!" and "War Eagle!" echoed back and forth, just as in the outdoor walkways at Homewood Junior High, where supporters of the rival schools tried to out-shout each other.

In the game, Namath solidified his reputation as a star quarterback. He threw for two touchdowns, and ran for another. Alabama won 38–0.

The next year Granddad again drove down to see Namath play at Legion Field. That made three years in a row that I attended a University of Alabama football game.

When my cousin Ron Poister visited us one time, the other college kids in Sunday school class at Shades Valley Presbyterian Church got excited when he said he lived in Beaver Falls.

"Do you know Joe Namath?" they asked.

"Slightly. We were in the same high school for a year or two."

"What's he like?" the Alabama fans asked.

Ron said: "I didn't really know him. He was a couple years older than me and from the other side of town."

They said it must have been exciting knowing such a famous athlete.

"Not really," Ron said. "He was always hanging out in pool halls, hustling kids, chasing girls. Not the kind of guy I wanted to know."

Someone else asked: "Why didn't he go to Penn State or some other Yankee school?"

Ron said: "He couldn't get in. Didn't have the grades."

This honest comment ended Ron's brief celebrity status as someone who knew Joe Namath. He saw angry expressions, heard muttered insults. Everyone drifted away.

As 1962 drew to a close, Paul Rilling announced that he had accepted a new job in Washington, D.C. Dad would report to a new Southern Regional Council field director, Paul Anthony. Dad wrote to Rilling, thanking him for his support and assistance. On behalf of ACHR, he wrote to Paul Anthony, offering congratulations and pledging the Alabama Council's full support.

Before leaving SRC, Rilling also wrote to ACHR President Nat Welch concerning finances. Although the council budget allocation could not be increased, he stated, "speaking personally and unofficially, I would hope there could be a little raise in Jimerson's salary," because "he is presently working within such a tight family budget that extra worries and pressures are present in a job which is at best a pressure cooker."

Likewise, shortly after assuming his new position, Paul Anthony wrote to the new ACHR president, Reverend Powers McLeod of Auburn Methodist Church, about his first Alabama visit: "I was impressed by your man and the work he is doing." He urged the Alabama Council to provide staff benefits for the executive director, such as travel and accident insurance, personal and family health and hospitalization, and a modest term-life policy. "With Jim's family situation these things should be done," he wrote. "I heard no complaints from him or his family, but there must be considerable financial straits."

Anthony also sent a memo to Southern Regional Council Director Leslie Dunbar. "For the environment and times, ACHR is in good shape," he wrote. "Jimerson is doing a good job, working hard, having some success in his efforts to meet and work with the power structure." He continued: "For Birmingham, Jimerson's efforts are encouraging. He has access to some surprising places, often with people who disagree with him but trust him and see his work as valuable."

However, Anthony pointed out some potential problems: "Jimerson and family are showing signs of the strain. Fine family, nice wife, five attractive children including five-months-old baby. Still lots of pressure, some threats and harassment, financial strain. Jimerson shows signs of early Bob Hughes: nervousness, always tired, stomach trouble, 70 hour weeks. Urged him to slow up, stay home more. Felt like an ass with my pep talks but think they helped some. He likes his work. His wife supports him completely. He is neither a genius nor a martyr, but ACHR has a good man."

In concluding his report, Paul Anthony wrote: "Birmingham is a pathetic, sick, police-state kind of city. But there is real hope there—and good people. . . . ACHR is limping along but this outfit has the promise of being what it should be. Jimerson is better than I expected. Promise and spirit are great things, and these people have both." This assessment of conditions in Alabama indicated the progress Dad had made, and the challenges lying ahead for 1963.

In December 1962, Mom typed and mimeographed a Jimerson family Christmas letter for 1962. The letter showed the close interweaving of our family's lives and Dad's work. It began with a verse from a hymn we knew well:

> O Heart of God incarnate, So human, so divine
> From Thee we learn what love is, in Thee love's ways we find:
> God's love to earth Thou bringest in living deeds that prove
> How sweet to serve all others, when we all others love.

Dear Friends:

We eagerly anticipate the messages and the pictures we shall receive from you this year. Christmas, 1962, finds us all healthy and happy, especially with the new addition the year has brought us. On July 30th Mark Douglas arrived and has brightened our lives as we never dreamed he could. Randy, Ann, Paul and Susan hardly start a morning without first greeting their brother.

Jim's work continues to fascinate him and even led him into court for the first time in his life. During the sit-ins in Talladega last April he and several other individuals, along with the students of the Negro college, were enjoined by the State Attorney General (for political purposes) from staging any more demonstrations. So far nothing drastic has occurred other than the Council's outlay of several thousand dollars for court costs. And still the trial, after two sessions, has been postponed until early next year. Actually, Jim was in Talladega to propose peaceful settlement of differences.

Our families are well. Melva's mother was with her after the baby arrived and her father took the boys for a short trip to Florida, since the girls had spent June and July in Pennsylvania. Jim's mother is spending December with us.

May you have a year filled with love and peace.

Sincerely,

The Norman C. Jimersons

14

Peacemaker in Birmingham

The "Year of Birmingham" began inauspiciously. The importance of Birmingham's civil rights revolution of 1963 couldn't be predicted as the year began. Fearing the loss of support from southern Democrats, President John F. Kennedy rebuffed appeals for a dramatic gesture to mark the centennial of Lincoln's Emancipation Proclamation, issued January 1, 1863. Despite his 1960 campaign pledge to address equality of opportunity with a stroke of the pen, the president who forced Khrushchev to back down during the Cuban Missile Crisis in October 1962 flinched two months later at the expected backlash over civil rights from southern senators and governors in his own political party.

Martin Luther King Jr. had led civil rights spokesmen in calling for a bold gesture from President Kennedy. In May 1962, on the eighth anniversary of the Supreme Court decision declaring segregated schools unconstitutional, King and other civil rights leaders issued a manifesto calling for a "Second Emancipation Proclamation." The statement declared: "The time has come, Mr. President, to let those dawn-like rays of freedom, first glimpsed in 1863, fill the heavens with the noonday sunlight of complete human dignity." But Kennedy dared not risk alienating southern voters and thereby likely losing his chance for reelection. Instead of celebrating the Emancipation Proclamation centennial, he quietly held a reception for black leaders in February 1963, on the anniversary of Lincoln's birth.

One of the southern Democrats Kennedy did not want to antagonize, George C. Wallace, took office as governor of Alabama on January 14, 1963. After defeating the more moderate Ryan De Graffenried in the 1962 Democratic primary, Wallace handily won the November election.

As my father later stated in his Alabama Council quarterly report: "Early in December of 1962 the general mood in Alabama was calm. Governor-elect George Wallace was making very few statements, although the statements that he made promised that his campaign speeches to prevent desegregation of the schools would be kept. Those who had hoped that Wallace would be a little more quiet in his defiance of the Federal Government were greatly disappointed when he made headlines with his extreme remarks at his inauguration."

The vicious side of Wallace's pledge to defy federal authority in order to maintain segregation soon became apparent. His campaign vow to "stand in the schoolhouse door" to prevent integration of the University of Alabama offered a preview. His inauguration speech dramatically began his attack on the civil rights movement. Wallace took the oath of office as governor on the front steps of the Capitol—the same spot where Jefferson Davis became president of the Confederate States of America in 1861. Wallace quoted General Robert E. Lee, invoked the Confederate heritage, and declared: "In the name of the greatest people that have ever trod this earth, I draw the line in the dust and toss the gauntlet before the feet of tyranny . . . and I say . . . segregation today . . . segregation tomorrow . . . segregation forever." He denounced the country's "ungodly government"—which imposed "the heel of tyranny" over the South—and the "propaganda" of appeals for "human rights." Wallace then attacked the Supreme Court, communism, and Harvard intellectuals, among others. He ended by repeating his campaign slogan, "Stand up for Alabama."

As we watched television news reports of Wallace's inauguration, I could see Dad's muscles tense. As he scowled, Mom quietly wept. I felt a chill run up my backbone. We—all of us in Alabama—would be in for a difficult time ahead.

The next day, Dad told Mom during supper: "Chuck Morgan is delighted. He says Wallace's complete defiance helps our chances of putting him in jail." He took another bite of fish sticks, chewing vigorously. "Wish I could share his confidence."

Two days after Wallace's inauguration, one hopeful sign appeared. Eleven Alabama religious leaders issued a public statement, printed in the Birmingham newspapers, appealing for law and order and common sense. Acknowledging that court decisions would soon bring about desegregation of schools and colleges, they decried defiance and stated that "inflammatory and rebellious statements can only lead to violence, discord, confusion and disgrace for our beloved state."

In the polarized atmosphere of January 1963, this public statement required immense courage. As we had seen while trying to find a church home, religious leaders who spoke out on racial issues—even indirectly—risked losing their pulpits or being shunned by their communities. That had happened to Bob Hughes and many others. Dad pointed out that one of the signers of this appeal, Reverend Edward V. Ramage of Birmingham's First Presbyterian Church, had become a close friend of his. Dad had also worked closely with three others: Episcopal Bishop C. C. J. Carpenter, his assistant, Bishop Co-Adjutor Reverend George M. Murray, and Earl Stallings, pastor of Birmingham's First Baptist Church.

The religious leaders' appeal suggested that Wallace's extremism might, perhaps, awaken the white moderates in Alabama to oppose radical segregationists. The Alabama Council on Human Relations hoped to gain support from this group of reasonable people willing to deal honestly with the state's racial problems.

Birmingham's newly approved switch to a mayor-council government required spring elections for mayor and council members. In the race for mayor, the leading candidates were Bull Connor, former Lieutenant Governor Albert Boutwell, and attorney Tom King, who had lost an earlier race for mayor. After a visit to Birmingham in mid-January, Paul Anthony, Dad's connection to the Southern Regional Council, reported to SRC head Leslie Dunbar: "Most cautiously predict Connor will be defeated. The money, Chamber of Commerce, and newspapers will support Boutwell. White moderates—as always—are fearful of Negro demonstrations, which will help Connor."

Anthony observed that "Some unity is being achieved in the Negro community." Miles College President Lucius Pitts had recently persuaded black business mogul A. G. Gaston to insist that Fred Shuttlesworth be brought into meetings with white business leaders, as Dr. King prepared to come to Birmingham. "This is a situation in which local leadership should be allowed full control," Anthony advised. "If they are not, King will be just above Bull Connor in popularity with them."

Since late 1962 my father had worked diligently to urge continuing communications between the Senior Citizens Committee and black leaders, but with little success. During the first three months of 1963 he talked frequently with prominent white leaders, urging negotiations to achieve peaceful desegregation. He also conferred with several downtown merchants, warning them that the black community would probably stage demonstrations after the mayoral election on April 2. Only frank negotiations could avert renewed problems.

Violence against blacks continued. As Dad stated in his quarterly report to Paul Anthony: "On December 14, a Negro church was bombed in Birmingham and several homes were damaged. On December 17, Negro ministers held a protest meeting. Persons present at the meeting accused the local police of showing more interest in destroying clues than in gathering evidence. One minister made the remark 'It is difficult to catch your own.'" Birmingham seemed determined to live up to its reputation as "the meanest city in the South."

Yet a Southern Regional Council press release indicated some signs of hope for the city. The SRC cited the work of attorney Charles Morgan Jr., the influence of Dr. Lucius Pitts, and the new leadership of A. G. Gaston. The press release also stated:

> There are a few white liberals whose very survival marks them as at least remarkable and/or persistent. Notable among them is the Rev. Norman Jimerson, Executive Director of the Alabama Council on Human Relations . . . who has access to some strange and high places, frequently with people who disagree with him but respect him and see the value of his presence.
>
> A small band of women are quietly starting a Save-the-Schools movement. They are timid and frightened, but chances are they will last and be an effective community force. . . .
>
> Birmingham represents real Deep South defiance. If it is changing—and I think it is—that is quite a story. Whatever happens, the people of Birmingham are quite a story.

Dad continued to meet with white businessmen and black community leaders, seeking to open lines of communication in order to reduce tensions and prepare for substantive negotiations regarding desegregation. In March he and other members of the Alabama Council talked with Robert S. Jemison, owner of the Birmingham Transit Company. Jemison had received letters from many white people saying that they did not ride the recently desegregated buses because blacks were jostling whites on them. Jemison also stated that many incidents of bus drivers and whites antagonizing blacks riding in the front seats of buses contributed to lost revenue.

Yet through the first months of 1963, the upcoming election for mayor and council positions created a sense of uncertainty regarding future developments in Birmingham's race relations. People seemed to be waiting for a new mayor to take office. The possibility of large-scale demonstrations added to this sense of suspended animation.

As in the previous fall, civil rights leaders hesitated to launch direct action in Birmingham for fear it would strengthen Bull Connor's chances of winning the mayor's race. In February, my father cancelled an Alabama Council workshop concerning merit employment, scheduled for March 8–9 in Birmingham. Businessmen and other white leaders requested this step because Connor might use this event in his campaign speeches. Dad explained: "Perhaps one has to live in Birmingham to understand the degree of concern that businessmen feel concerning any action in the area of civil rights that might give Eugene 'Bull' Connor ammunition in his attacks upon the other candidates."

On Tuesday April 2, Albert Boutwell defeated Bull Connor and became the elected mayor of Birmingham. The election inspired the largest turnout ever for a city election. Boutwell beat Connor by 8,000 votes, winning nearly all of the 10,000 black votes. Dad observed: "Most people feel that the council members elected on April 2 will be able to deal realistically with Birmingham's problems. All of those elected to the council campaigned to open the city's parks."

The next day after the election, the *Birmingham News* carried a front-page drawing of a golden sun—a rare use of color—rising over the city skyline, dominated by the Vulcan statue. The headline proclaimed: "New Day Dawns for Birmingham." However, Bull Connor vowed not to let the minor matter of an election end his dominance over city government. Connor refused to vacate his office in City Hall. As Martin Luther King Jr. arrived in Birmingham, he found a city with two mayors, two city governments, and a political tangle to unravel.

At its annual meeting in Tuskegee, February 1–2, 1963, the Alabama Council on Human Relations had reelected Reverend Powers McLeod as president. The board took two steps toward racial equity in its leadership and staffing. The Alabama Council had always included both black and white members on its board of directors. Now they decided that in 1964 they would have a black president. They also agreed to hire a black secretary immediately, replacing a white woman who had not performed well and whose loyalties to the civil rights movement seemed uncertain.

During the board meeting on February 1, the council agreed to accept a student intern from Kalamazoo College to work with the executive director for a period of three months beginning April 1, 1963. This move would provide some additional support for Dad's daily responsibilities, and perhaps open opportunities for special projects.

Thus, on Monday April 1, Dad hired a black secretary, Myrtice Woods, to begin work a month later. The next day, as Birmingham voters went to the polls to elect a new mayor and city council, Michael Morden, a student intern from Kalamazoo College, arrived in the Alabama Council office.

On the following day, Wednesday April 3, Dad's office phone rang at 8:30 or 9:00 in the morning. A reporter for the *Atlanta Constitution* wanted to know if demonstrations were going on in Birmingham. He got a similar call from New York. *Newsweek* also wanted to know if there would be demonstrations. To both inquirers, Dad said, "I sure don't know, but I'll soon find out."

Dad walked two blocks from his office in the Comer Building on Twentieth Street, over to Twenty-second, and saw that there were demonstrators at Newberry's Department Store. He arrived as police made their first arrest. Dad spoke briefly with two FBI agents and a black minister. Then he went back to the office, contacted some of the Birmingham leaders to tell them that demonstrations were underway, and confirmed this with the newsmen in Atlanta and New York.

(A few months later, one of the store owners told him that the merchants assumed that because they had seen him on the corner, they told people that Jim Jimerson was masterminding the demonstrations. Dad commented: "That's probably the most glory I've been given. All undeserved!")

The Birmingham campaign, which began on April 3, became a major nonviolent confrontation with the entrenched forces of segregation in the city. Wyatt T. Walker, King's executive director and Dad's former associate in Virginia, had quietly scouted out possible locations in Birmingham for sit-ins, marches, and demonstrations. Walker developed detailed plans for "Project C," his code for the Birmingham direct action "confrontation." The demonstrations began with some quiet sit-ins. "Many Negro leaders in Birmingham did not know that the demonstrations were going to take place," Dad reported. "King and Shuttlesworth had not been in touch with people who did not belong to the Alabama Christian Movement for Human Rights."

At first Dad was not sure who had initiated the sit-ins, but the blacks in Birmingham assumed that King could not come into Birmingham without Shuttlesworth's support. My father was not involved in the demonstrations, but he immediately started visiting people in the black community to learn what was going on. He quickly found out that Andrew Young was King's lieutenant in charge of planning the details of demonstrations—what stores they would picket, and what day and time.

While King stated that Birmingham was the worst city in the South, Dad noted, Young admitted privately that "demonstrations were held only because Birmingham's climate had improved to the point that they felt demonstrations could be held without anyone being killed." King arrived on election day, April 2, and set up headquarters at the Gaston Motel. During the early stage of demonstrations, Dad observed, "King, Abernathy, Andrew Young, Shuttlesworth, and a few others, probably, were the ones who made the decisions."

If many of Birmingham's black leaders expressed surprise that demonstrations had begun the day after the mayoral election, the white community was shocked. White moderates felt betrayed by "outside agitators" intervening in local political concerns. David Vann, the liberal white leader who had worked actively to change the form of city government, said on April 3: "This is the most cruel and vicious thing that has ever happened to Birmingham." Vann argued that the incoming mayor and council should be allowed time to change Birmingham's climate. Dad said that Vann and other sympathetic whites and moderate blacks "assume that the new government is fully aware of the urgency of dealing constructively with discriminatory practices in Birmingham." Vann thought that Mayor Boutwell and the new council would be friends of the black community if given a chance.

On the same day that demonstrations began, Father Albert S. Foley—the long-time Alabama Council board member who had offered the executive director position to Dad two years earlier—arrived from Mobile. At the Gaston Motel early that evening, Foley criticized King and Shuttlesworth for intervening at the moment that Bull Connor had been defeated. "Do you Negroes want progress or attention?" he asked. Shuttlesworth responded: "Go over to the city jail and ask twenty-one Negroes in jail what they want."

Later that evening, as Shuttlesworth led a mass meeting, Foley addressed a gathering of the conservative black businessmen's club Frontiers International. As someone told Dad, Foley argued that "the demonstrations are ill-timed and disrupting negotiations already under way." The press carried stories that Father Foley also charged that Martin Luther King's actions were motivated by the desire to raise money.

Coming from a prominent leader of the Alabama Council on Human Relations, such accusations could undermine Dad's efforts to mediate between the demonstration leaders and the white business community. He had to distance himself from Foley's criticism of King. So Dad and Powers McLeod quickly talked with demonstration leaders and others to make it clear that Father Foley did not represent the council.

In addition to putting out this fire before it caused too much damage, immediately after the demonstration started my father went to the white leaders and said, "This will be going on and on and on until they get negotiations." Dad wasn't aware of all the moves by the black leaders. But he did know they were trying to contact Attorney General Robert Kennedy to ensure protection. The beginning of King's Birmingham campaign placed everyone on high alert. Some white civil rights supporters hoped for a major breakthrough. Others feared disaster, violence, deaths.

After three days of sit-ins, Fred Shuttlesworth led the first protest march of the campaign on Saturday April 6. The next day, Palm Sunday, Reverends A. D. King (a Birmingham minister and brother of Martin Luther King Jr.) and John T. Porter led another march. Birmingham police brought in their trained K-9 corps. Black spectator Leroy Allen and several others sustained minor injuries. This was the beginning of more than a month of demonstrations in Birmingham.

Throughout this period, my father spent considerable time at the Gaston Motel with leaders of the movement. He also communicated frequently with business and civic leaders in the white community. Dad repeatedly urged white and black leaders to sit down for informal talks, long before they were ready for formal negotiations. As he explained, "I keep saying to the Negroes that they need to decide what they really want. Then I talk to people like Sid Smyer and Jim Head in the white community and say, 'You've got to start communicating with the Negroes.' I keep asking David Vann to help me convince these white businessmen to negotiate."

During the first week of demonstrations, Reverend Ralph Abernathy called my father and said that Dr. King wanted to sit down and talk with the white ministers from downtown, along with some of his own staff. As Dad said later, "King wanted me to help get people together, so he could interpret and explain his philosophy and why they were having demonstrations."

Dad arranged a meeting of white clergy including Bishop Coadjutor George Murray, the Episcopal assistant bishop; Ed Ramage of the First Presbyterian Church; and Earl Stallings of First Baptist. King brought his brother A. D. King, Andrew Young, J. L. Ware, Fred Shuttlesworth, and other black ministers. This group met twice, so that King could explain the need for demonstrations and why they couldn't wait any longer. Two white ministers said they were upset because people in their congregations were putting pressure on them, and the outside forces coming into Birmingham placed them in a difficult position. Dad said: "The meetings were really interesting, because white ministers who were liberal about wanting to see advances in human relations—such as Bishop Murray, who was not out in front or saying much, but who wanted to see progress in race relations—became, at this point, antagonistic toward King and the demonstrations."

In addition to this request by Dr. King to meet with white ministers, my father tried to bring together white business leaders and King's advisors. After talking several times, separately, with David Vann and Andrew Young, Dad convinced them to get together on Sunday night, April 7, to discuss the developing crisis. They met in the parsonage of Reverend Joseph Ellwanger, the white pastor of a black Lutheran church on the south side of Birmingham, not far from downtown. Ellwanger said he would be gone, but he made arrangements for the house to be unlocked. Dad, Vann, and Young agreed to meet at midnight. Only the three men would be there. Each of them parked a block away from the house so that nobody would see them coming and going. In this secret meeting Young and Vann agreed that each of them would find five or six people to represent the black community and the white community for informal discussions. This would provide communication channels in preparation for full negotiations.

Two days later—April 9, my fourteenth birthday—Dad and Father Foley arranged a meeting between Reverend Fred Shuttlesworth and three other members of his group with Sidney Smyer and two other white leaders. Smyer had said he would not meet unless the director of the Alabama Council called the meeting. In part this marked a tribute that he trusted Dad. It also averted public embarrassment that might arise for Smyer if he assumed responsibility for opening discussions with the black activists.

Held at the Episcopal Church of the Advent, this meeting included Bishop George Murray, Shuttlesworth, Smyer, Chuck Morgan, A. D. King, and

Andrew Young, who represented SCLC. Foley had been unable to convince Dr. King to participate. During the meeting, Shuttlesworth made it clear that he did not want to end the demonstrations until Birmingham's white leaders accepted all of his demands. The meeting became a confrontation and ended in a stand-off, but both sides agreed to meet again two days later.

Despite this inauspicious beginning, Dad remained hopeful. At the very least, he enjoyed being at the center of things and meeting important people. He told us again about the leading white businessman at the meeting:

> Sid Smyer is an interesting guy. He's president of the Birmingham Realty Association. I thought they sold houses, but I found out they own huge tracts of land—coal mines, limestone mines, iron mines. He was at an International Rotary meeting in Tokyo, when the freedom riders were beaten up in Birmingham, and the bus was burned in Anniston. People from different parts of the world would say, "Birmingham. Wow! What a horrible place! How do you live in a place like that?" This was quite shocking because he was the president of the Rotary Club in Birmingham—and later the Chamber of Commerce. He has loads of power and influence, and he's involved in all kinds of things. Now I find out that I am as close to him as any white person—white businessman—in Birmingham. Jim Head is a little bit more warm and receptive, but Jim Head and I never talk hard realities about negotiating and stuff like that, as I do with Sid Smyer. I'm told he has a lot of respect for me.

The group met again on April 11. When they gathered, one new white businessman—attorney George Peach Taylor—joined the group, but Shuttlesworth brought only the same people. Dr. King had promised that he would attend, but did not. This meeting didn't accomplish much, but they planned a third meeting for April 16, a Tuesday evening. This would engage a larger, more representative group of ten or twelve whites and the same number of blacks, representing a broader cross-section of the community.

Meanwhile, on Good Friday, April 12, King and Abernathy led a game-changing march. Their arrest and jailing greatly raised the stakes of the Birmingham campaign and gained national news coverage. That very day, seven white ministers and a rabbi published an open letter in the *Birmingham News* criticizing the timing of the demonstrations. The eight religious leaders signing this letter had all signed the public "appeal for law and order and common sense" following George Wallace's inflammatory inaugural address less than three months earlier. Dad knew and had worked with four of the eight men who signed this public letter. He had invited Bishop Murray and several others to meet with King just days before. He had also worked closely with Bishop C. C. J. Carpenter and Reverend Earl Stallings on several occasions. In particular, Dad said he had "a good warm personal friendship" with Reverend Ed Ramage.

The Good Friday letter acknowledged the impatience of "some of our Negro citizens," but criticized the "unwise and untimely" demonstrations led "in part by outsiders." After commending local news media and law enforcement officials for calmly handling the situation, the letter declared: "We further strongly urge our own negro community to withdraw support from these demonstrations, and to unite locally in working peacefully for a better Birmingham." The statement called for negotiations and for resolving problems in court "and not in the streets."

This moderate statement of concern by well-intentioned religious leaders, sympathetic to King's goals of civil rights and improved race relations, soon became infamous as the catalyst for King's eloquent "Letter from Birmingham Jail." In this letter—not published in full until months later—King articulated the goals of nonviolence and the deeply felt reasons that African Americans could no longer accept pleas for patience, delay, and forbearance. However, by harshly criticizing those who advocated caution and restraint, King inadvertently damaged the reputations of fellow religious leaders who thought they were on the same side, and who had risked a great deal in publicly speaking on behalf of tolerance and common sense.

King's arrest changed the dynamics of the meetings my father had been organizing. After a great deal of discussion, the blacks were able to appoint a negotiating committee and were ready to meet on Tuesday, April 16. But as Dad reported to the Southern Regional Council: "At this point the white leaders backed down and said that they did not feel that they should meet until there was a court decision on the suit brought by the three former commissioners of Birmingham in their attempts to prevent the new city government from being installed." Since the white business leaders could speak only for themselves, they argued that it would be pointless to continue private negotiations until they knew who would be running city hall, the newly elected Boutwell administration or the old-line commissioners led by Bull Connor. There would be no more negotiations until early May. Meanwhile demonstrations continued.

If Dad hadn't talked with us about the demonstrations, we would hardly know anything unusual was happening on the other side of Red Mountain. The newspapers carried only brief reports. The demonstrations didn't reach the front page of the *Birmingham News* until May 7. However, the *News* did cover local political developments, including the city commissioners' announcement that they intended to complete their full four-year terms, which would end in 1965. Bull Connor would not acknowledge the validity of the recent elections. In Homewood, meanwhile, our teachers, schoolmates, and neighbors rarely mentioned anything about the protests, which could have been taking place hundreds of miles away for all we knew.

In the Alabama Council newsletter for April 1963, Dad made only indirect reference to the Birmingham campaign. He wrote about the need for common sense: "If you criss-cross Alabama, you get the impression that rational people realize that *change* is the law of life, and technology is accelerating the tempo. Alabama's changing too, from an agricultural state to an industrial state. Hand in glove with this change is the Negro's desire for change in human relations, and now that the courts are closing up legal loopholes, change in this vital human area appears inevitable."

He added a story about a businessman who had told him that "the Negro's desire for justice and equality of opportunity" stems from the teachings of Jesus. The businessman stated: "People have got to start thinking with their heads instead of their emotions, and face up to the inescapable fact that there are changes coming." Dad added, jokingly: "Maybe the next time I see him, he'll be ready to enlist with the Alabama Council on Human Relations."

Meanwhile, by the second week of demonstrations, it became clear that divisions among the black factions threatened to undermine the success of the entire Birmingham campaign. In an effort to unify activists and moderates, on April 8 Dr. King spoke to the newly created Jefferson County Interdenominational Alliance, a group of moderate black clergymen led by J. L. Ware. Despite his plea for the 125 black ministers attending to support the SCLC initiatives, they would only express general support for desegregation. Speaking to a group of prominent black professionals and businessmen that evening, however, Dr. King proposed to allow the protests to be directed by a three-part committee representing SCLC, Shuttlesworth's Christian Movement, and the local black moderates. This concession began to create a more unified support for the demonstrations.

Dad told us that he had attended the morning meeting with the black ministers before having lunch with Dr. King. He explained that some of the local black leaders opposed the demonstrations. For example, Reverend J. L.

Ware, president of the black ministers group in Birmingham, had spoken out against King's direct action campaign.

Dad said: "Ware's group of Negro Baptist ministers is a real powerhouse. Most of them haven't supported the demonstrations. But Ware did allow King to speak at the meeting today. I heard King was going to speak—he asked me to have lunch with him—and I went over to see what would happen."

Mom asked: "Did they argue about the protests?"

Dad said: "Not really. That's the funny thing. Ware is strongly opposed to the demonstrations. King gave all the reasons why the demonstrations were happening. Then after King spoke to them, the ministers association voted overwhelmingly to support King and the demonstrations. King took the leadership of the group away from their powerful president. All Ware could do was go along. You see they're heading off in another direction, and you run to get ahead of them."

Dad thought for a moment, then added: "Right after the meeting, I had lunch with King at the Gaston Motel. We set that up before the ministers meeting. While we were talking, John Drew—he's a Negro insurance man, you kids might have heard me mention before—came up and said to King, 'Marvelous talk, marvelous talk! It really took the leadership away from the president.' Meaning Ware."

Mom asked, "What did King say?"

Dad answered, "Oh, he just said, 'It's good to have him on board.'"

Mom said: "But isn't Reverend Ware a friend of yours?"

"I think so," Dad said. "I've talked with him on occasion. He's always friendly. He invited me to preach at his church one Sunday. I enjoyed that." He paused. "But one time I went to his home and knocked on the door. I knew he was inside, but I realized he wasn't going to answer the door."

"Why not?" Susie asked.

Dad said: "Well, Pitts—or somebody—told me that unless you have an appointment, Negro pastors just don't come to the door. It's too dangerous. One way they deal with whites is they never answer the door."

"But that's not polite!" Paul said.

Dad replied: "Maybe not. But they don't want trouble. Another thing is, Negro ministers always go by their first two initials, so nobody can make a nickname out of it. If you say your name is Robert, the whites'll call you Bob instead of Mister. It doesn't mean the whites will use their last name, but at least they can't use some nickname that Negroes would want only their friends to use."

Mom said: "You can't blame them for not wanting to be insulted all the time. They're treated like children!"

❖

Throughout the demonstrations, my father tried to maintain good relations with all sides: demonstration leaders, black moderates, and white moderates. He knew the rabid segregationists would not listen to him. As he worked behind the scenes, he relayed messages from one group to the others and advised all parties to communicate and negotiate, rather than escalate racial tensions.

During the early stage of demonstrations in April, Reverend Fred Shuttlesworth said he wanted to talk with my father. Dad told us about it the next day. "This was rare for Shuttlesworth to want to talk to a white person," Dad said.

We had to meet at eleven o'clock last night. He had another meeting before then. Shuttlesworth said, "Where can we meet without drawing attention?"

So I said, "The only place I can think of is my office in the Comer Building." The front door would be open and the elevator operator would be off duty, so it would be on automatic.

We talked for a half hour or an hour about what I'd do for King and what he's doing. Very interesting. Then this morning, the Negro elevator operator, an older woman said, "You were here last night? The police were all over the place."

She has always been very friendly, and I enjoy talking with her. But now her eyes lit up when she saw me, like "Well, you really are *somebody*."

She made sure nobody else could hear her. We were alone in the elevator. She said, "I understand you had Reverend Shuttlesworth in your office last night?"

I said, "Yes, as a matter of fact I did. How'd you know?"

She said, "The police came by and told me." They'd been following Shuttlesworth, and they knew he came to the Comer Building. So she has a special sparkle for me now, 'cause I know Shuttlesworth.

Paul said: "Did the police chase you?"

"No, Butch," Dad said. "Haven't heard from them yet! But it's interesting to know that what I do is important to the police."

15

Celebrities

The world had flocked to Birmingham for the big showdown over segregation. Dad met with more journalists and writers than he could remember, including some already famous and others who would later become household names.

One school-day afternoon during the April 1963 demonstrations, Dad telephoned Mom from a pay phone. He excitedly urged her to take the bus downtown to the Gaston Motel, where comedian and activist Dick Gregory was holding forth at a table full of movement folks. Gregory had come to Birmingham to join the demonstrations. For civil rights activists like Dad, Dick Gregory had long been a favorite. His cutting-edge humor relieved some of the daily stress of fighting against segregation. Dad had been retelling Gregory's jokes for more than a year.

As she left the house, Mom had the foresight to take Ann's new autograph book with her to the Gaston Motel. Dick Gregory's signature became the only "famous person" autograph in Ann's little book. But Ann soon realized that she always had to explain to her friends at school who Dick Gregory was.

(In 1996, at a Martin Luther King Day celebration in Washington, D.C., Ann finally caught up with the comedian and activist. She trailed after him as he left the dais. "Mr. Gregory!" He ignored her call. "Mr. Gregory! My parents got your autograph for me in 1963 at the Gaston Motel. . . ." He turned on his heel and locked eyes with her. ". . . and I'd love to have another autograph to pass on to my kids." He smiled, shook Ann's hand and signed her program.)

On Sunday May 5, as the children's crusade continued to fill Bull Connor's jails, Mom asked Ann to drive into Birmingham with her.

"Come on, Ann, it'll be fun. She's a young girl who plays the guitar and sings beautifully. Why don't you come to Miles College with me to hear her?" Mom asked.

Ann said: "Nah, that's okay, Mom. Maybe next time."

Having come to Birmingham to express solidarity with the civil rights demonstrators, Joan Baez performed an evening concert at the black college, whose students had led earlier sit-ins and marches. Mom went alone, enjoyed the combination of folk songs and movement anthems, and clapped along with the music. During breakfast, as we prepared for school, she raved about the concert.

"This thin young girl walked onto the stage barefoot, carrying a guitar!" Mom exclaimed. "With almond-shaped eyes, black hair hanging down her back, dark skin—Mexican, I think."

"The audience was integrated, and I could feel electricity in the air," Mom said. "She has the most beautiful high soprano voice." She looked at Ann. "You would have loved it!"

I said: "Mrs. Kraus has her first album. She played some of it for me after German lessons. My favorites are 'Silver Dagger' and 'East Virginia.' The high notes made me shiver."

Mom said: "When she sang 'We Shall Overcome,' everyone sang along, holding hands—arms crossed like this—and swaying side to side. It was incredibly moving. Especially with an integrated audience—right here in Birmingham!"

Ann said: "Oh, Mom! I wish I had gone with you!"

(Later that year, the album *Joan Baez in Concert, Part 2,* included her rendition of "We Shall Overcome." The liner notes said the song was recorded at Miles College in Birmingham, Alabama.)

In an ironic coincidence, the motion picture *To Kill a Mockingbird* first premiered in Birmingham on April 3, 1963—the very day that the Birmingham campaign ("Project C") began. This sensitive portrayal of racial controversies in 1930s Alabama, released nationally late in 1962, had seemed too unsettling for the white power structure of the Magic City. The Junior Chamber of Commerce finally persuaded city authorities to allow the movie to be shown locally. After all, the two young co-stars, Mary Badham and Philip Alford, came from Birmingham. Now the controversial film about racial injustice arrived in their hometown on the very day that Martin Luther King Jr. and the Southern Christian Leadership Conference began their effort to overthrow segregation.

Based on Harper Lee's Pulitzer Prize–winning novel, *To Kill a Mockingbird* told about the unjustified conviction of a black man falsely accused of raping a white woman. From Atticus Finch's principled defense of Tom Robinson to his daughter Scout's disarming greeting of a white man leading a would-be lynch mob, the novel and film went against the prevailing racial climate in Alabama. Gregory Peck gave Atticus Finch a solid dignity even in the face of threats from his neighbors. Atticus even told his daughter, "Don't say nigger, Scout."

In one climactic scene, as Atticus walked out of the courtroom after hearing the guilty verdict against Tom Robinson, all of the black spectators in the balcony stood in tribute. Scout sat next to Calpurnia, the family maid, and Reverend Sykes. As she watched the black people paying silent tribute to her father's courage, Reverend Sykes said: "Miss Jean Louise, stand up. Your father's passin'." When I saw the movie—and again later, when I read the book—tears came to my eyes at that simple line. Atticus Finch reminded me of my father.

By fall of 1962, Ann said, Birmingham's sixth graders had been abuzz with the news that "one of our own"—Mary Badham, a private-school girl her age—would play Scout in *To Kill a Mockingbird.* Ann said: "My friend Janet Mowry transferred to Mary's school after fifth grade. She said that Mary was stuck up and not very nice. At first I was crushed. Then I decided that it just confirmed that I should have had the role."

When Mom and Dad let Ann read their paperback *To Kill a Mockingbird,* she decided that her life was pretty much the same as Scout's. They both: lived in Alabama, shopped at Elmore's five-and-dime, made papier-mâché Halloween costumes, took a child's-eye view of racial injustice, and—above all—had fathers who had been in court about the race question. On the other hand, she admitted, Scout was considerably bolder and more reckless. Scout got into fights, took risky chances, and startled the relatives by calling out, "Pass the damn ham, please!" at Sunday dinner. "That's the line that got me noticed reading the book at school," Ann said. "I was so shocked by the utter humor of that rhyming line that I passed it around at the back of row one."

Sometime after the Birmingham premiere of *To Kill a Mockingbird,* our family attended a play at the Town and Gown Civic Theater. Before the performance began, an announcer welcomed Philip Alford, the Birmingham boy who portrayed Jem Finch in the movie. He was about the same age as me. During the intermission, a woman approached me excitedly. "Oh, my!" she said. "I just *loved* you in that movie!" I had to explain I wasn't the actor.

Because our parents mingled with some of Birmingham's art-scene figures, after the play Ann did manage to meet Philip Alford backstage. Dad's Alabama Council friend Bette Lee Hanson, a local television celebrity, introduced them. Ann told us: "He was polite and even cuter than he looked on the big screen."

Although we did have a few brushes with famous people—connected at least indirectly with the civil rights movement—our lives followed paths and experiences more typical of other children our age. Until the beginning of summer vacation, most of our time centered on school, homework, and related activities.

Only in looking back later did I realize that my eighth-grade history assignment to create a booklet on the history of Birmingham coincided with the start of the city's most traumatic civil rights confrontation, in April 1963. In writing about "'The Magic City': Birmingham, Alabama," I played it safe. Nothing controversial under the headings "Birmingham's History" or "Birmingham's Industry." Under "Birmingham Today" I began: "Birmingham, Alabama is the South's largest industrial city and is often called the 'Pittsburgh of the South.'" A page of prose that could have been written by the Chamber of Commerce concluded with an understated recognition of political change: "Birmingham's form of government was changed in a popular election last November. The newly elected mayor, Albert Boutwell, and the nine councilmen have been sworn in, but are awaiting the verdict of the Alabama Supreme Court to take office. At present, Birmingham is being ruled by two mayors, nine councilmen, and a three-man commission."

I resisted the urge to include comments about Birmingham's darker aspects, including anti-union violence, lynchings and beatings of blacks, and racial animosity. Nothing at all about segregation, civil rights, or chucking rocks at a Bull Connor campaign poster. I knew that would get me in trouble with the teacher. And I wanted a good grade.

Meanwhile, in eighth grade I was tracked ahead into Algebra I, designed for college-bound students willing to respond to the Sputnik challenge of learning math and science. The homework proved frustrating, and I struggled through the year. Fortunately, Dad's early college background in engineering enabled him to help me with algebra. When he was home, he often explained the problems and showed me how to use his old ivory-faced slide rule, kept in a protective leather case. The next year, in geometry, Mom—with a background as an architect—helped me more than Dad.

Mom thought that I should start learning a foreign language. Since

Homewood Junior High didn't offer language classes until ninth grade, she suggested taking German lessons from her friend Anny Kraus. Born in Austria, Anny Wiener had married Frederick Kraus in 1935. As Jews, they escaped the Nazis in the late 1930s by moving to Paris and, again in 1940, by crossing the Pyrenees on foot to Spain. After moving to Birmingham in 1953 so that Dr. Kraus could take the lead in establishing a new University of Alabama dental school, they both helped to form the Birmingham Council on Human Relations, the local chapter of the Alabama Council.

I enjoyed walking to their house, across Montgomery Highway, on Saturday mornings to struggle through a complicated new language. Anny Kraus told stories about her life in Europe, introduced me to the music of Joan Baez and other folk singers, and smiled patiently at my stumbling efforts to learn verb conjugations and vocabulary.

Mrs. Kraus guided me to what surely remained an imperfect Mother's Day greeting note: "Samstag der 11.5.63, Liebe Mutter, Ich haffe dass Du hast einen Schönen Muttertag. . . . Mitt liebe, Dein Sohn, Randy." As I struggled with this greeting, I barely thought about the critical climax of the civil rights campaign taking place on the other side of Red Mountain.

The beginning of the Birmingham campaign had coincided with the arrival of a Kalamazoo College intern in Dad's office. A distinctive feature of the western Michigan college's curriculum, called career-service, placed interns around the country in positions related either to their academic and professional career plans or to public service. Mike Morden spent the spring-quarter term, from April to June 1963, working with Dad. He assisted in the office with administrative details and secretarial work. But he could not have chosen a more dramatic time to observe firsthand the turmoil and excitement of Birmingham's dramatic confrontation between civil rights activists and entrenched segregationists, led by Bull Connor.

Mike became another of our favorite houseguests. Ann thought he was cute, earnest, and fun to be around. He talked about President Kennedy's new Peace Corps, and after his term in Birmingham, he joined one of the first groups to Africa. Ann later said: "I credit Mike with saving me from becoming a missionary to Africa. All alone on a sunny Easter afternoon when I was eight or nine, watching a movie about Albert Schweitzer on TV, I had made a solemn commitment to serve God on the dark continent. I altered my pledge. Fifteen years later, when my Peace Corps buddies in Honduras asked why I had joined up, they thought I was joking when I said I was fulfilling a childhood dream."

During the summer of 1963, Dad welcomed a second student intern. George McClain, a student at Union Theological Seminary in New York, worked part-time in the Alabama Council office. The Student Interracial Ministry arranged with Dad for George to work with the Alabama Council during the week. He also assisted Reverend Nathaniel Linsey, the black pastor of Thirgood C.M.E. Church, on weekends. This met the purposes of the Student Interracial Ministry, which provided opportunities for white students to work for a summer in black churches and for black students to serve as assistants to ministers of white churches. Dad liked this arrangement: "Congregations that have had students from SIM have shown real enthusiasm for this effort of building bridges of understanding between Christians."

George McClain described his experiences in Birmingham in an article written for *The Grain of Salt,* a Union Theological Seminary publication:

My first direct encounter with the reality of segregation and its accompanying fear came just four days after my arrival in Birmingham. Rev. Norman Jimerson, director of the Alabama Council on Human Relations, whom I served as an assistant this summer, invited me to ride with him and his Negro secretary to an integrated meeting of church women at Tuskegee Institute. Along the way I soon learned from my companions that integrated travel through the Black Belt of Alabama was not without its risks. We experienced no incidents, just the fear and uncertainty. But when on the return trip we became hungry, we felt it necessary to exercise such extreme precautions as to drop me off—after dark—in front of a drive-in restaurant to buy sandwiches while the others circled the block. After they picked me up, we then parked along an unlighted side street and supped surreptitiously in total darkness!

As a teenager, I found these encounters with exotic people from far away fascinating and exhilarating. Being at the center of action for civil rights meant hearing about and seeing celebrities as well as volunteer activists who would never reach headlines or public recognition. Most of this contact remained indirect. It was Dad—and sometimes Mom—who met Dick Gregory,

Joan Baez, Martin Luther King Jr., Fred Shuttlesworth, and other famous people.

But there were plenty of exotic visitors coming to our house as well. In June 1963, for example, Mom wrote to Aunt Julie about our busy social calendar. "It's been very exciting with reporters in and out," Mom wrote. In addition, "Tomorrow a member of India's Parliament will arrive and Jim is to be his host. We're planning to have some businessmen and wives in Tuesday night. Sunday a minister (white) of the government of Nyasaland arrives and again Jim will host him." Whenever such guests came for dinner, Susie always wanted to sit next to them at the dining table.

Even when visitors from far away didn't come to the house, hearing Mom and Dad tell stories about them enabled us children to share the excitement. Such celebrities added glamour and mystique to our lives. If Ann hadn't realized her dream of portraying Scout on film, and I would only mistakenly be greeted as Philip Alford, we could at least indirectly be part of important events taking place in our own community. Our experiences, our brushes with famous people, might not compare to the dramatic events in *To Kill a Mockingbird*. But we felt proud of our father for his courage in standing up for justice and equality. Our Dad was not Atticus Finch, but he seemed heroic in our young eyes.

16

Gaston Motel

As the Birmingham campaign continued during April and May of 1963, the police—under the on-scene control of Bull Connor—used trained attack dogs to control the crowds. Images of police dogs snarling on their chains, lunging at demonstrators, and ripping their clothes appeared repeatedly in television news broadcasts and newspaper coverage around the world. The first use of police dogs occurred on Sunday, April 7, 1963.

On April 19 the Alabama Advisory Committee of the U.S. Civil Rights Commission conducted hearings regarding charges of police brutality. Chaired by Father Albert S. Foley—who had earlier criticized King for the timing of demonstrations—the committee heard testimony gathered by Reverend C. Herbert Oliver, founder of the Inter-Citizens Committee. For several years Oliver and his organization had investigated and cataloged incidents of police brutality toward black citizens. In this hearing he read testimony from several blacks—both demonstrators and innocent passersby—regarding their injuries from dog bites and police batons.

At the conclusion of the hearing, Father Foley reminded witnesses that the Advisory Committee had no authority to act, other than to send a report to the Civil Rights Commission. The commission could then recommend that the Justice Department investigate these charges of "misuse of police power." Foley then advised anyone who witnessed police violence to get accurate descriptions of the officers, including names and badge numbers if possible.

Throughout the Birmingham demonstrations, civil rights leaders held mass meetings to motivate people and recruit volunteer marchers. Held at various churches, these meetings provided the focal point for the local campaign. Curious to see what occurred during these events, Dad attended several mass meetings.

One evening during supper Dad told us about the day's activities.

"The mass meeting this morning was fascinating," he said. "The church was almost full. People were standing up, swaying back and forth, and singing. I looked around, and the only other white people there were a couple of police detectives."

Ann asked: "Why did policemen go to the meeting? Do they want to demonstrate?"

Dad laughed and said: "No. That'd be the last thing—." He paused, frowned. Now he looked serious. "Bull Connor sent them to spy on the meeting. He's still in charge of the police and firemen."

Paul said: "Did they let the police stay?"

"Yes," Dad said. "The cops didn't stop the meeting. So after some singing, Abernathy—he's King's top assistant—got up and gave a rousing speech. He tried to get people fired up. Very emotional rhetoric, to build up excitement before King spoke."

I said: "Like the opening act for a concert?"

"Exactly!" Dad said. He dished up more mashed potatoes. Then he continued: "King started with a very quiet voice. Calm and soothing. A simple message. Then he built, idea upon idea, a strong appeal for support. The volume and intensity kept increasing."

Dad ate quietly for a minute. His eyes moved back and forth as he chewed. "During King's talk, people called out 'Amen!' and 'Say it, brother!' One woman stood and yelled, 'SWEET JESUS!'"

"Just like the churches we visited," Ann said.

Susie asked: "Why did she yell so loud?"

Dad said: "Well, Susie, she felt Jesus was there. She really sees Jesus when she looks at Reverend King. Vincent Harding—one of the Negro reporters I met—says that a lot of Negroes talk about King as the Messiah."

Mom said: "Jim, I admire King and the other civil rights leaders. But it isn't right to compare people to Christ."

"Yeah, you're right," Dad said. "But for some Negroes, King seems like the promised leader." He picked up a piece of fried chicken, chomped a big bite, and waved the drumstick as he chewed and looked around the table at each of us.

When he knew we were listening, he went back to his story: "Before the demonstrators left the church, they all filed by big baskets. They had to empty their pockets of knives and guns, and whatever weapons they might have. To make sure they practiced nonviolence."

I asked: "Did you join the demonstration?"

Dad said: "No, that's not part of my job. I'm trying to get communication started. Negotiations. I went to the mass meeting just to see what's going on. So I can understand what they're saying and doing."

He took another bite and then laid the drumstick on his plate. He was looking past us out the window where a flame-red cardinal perched in the mimosa tree. "They do a thorough job of inculcating attitudes among blacks. Nonviolence. Courage." Now he looked at us again. "It's a wonder there haven't been blacks who break ranks and cause violence during the demonstrations." He peeked at Mom, cautiously. "Let's hope it stays that way."

As the demonstrations continued through April and into May, Dad kept going to his office, handling mail, and monitoring news about racial issues around the state. His job with the Alabama Council had always included research, keeping up with what was happening across the state, from the Tri-Cities and Huntsville to Mobile and Dothan. During the five weeks that the demonstrations were going on, he still traveled, visiting local chapters. But his main focus remained on Birmingham. He kept in touch with many people he knew in the black community to talk about their plans and concerns, then made appointments to talk with white people such as Sid Smyer, David Vann, and Jim Head.

The central problem for most people in Birmingham—black and white—as my father concluded, had been a breakdown in communications. Sympathetic white people couldn't discuss, even with other white people, their feelings about racial equality. One minister told him: "Many young people say they want to talk with me about this situation because they cannot discuss it at home with their parents."

As Dad wrote in the May 1963 Alabama Council newsletter: "Private conversations between colored and white people help each to understand differences and to see the errors in generalizations relied upon for so many years. Recently Birmingham people have been saying, 'At least we ought to have some conversations, which may lead to understanding and respect. This could prepare the way for serious negotiations.'" Dad thought this process of informal conversations, followed by formal negotiations, would be necessary to resolve the Birmingham crisis. Activists such as Fred Shuttlesworth sought to compel the white power structure to accept their demands for civil rights, whereas black and white moderates sought to persuade whites to recognize the injustice of segregation. The Alabama Council leaders believed that communication and negotiations would lead to interracial peace. Shuttlesworth and King argued that only confrontation would force whites to bargain in good faith. Same goal, different strategy.

Birmingham soon became the focus of national press coverage, and even more reporters than usual contacted Dad for background information or to make contacts with key people involved on both sides, blacks and whites. Seldom did Dad's name appear in reports for which he had provided valuable information. But he also taped interviews with reporters for radio stations, including the Westinghouse Radio Network, the radio station operated by Riverside Drive Baptist Church in New York, and Canadian stations. As Dad later reported, "at the height of the demonstrations, I found myself in the unique role of interpreting to newsmen and national magazine writers the larger context of the Birmingham situation, seeking to point out the subtle progress being made, along with the massive problems."

Dad told us about some of his connections with reporters, but often he seemed too busy to describe everything he was doing. One reporter he did talk about, Vincent Harding, was a young black author, now covering Birmingham for *The Reporter.*

"Harding and I were moaning and groaning that the demonstrators and the leaders of the demonstrations are only saying, 'We want three hundred years of segregation to disappear. We want all our rights now. We will not compromise. We're not gradualists.'"

As he said this, Dad chuckled. "It's very interesting," he said. "One of the black ministers—Reverend Porter in the Baptist church on the south side of Birmingham—said, 'I'm no gradualist, but I know you have to take one step at a time.'" Telling this made Dad laugh.

"So I kept saying, 'What is it that you need to have happen before you end the demonstrations?' Their response was, 'We want everything. We won't deal with that question.'

"I told Harding I was frustrated, and he said, 'Well, actually, that's the same response I'm getting, and I'm getting pretty frustrated with it.'"

Shortly after the Birmingham campaign ended, Vincent Harding published "A Beginning in Birmingham" in *The Reporter* issue of June 6, 1963. The article provided a succinct account of the behind-the-scenes negotiations taking place during the demonstrations. It didn't mention Dad by name, but referred to "the help of a white member of the Alabama Council on Human Relations" who had worked to establish contacts between the demonstrators and white leadership. Anonymous credit at least felt better to Dad than no credit.

One of Dad's friends from Pennsylvania sent him a letter: "I have just finished reading the most recent issue of *The Reporter,* which has a run-down on the Birmingham situation. I was pleased to note the credit given to your Alabama Council on Human Relations. This is probably as close as you will come to celestial stars in your crown. Certainly, this is one of the purposes for your organization and the fact that you are able to work effectively in this situation underscores the urgent necessity for groups such as your own."

By mid-April the demonstrations began losing momentum. On some days fewer than ten volunteers stepped forward to march, knowing they would end up in jail. Negotiations also bogged down. Neither side expressed willingness to make significant concessions. Working behind the scenes, Dad continued to seek common ground for an agreement. As he said, "My role is to say, 'Sit down and negotiate.' And of course, at that point, I'm treated with equal contempt by the Negroes, as well as the whites."

Dad kept telling the black activists that they had to find something that they could settle on. As he observed: "There's no way that everything will be turned upside down immediately. Progress can only come one step at a time."

He continued to meet with Sid Smyer and other white leaders, saying to them: "You know, these demonstrations are going on and on. The Negroes won't be mollified by some small token gestures. There's going to be more escalating violence, and if you don't do something—." But the white businessmen assumed that, the longer the demonstrations went on, the more difficult it would be to recruit demonstrators, so it would just be a matter of time. They'd just wait it out.

As Dad said: "The whites think time is in their favor. But it won't work that way."

By late April, Reverend James Bevel, a Mississippi native and former SNCC worker, began arguing with King, saying that the demonstrations would only succeed if children could be mobilized to fill Bull Connor's jails. With Andrew Young's assistance, Bevel organized a youth rally, which drew an enthusiastic crowd. Despite his initial resistance, King finally relented. On May 2—"D-Day" as Bevel called it—nearly eight hundred children skipped school and gathered at the Sixteenth Street Baptist Church, behind the large stained glass window showing Jesus, holding a shepherd's staff, knocking on a door.

Over the next week the "Children's Crusade" overwhelmed the Birmingham police, filled the jails, and provoked police violence against demonstrators. Startling photographs and television news footage of snarling police dogs and children and adults knocked to the pavement by high-pressure fire hoses reached people around the world. Although many condemned demonstration leaders for placing young children at risk, these scenes gained worldwide sympathy and support for black protestors.

The children's marches began to change people's minds in Birmingham as well. Conservative black businessman A. G. Gaston, while talking on the telephone with David Vann about their shared desire to see King's SCLC forces leave town and allow the new city government to handle the city's problems, looked out his office window to see a young girl being slammed down the sidewalk by a torrent of water from a fire hose. He blurted out: "Lawyer Vann, I can't talk to you now or ever. My people are out there fighting for their lives and my freedom. I have to go help them."

On the other side of Red Mountain in Homewood, we saw the television news coverage as though the events were taking place half a world away. It hardly seemed possible that this was our own city, just a few miles from our house. In fact, the *Birmingham News* barely mentioned the local events that made front-page headlines in New York, Detroit, and around the world. The story of Birmingham's most profound crisis could only be found on the inside pages, without the iconic photographs shown everywhere else. A typical back-pages report, headlined "Police Use Water, Dogs on Marchers," ran only a head shot of Mayor Boutwell.

More than a thousand children—the youngest eight years old—quickly filled the city jails. Bull Connor ordered hundreds to be held in rooms under the pavilion at the state fairgrounds. The pressure of being pictured as so inhumane as to lock up children finally aroused public opinion. White people began to tell Dad, "We've got to negotiate. We've got to do something to stop this."

Dad said: "A lot of people in the white community—most of the white community—deeply resent involving the children. Partly because it works. They're not really that concerned for the kids!"

As hundreds of children huddled in makeshift detention facilities, city officials refused to budge. Moderate white business leaders finally took the initiative of forming a negotiating committee to seek a resolution of tensions and an end to demonstrations. The Senior Chamber of Commerce voted strong support for the negotiations, but the Junior Chamber of Commerce continued to oppose the negotiating sessions. Dad commented: "This is just the opposite that you'd expect. You expect the younger men to be more realistic than the older people. But they carry more prejudice than their parents."

The formal negotiating committee brought together white and black leaders believed capable of speaking for their respective communities. Following his persistent behind-the-scenes efforts to start negotiations, Dad hoped to be asked to join this group. Instead he was excluded. He told us: "It might have been interesting to be on the negotiating committee, but that isn't my role. As long as it gets started, that's what counts. My goal is to achieve a resolution, not direct what the outcome will be." David Vann, his close friend—who had earlier resigned from the Alabama Council board rather than be publicly identified—served as one of the whites on the negotiating team. He kept Dad up-to-date on what was happening.

Following Bull Connor's use of police dogs and fire hoses against school-children, Attorney General Robert Kennedy sent Burke Marshall and Joseph Dolan to Birmingham in an effort to renew negotiations. By the time Marshall and Dolan arrived on May 4, the downtown merchants and white progressives were ready to resume discussions with civil rights activists. The merchants' Downtown Improvement Association asked David Vann to represent them in negotiations, and the Senior Citizens Committee authorized a subcommittee headed by Sid Smyer. On Sunday May 5 these two groups of white businessmen met with black leaders, who presented proposals for a settlement that were less aggressive than Fred Shuttlesworth's demands made in the previous negotiations on April 9. Rather than requiring immediate hiring of black policemen and other concessions—many of which the merchants had no power to grant—the black negotiators now requested the businessmen to pressure city government to create a biracial committee to develop specific plans for integrating the police force, desegregating schools, removing obstacles to voter registration, reopening municipal facilities on a desegregated basis.

Despite these more limited demands by black negotiators, the white leaders argued that they could not support desegregation without city government backing. This could not happen until the courts determined which of the two rival municipal administrations would prevail in the legal contest over the change of government. As negotiations continued over the next two days, the escalating tensions created by the children's marches and Bull Connor's harsh response led to fears that Governor Wallace would respond by escalating the danger of violence.

On May 7, Fred Shuttlesworth received a concussion from high-pressure fire hoses while leading a group of marchers. This left the local black negotiating team in the hands of moderates, including Lucius Pitts, Arthur Shores, A. G. Gaston, and John Drew. Andrew Young represented SCLC. During late-night negotiations, black representatives agreed with the white negotiators' demand to link store integration with settlement of the state supreme court's decision on the Birmingham change of government lawsuit. By the early morning hours of May 8, the basis of a settlement seemed secure. The only problem was that Fred Shuttlesworth had not been consulted.

As the white negotiators met with the Senior Citizens Committee and the DIA to secure approval of the settlement, Martin Luther King Jr. urged Shuttlesworth to leave the hospital for an emergency meeting at John Drew's home. During this meeting a still-groggy Shuttlesworth expressed his distrust of the black negotiators, Burke Marshall, and especially the white businessmen. He resisted the call to suspend demonstrations on the terms proposed. Without Shuttlesworth's support the agreement seemed dead. Only after a telephone conversation with Robert Kennedy, who suggested that the suspension of demonstrations could be simply a temporary concession pending good-faith action by the white community, did Shuttlesworth acquiesce.

This led to a press conference at the Gaston Motel on Friday, May 10, at which King, Ralph Abernathy, and Shuttlesworth announced a settlement of their demands and a suspension of demonstrations. In a turbulent racial climate, Birmingham's black and white moderates had found a resolution to the crisis. The majority of the city's residents, however, felt that they had not been consulted. In the coming months, many blacks would express disappointment over the limited gains. Segregationists immediately responded angrily to the "sell-out" of white business leaders. As historian J. Mills Thornton III later concluded: "The destiny of the masses of black and white Birmingham had been determined by a handful of essentially self-appointed negotiators, meeting in secret." The May 10 settlement provided only a quick fix, a beginning of a resolution of Birmingham's civil rights crisis, but not its ending.

In his quarterly report for the Alabama Council, Dad summarized the negotiations leading to this settlement of the Birmingham crisis:

In May the demonstrations got larger and larger. On Friday, May 3 one of the leading merchants ardently said that neither he nor any merchant would sit down and negotiate with the Negroes at any time. Assistant U.S. Attorney General Burke Marshall came to Birmingham on May 4, and his presence was helpful in getting negotiations under way. On Sunday morning May 5 in a lawyer's office there was a meeting of merchants and businessmen. A committee of three was appointed to meet that evening with a group of Negro leaders. On May 7 there was a 24 hour truce, and on May 8 it was extended again. Finally on May 10 there was a public announcement by Dr. Martin Luther King, Reverend Fred Shuttlesworth, and Reverend Ralph Abernathy that negotiations had successfully been concluded. They declared that there was an agreement that lunch counters would be desegregated, an official biracial committee would be established, a committee on employment would be established, and one Negro clerk would be hired in one store. This was to take place in a period of 60 to 90 days.

Newspaper stories, magazine articles, TV programs have carried innumerable accounts of the demonstrations in Birmingham, and the effect that this has had on the rest of the country. Negroes in Birmingham began to be upset that there were no visible changes while other communities were making real progress in reducing discrimination because of the demonstrations in Birmingham. It is doubtful if anyone predicted that demonstrations in Birmingham would touch off such nationwide concern. People have been saying that this is a revolutionary movement. Birmingham has made it crystal clear to the country that gradualism is no longer a possible approach to our racial problem.

In the Alabama Council newsletter, describing events during the Birmingham campaign, Dad stated: "The Council's role, behind the scenes, we hope played a significant role in the complicated proceedings in Birmingham. In my opinion, the pressing reason for men and women of good will to step forward now—in Alabama—is that failure to step forward creates a vacuum that lunatics will fill up. They want only to deprive Negroes of their human rights."

Just before announcement of a settlement, I had my own direct experience observing the unfolding downtown drama. On Tuesday May 7 the Senior Citizens, Sid Smyer's group of white community leaders, met and agreed to come to terms with King and Shuttlesworth. Final details needed to be worked out, but the demonstrations ended. This was also the first day that the *Birmingham News* mentioned the "Project C" campaign on its front page. The city's dark secret could finally be mentioned.

On Thursday night Dad asked if I wanted to drive into the city with him. He had to drop off something. The VW chugged to the crest of Red Mountain, with the lights of Birmingham spread across the valley below. Down into the city and into the black neighborhood, where I had seldom ventured. We parked in front of the Gaston Motel, where Dr. King and Reverend Shuttlesworth used a second-floor office room as campaign headquarters. It was already past my usual ten o'clock bedtime, but crowds of people—mostly black, but a few whites—jammed the small lobby.

For the first time I saw black people wearing colorful African clothing—dashikis, I later learned. One thin figure stood out. A man wearing bib overalls, with a shaved head topped by a skullcap. "That's Jim Bevel," Dad said. "A real charismatic young guy."

Dad told me, "Wait here. I'll be right back." Clutching a large envelope, he disappeared into the sea of black faces. I stood next to a wall, trying to look inconspicuous. Trying not to look shocked. Or afraid. It felt as though I were watching a play, with exotic and colorful characters walking quickly through the lobby, or pausing to greet each other, or earnestly talking. Men with thin beards or goatees, shaved heads, long flowing robes, or head coverings unlike any I had seen before.

Soon Dad reappeared, without the envelope. He didn't explain what he had delivered, or to whom. It must have been something about the negotiations or the agreement, but I could only imagine. I didn't ask. "Busy place," he observed. "Let's get you home before I get in trouble with your mother!"

The next day, Friday May 10, Dad returned to the Gaston Motel. King, Shuttlesworth, and Abernathy held a press conference in the motel courtyard to announce the resolution of their five-week campaign. That evening Dad described the scene: "Media people were called in, and I was there, along with maybe a couple of hundred people. They announced the terms of negotiations—that demonstrations would end, that blacks would be hired as clerks in some of the stores, that lunch counters would be integrated, and a few other things. Four or five points."

Dad continued: "Afterwards, Vann told me that the problem the whites had was to find enough things that King could have as face-saving accomplishments, so that he would not be going empty-handed to the Negro community. So at least the demonstrations accomplished something positive. One of the Negro leaders said that the informal talks between whites and Negroes cleared the air and, in his words, 'allowed the actual negotiations to proceed in a spirit of love.' That might be overstatement. But I feel good that I helped make it possible."

Then came the white backlash. Late Saturday night the Gaston Motel was bombed in response to the whites caving in to black demands. When I heard the news on Sunday morning, I thought: "I was just there two days ago!"

Dad said: "I was down there at the motel last night trying to see Abernathy, and he said he would see me in a little while. He kept me waiting two hours. I talked to one or two people in the lower echelon, and then left at midnight. At two o'clock in the morning, a bomb went off at the corner of the motel."

The bomb exploded underneath the large second-floor corner suite where King and his colleagues had planned the Birmingham campaign for the past month. King had already left town, and no one was injured. Everyone assumed the Klan was responsible for an assassination attempt on King. The bombing sparked rioting downtown. The pent-up frustrations and animosities of almost six weeks of protests and police attacks boiled over. The black mob burned cars, stores, and a nearby house before the riot ended. Black leaders, including Wyatt T. Walker, tried to calm the crowd before state troopers arrived. By daylight the rioting had stopped. The nonviolent protests of the Birmingham campaign thus ended in violence. Blacks at last unleashed their anger and resentment.

A week or so after the Birmingham settlement, John Brush, one of Dad's former professors at Andover Newton Theological School (ANTS) sent a postcard to Dad: "As the storms lower over the South, I think of friends down there who carry concern and responsibility. We of ANTS don't forget our own men on these frontiers. You are in our thoughts & prayers."

Shortly after the Birmingham demonstrations ended, Dad's close friend from Hopewell, Reverend Gene Ensley, wrote: "We don't read the newspaper these days without thinking of you and Melva and whispering a prayer for you and the work you are doing for us all." He added that twenty people in Hopewell now planned to organize a local chapter of the Virginia Council on Human Relations, the sister organization of Dad's ACHR.

But even this sympathetic friend criticized the methods and timing of the Birmingham campaign. "There is no need for me to indicate where my sympathies lie in this crisis, but I can't help but wonder why Dr. King did not exercise a little more patience and hold off on his demonstrations until after this new government was in power," Ensley stated. "I fear that the real danger now is that the immediate goal of integration may be realized but that the relationship between the races will deteriorate as a result of the timing and methods that were used."

Dad even faced criticism from within his family. He felt disapproval of his involvement in civil rights from his mother and some of his in-laws. On May 7 he wrote to Grandma Jim: "More demonstrations today—the situation is extremely complex—but Birmingham has improved tremendously in the past 18 months." He apologized for not writing often enough, then stated: "I believe that God wants me in Alabama doing what I can to encourage people to deal justly with each other. And you know that you brought me up to trust in God. I know in times past you have worried that I was going to lead people astray and you would be held responsible—but you should have great confidence that you gave me and Junior, Ced and Marian a good bringing up. I don't know too much about what's right—but I'm trying to learn." After saying he would visit her in summer, he added: "Mother, I do appreciate what you have done for me. I know I am not always too thoughtful but in my better moments I realize how deeply indebted I am to you."

If Dad did not always enjoy full support from his own mother, he did receive reassurance from friends and colleagues. Joseph Ban of the American Baptist Home Mission Societies in Valley Forge, Pennsylvania, wrote to thank Dad and Mom for their hospitality during his visit to our house: "We have a great deal to thank you for, not the least of which is the kind of Christian courage you and your family display in the midst of your ministry there. You are carrying on a very important work and all of us owe a great debt to you, doubly so, because you are doing it with the kind of Christian spirit that you bring to the task."

Throughout the many weeks of Birmingham's crisis, people had called my parents—and their social friends, including white people in the Alabama Council—to express concern for their well-being. Friends received phone calls from as far away as Lebanon wondering, "Are you safe?" They replied, "What do you mean, safe? We're out here in the suburbs." The violence against black demonstrators—the police dogs and fire hose blasts, even the bombings—happened downtown, but many white people in the suburbs hardly noticed. We continued to receive hate calls and threats, but that simply felt normal by now.

However, one day when Dad was out of town during the demonstrations, a green state-owned vehicle parked in front of our house. No one got out of the car or said anything, but it felt intimidating to Mom. But when Dad called her, she said, "Oh, no, no. Everything is fine." After Dad returned, though, his black secretary, Myrtice, told him it had been a very frightening experience for my mother.

Mom had good reason to worry. The threat of violence cast a dark shadow over Birmingham. One never knew when an ominous threat would be carried out, or when the possibility of danger would become tangible.

As Birmingham continued to grapple with the aftermath of the spring demonstrations, on June 11, 1963, national attention shifted to Tuscaloosa. At the University of Alabama, Governor George Wallace kept his campaign promise to "stand in the schoolhouse door" to prevent integration. Alabama was the only remaining state in the union with an all-white state university. Two black students, James Hood and Vivian Malone, had been admitted to enroll for summer classes, and Wallace vowed to block their way physically.

I watched the scripted drama unfold on live television. After a long wait, the car carrying the two students approached. As the black students waited in the car, Deputy U.S. Attorney General Nicholas Katzenbach, representing the Kennedy administration, lumbered slowly towards the auditorium where the students would register. Governor Wallace waited for him, standing behind a podium placed in front of the building for dramatic effect. As Katzenbach approached, visibly sweating in the 95-degree heat, Wallace stiffly raised his hand, elbow by his side, to signal stop.

During a brief confrontation, Wallace read a prepared statement. His jaw jutted out as he said: "The unwelcomed, unwanted, unwarranted and force-induced intrusion upon the campus of the University of Alabama today of the might of the Central Government offers a frightful example of the oppression of the rights, privileges and sovereignty of this State by officers of the Federal Government. . . . I stand here today, as Governor of this sovereign State, and refuse to willingly submit to illegal usurpation of power by the Central Government."

Katzenbach replied that the United States government had no choice but to enforce the court order requiring the university to admit Malone and Hood. He spoke clearly and slowly, directly at the defiant governor, stating that the two black students "will register today to go to school tomorrow and go to school this summer."

After concluding this camera-ready drama, Wallace and Katzenbach left in opposite directions. Vivian Malone and James Hood enrolled that afternoon at the University of Alabama, and George Wallace eventually rode his moment in the spotlight to presidential campaign efforts in 1968 and 1972.

That evening, following the Tuscaloosa confrontation, President John Kennedy delivered a televised message to the nation. Since the Birmingham campaign, we had heard rumors that he was planning a major civil rights announcement. When we turned the television on that evening, June 11, we hoped this would be such a message. Kennedy began by referring to the afternoon confrontation in Tuscaloosa, then asked every American to examine his conscience about the nation's founding principles "that all men are created equal, and that the rights of every man are diminished when the rights of one man are threatened." He insisted that this was not a sectional or partisan issue, nor even only a legal or legislative issue. "We are confronted primarily with a moral issue," the president said. "It is as old as the Scriptures and is as clear as the American Constitution."

I looked at Mom and Dad. They were smiling, joyfully but quietly celebrating a clearly significant milestone. Dad had often criticized President Kennedy for his timidity about taking a stand in support of civil rights and eliminating discrimination. As Kennedy announced that he would send Congress a new civil rights bill, which he hoped would soon become federal law, we began to rejoice. Finally, the U.S. government seemed ready to put its power behind the movement to end segregation and oppression.

Kennedy said the proposed legislation would give all Americans the right to be served in facilities which are open to the public—hotels, restaurants, theaters, retail stores, and similar establishments—as well as greater protection for the right to vote. The bill he publicly announced on June 11 became the basis of the Civil Rights Act of 1964, passed after President Kennedy's death by an assassin's bullets. The Birmingham campaign had paved the way for this important initiative. As historian J. Mills Thornton III concludes, the 1963 demonstrations "are almost solely responsible for moving the Kennedy administration to propose and endorse what became the Civil Rights Act of 1964."

On the same evening that Kennedy announced his support for federal legislation—and declared civil rights "a moral issue"—a tragedy took place in Jackson, Mississippi. Medgar Evers, the beleaguered head of the NAACP in Mississippi, returned home from a strategy session seeking to achieve desegregation in the state's capital city. As he walked from his car toward the front door of his home, a White Citizens Council member named Byron de la Beckwith shot Evers with a deer rifle. He died before he could be taken to a hospital.

As if these were not enough momentous events for one day, in Saigon, South Vietnam, a Buddhist monk protesting government oppression of Buddhists set himself on fire. The haunting photograph of a man sitting amidst roaring flames reached American newspapers within a day or two. I stared at the grainy newspaper photo, transfixed, appalled, and fascinated at the same time. What could possibly happen next, I wondered.

It didn't take long to find out. The Gaston Motel bombing marked another link in the chain of violence that anchored Birmingham to its violent past. In the months following the 1963 civil rights campaign in the "Magic City," the Klan renewed its threats against black people and their white sympathizers. The violence unleashed in Birmingham also attracted another group of right-wing extremists, the National States Rights Party.

This anti-Jewish political organization, led by Dr. Edward Fields, had moved its office from Louisville to Birmingham in the wake of Harrison Salisbury's 1960 *New York Times* exposé of the city's racial tensions. On his 1952 draft registration form Fields had listed his occupation as "Anti-Jewish Crusader." In Birmingham the National States Rights Party (NSRP) turned its attention to attacks against blacks as well as Jews. Fields had advance knowledge of the 1961 Mother's Day attacks on the Freedom Riders in Birmingham, and the NSRP likely collaborated with the Klan on bombings and other acts of violence against blacks.

In July 1963 the National States Rights Party began mimeographing a hate sheet called the "Birmingham Daily Bulletin." One flyer dated July 26 carried a handwritten headline, "Lunch Counter Race Mixing—When?" The writer threatened to disclose the beginning of desegregation at five downtown stores, as a means of intimidation. He thanked anonymous employees at each store who had promised to alert NSRP when this "race mixing" began. The reverse side of the flyer carried a full-page diatribe, "Science Proves: White and Negro Races are Not Equal."

Another NSRP "Bulletin" dated July 31 announced in a hand-lettered screed under the heading "Birmingham Betrayed!" that six stores had integrated their lunch counters the day before: "*Black* day in history! This is the day white people were stabbed in the back!" A typed message on the reverse side listed the stores, and declared: "Never forget these stores which joined hands with Martin Luther King to destroy our way of life. No decent, self-respecting whiteman will have anything to do with these mongrelized stores."

When desegregation of the lunch counters began, white members of the Birmingham chapter of the Alabama Council waited at the counters to sit near the blacks when they came in. One store hired a black clerk, but the store owner told Dad he was allegedly caught stealing and fired. The store manager said he was highly disappointed, because he felt that it was inevitable that blacks would be hired and he wanted their confidence.

Despite the apparent success of the Birmingham campaign for desegregation, the extremists seeking to maintain white supremacy clearly had not given up. More violence appeared to be in store for Birmingham's black community, and perhaps for any white people sympathetic to integration.

17

Summertime

The excitement and tension of Birmingham's spring 1963 civil rights campaign eventually gave way to summertime exhaustion. The entire community seemed to need rest and time to catch our breath. For the Jimerson children summer meant, as well, a constant effort to escape the oppressive Alabama heat. Without home air conditioning, we resorted to visiting the library, stores, movie theater, and any other place that promised "air cooled" comfort. Mrs. Walbert again offered her backyard swimming pool as a welcome respite.

Dad moved his office from the Comer Building to a modern high-rise called the 2121 Building (said as "twenty-one twenty-one"), located a few blocks from the city center. On some weekends—especially Sunday after church—Dad would decide he had "work to do" and take us all to the quiet air-conditioned office building. We played on the office desk chairs, pushing each other around the room. I enjoyed reading the exotic black-oriented magazines stacked on a table, especially *Ebony* and *Jet*. They showed images of black life that I never experienced directly. *Jet* even carried photos of light-skinned black bathing beauties along with "social register" news of black communities around the country and political reports and commentary.

One day while working on my homework at Dad's office I opened a drawer looking for a pencil. What I found surprised me: a cigarette pack with only a few cigarettes left. I didn't say anything. But I realized I had seen an unsuspected side of my father. He was a closet smoker. We never saw him smoke, but I now knew one secret he kept from his children.

At home I enjoyed listening to AM radio, especially WSGN, "the South's greatest newspaper," the slogan their call-letters supposedly represented. Doo-wop was fading out, as surfing music gained popularity.

"Who do you like better," I asked Tony, "the Beach Boys or Jan and Dean?"

Tony replied: "Naw, I like fast cars. Gimme a 'Vette or T-Bird." He grinned. "Please? Pretty please with sugar on it?"

The WSGN disk jockeys played "Surfer Girl" by the Beach Boys, Jan and Dean's "Surf City," and the "surf guitar" instrumental "Pipeline" by the Chantays. They played sappy songs like "Hey, Paula" as well as records I liked, including "Sukiyaki" and "Louie, Louie." Without identifying the musicians' race, they also played music by Ray Charles, Little Stevie Wonder, the Shirelles, and other black Motown and soul artists. Even Peter, Paul and Mary singing "If I Had a Hammer," with a final stanza that echoed civil rights movement goals: "It's the hammer of justice. It's the bell of freedom."

Frustrated the summer before by my inability to hit curveballs, I had given up baseball. This left a gaping hole in my summer schedule for 1963. For reasons inconceivable to me now, I decided to join marching band "camp" at Shades Valley High School. Every morning I rode my bike to the high school for practice. We spent an hour or so learning to march in formation on the school parking lot. As a trombone player I marched in the front row. The older high school band members took this very seriously. It almost seemed like army boot camp marching drills.

As the morning heated up, we retreated to the somewhat cooler band room, where we rehearsed both marching songs and concert pieces. Every Thursday evening, for the five or six weeks of band camp, we played an outdoor concert in Central Park. We sat on folding chairs, while people—mostly parents of band members—brought lawn chairs or blankets. Some families tried to enjoy picnic meals while we tweeted, blared, and squeaked through ten or twelve selections.

One thing playing trombone teaches you—even if, like me, you're not very talented—is to wait patiently for your turn. Another is to be satisfied in a background role, providing a (somewhat) rhythmic bass line accompaniment to the real stars, trumpets and clarinets. But one Monday the other trombone players whispered excitedly that it was "our turn." One of the selections for the week's concert would be "Shoutin' Liza Trombone," a song they had played before. It turned out to be a Dixieland-style trombone solo, full of trombone bravado and long sustained glissandos (the smooth gliding notes played moving the slide forward and back). The eight trombonists would play in unison.

For once I had something actually worth practicing at home that week. Normally I spent only as much time practicing as Mom could coerce me into.

But that week I drove everyone crazy with my honking, gurgling efforts to conquer "Shoutin' Liza."

Then at dusk on Thursday in the park, when the band conductor announced our trombone solo, the band quickly went into the song. At the first note all the other trombonists stood up and began the first loud glissando. I stumbled to my feet, lost sight of the music sheet, and never caught up. Not knowing we would be standing to play, I didn't know I should memorize the piece. I felt lost and embarrassed. I hoped Mom and Dad wouldn't notice that I was faking my way silently through the trombone solo.

Ann at least wasn't in the park to see my blunder. She had already left for summer camp, far away in New Hampshire. Her solo trip to camp provided a sometimes bewildering adventure for a twelve-year-old girl. This is her story to tell.

When Mom and Dad sent out a mimeographed Christmas letter describing Dad's work in Alabama, Ed Clark, one of Dad's seminary classmates, wrote back, offering Randy and me scholarships to the New Hampshire summer camp he directed. He thought we could use some relief from Alabama's hot summer, and that our parents would appreciate having us far from the powder keg of Birmingham.

Camp Merrowvista's two-color brochure promised canoeing, hiking, sports, crafts, a little bit of religion (Christianity, naturally), and lots of good old-fashioned character building. Girls Camp was the month of July and Boys Camp the four weeks of August.

Along with shopping for camp shorts, rain poncho, flashlight, and jackknife, our parents considered the travel logistics. The end of the summer was simple. Since Dad had landed a summer-replacement ministry in Plaistow, New Hampshire, the family could drive up to pick me up from Girls Camp at the same time they dropped Randy off for Boys Camp. We'd still be there at the end of August to drive Randy home with us.

The tricky part was getting me up there before the Fourth of July. A round-trip drive would cost the family four days or more. Dad couldn't take off from work, and Mom was caring for baby Mark, not yet a year old. Flying was not an option. Only rich families flew. Greyhound bus looked like the answer.

I filled Dad's old Army footlocker to the brim and padlocked it shut. My handbag burst with chewing gum, a book, paper and pencils, a deck of cards, and my Greyhound ticket. The first leg of my trip would take twenty-four hours to Washington, D.C., where the family of an Episcopalian minister Dad knew from his travels to D.C., the Browns, would host me.

The entire family drove me to Birmingham's Greyhound station. We may have acknowledged the segregated status of the waiting room, but no one mentioned the showdown that had occurred at the nearby Trailways station in 1961 when the Freedom Riders came to town. Mom settled me into a seat midway back. For the first time, my stomach fluttered and my palms got clammy. They wouldn't really send me off alone, would they? What if I had a nose bleed? It must be all right if my parents thought it was okay, right?

The bus growled and heaved out of its berth. I checked my tears as I bravely waved goodbye. At one of the first stops, a girl boarded and asked me for the window seat. "I'm Margie," she said. Boy, could she talk! She was fourteen, on her way to spend the summer with some part of her family in North Carolina. I was shocked when she lit up a cigarette. Next, she lurched down the aisle to the restroom. Pale when she returned, she announced she'd thrown up. Margie needed a nap. Before she conked out, though, she extracted a promise from me: "Wake me up when we get to my stop, okay?"

This responsibility I took seriously. The bus grew quiet. My eyes were heavy. But each time the bus rocked into a station, I strained to read the town's name. Margie settled more comfortably into her sound sleep. At last, the sign for her stop shone back from the bus's headlights. Margie stirred, wakened herself, and was off the bus with barely a thank you. Finally I slept.

The Washington, D.C., bus station was abuzz at mid-morning, and Mrs. Brown and her girls hugged me and jostled me into their car. They made a bed for me in one of their decorated bedrooms. After a whirlwind of barbecues and family outings, two days later I took a deep breath as they shuttled me back to the bus station.

The trip to Dad's brother's home in Reading, Pennsylvania, was a breeze. Aunt Julie and cousin Doug, my age, met me. I was the only girl in a household full of three boy cousins. Doug played the piano and put together plastic models of songbirds. Bob had built a kayak that he steered down the creek that coursed through their property. The oldest, David, hardly noticed me. Late in the evening, Uncle Ced burst in from the hospital, where he had done surgery all day, and mobilized to grill steaks. He fussed over me. It was a whole vacation in three short days.

Uncle Ced made a long-distance call to my parents to confirm plans. What was I to do at Port Authority Station, and would I really be okay changing buses there? He looked worried as he handed me money for lunch in New York.

As the bus lumbered into the city, the huge apartment buildings seemed terrifyingly strange up close. The driver pulled my footlocker off the bus and there I was, alone on the boarding dock.

I heaved the footlocker to some phones marked "Information." I lifted the receiver and a voice snapped, "How can I help you?"

"When is the next bus to Newport, Rhode Island?" I choked out.

"Can't hear you!" barked the voice. I asked again. He said: "12:10, gate 8!"

"I thought it was at 12:20," I said hesitantly.

"You asked for the next bus to Newport. It's 12:10, gate 8." New York was a place where you could stand at the phone crying and no one would ask you what was wrong.

Cheeseburger in hand, I boarded the last bus of my trip. No room to sit. For two hours I stood in the aisle, grateful to be safe on a bus. My spirits buoyed. Progress was slow, as we pulled off the highway and purred into station after station. I consulted my watch.

I worked my nerve up to ask the driver, "Aren't we supposed to be in Newport at 6:30?"

"No," he replied, "that's the direct. You're on the local."

In Newport, Aunt Marian, Dad's sister, waited on the platform, smiling. She had figured out the problem. The next morning, we climbed back into her old car for the last leg—a gorgeous drive into the pine- and maple-covered mountains of New Hampshire.

Family cars covered the playing field outside Camp Merrowvista's old farmhouse. Ed Clark and his wife welcomed me to camp and made sure Aunt Marian would stay for supper in the dining lodge. Back in my "village" in the woods, with eleven new friends, I found we would live in hogans—raised platforms with waist-high walls and arched canvas tops. I pulled on a sweatshirt and planted my skinny bottom onto a log seat for our first campfire. At twelve, I wasn't the youngest girl in the village. But I sure had come the farthest.

Ann sent back a postcard or letter twice a week describing her adventures at Camp Merrowvista. I couldn't wait to go for Boys Camp. By late July, with the Birmingham crisis temporarily quiet, Dad felt comfortable taking his greatly needed vacation. He looked forward to spending August in Plaistow, New Hampshire, as interim minister while the regular pastor enjoyed his own vacation. First, we would make our annual visit to Beaver Falls so Mom could enjoy spending time with her family.

This was our first long-distance trip in our "new" 1960 Plymouth station wagon. One day when Dad parked the '55 Ford wagon on our steep rear driveway, he forgot to set the parking brake. It rolled downhill and wrapped the bumper around a small tree. The car could still be driven, but Dad decided to sell it, cheaply, to a black family that needed a car. Granddad insisted on picking out a replacement car for us, and he and Monty drove it from Beaver Falls to Birmingham—a good excuse for a car trip and a visit to their daughter.

The Plymouth made it back to Beaver Falls in good shape. Dad piled our suitcases on the top luggage rack and covered it with a large canvas tarp, securely tied. I always enjoyed Granddad and Monty's house—a quaint structure built twenty years before as a temporary cottage until the new house could be built (it never was)—overlooking a small pond. Their property covered seventeen acres, almost equally divided between spacious lawns and woods, with a rust-stained creek ("crick," Monty called it) meandering through. The long slag-and-ash driveway curved from the county road to the house, and beyond. Over a narrow hand-built stone bridge crossing the creek, it curved up the hill to a now-blocked exit back onto the road.

After a short visit in Beaver Falls, we drove all the way to central New Hampshire. The long dirt road to Camp Merrowvista curved up and down several hills before passing under a large sign hung from poles beside the roadway, with the camp's name carved on a wide dark-stained plank.

When we pulled up to the white farmhouse that housed the administration offices and parked nearby on the grass, Ann ran up and hugged Mom and Dad. In the evening the closing ceremony for Girls Camp took place in the woods, at a circular structure with several rows of rough plank benches. Camp director Ed Clark presided from a ceremonial seat with Indian symbols carved on a backrest. Camp girls lit a large bonfire in the center of the circle. The ceremony included lots of camping songs, skits presented by each of the camp villages, a speech and prayer by Mr. Clark, and awards given to girls for swimming-class certificates, athletic feats, and other achievements.

After the end of Girls Camp, I stayed on for a few days until Boys Camp began. The rest of the family drove south to Plaistow, where they spent the month living in the church parsonage.

As the other campers arrived on July 31, I learned that I would be in Village 5. Instead of the hogans where Ann stayed, my village had teepees. Eight fourteen-year-old boys would live in two teepees, and our two counselors shared a third. Each teepee formed a circle just large enough for four cots to fit, end to end, with our footlockers between. The other boys in teepee B were Dave Zentmyer from Lancaster, Pennsylvania; Ricky Palmer, Dover, Delaware; and Tom Hawthorne, Statesville, North Carolina.

In teepee C, Richard Walker—also from Dover—was one of several black kids in camp. After living many years in the South, joining an integrated summer camp felt exciting. It provided an opportunity for me to overcome some of my own stereotypes and prejudices. I had difficulty admitting to myself that skin color did affect how I responded to people. No matter how much I knew it was wrong, I still had feelings of different-ness. When such emotions surfaced, unintentionally, I tried to hide my reactions and remind myself not to act on these subconscious responses.

From the start I liked our counselors. Jim O'Brien, from Webster Groves, Missouri, was a student at College of Wooster in Ohio. Ed Hamlett, from Jackson, Tennessee, took a special interest in the son of a civil rights worker. When Dad visited camp, Ed asked him to talk to our village group about his experiences in Alabama. Ed told Dad he was interested in joining SNCC, but knew his family and friends would disapprove. While Ed seemed serious and Jim energetic and athletic, both had good senses of humor. They helped us learn camping techniques, such as pitching tents, lashing sticks together to form a rustic table, and cooking over a campfire. We even learned how to bake a cake in a cast-iron "Dutch oven" buried in glowing fire embers.

Camp Merrovista provided a perfect respite from Birmingham's heat and tensions. No threatening phone calls for one thing. The motto for Camp Merrowvista—and its sister camp in Michigan—was "MPRS": Mental, Physical, Religious, and Social. These four components of a healthy life formed the basis of camp philosophy. We got a workout in each of them—especially Physical.

Mental elements of camp life included "interest group" classes, nature walks, and frequent discussions about biology, geography, local history, and other topics. The Religious component of camp included Sunday church services, evening vespers, private meditations, and discussions about religion, ethics, and personal values. Living in small teepee groups in a village deeply embedded in the woods taught us social relationships and skills. The Physical emphasis included swimming lessons, sports, athletic competitions, hiking, and camping trips.

On Saturdays we had track-and-field events, or "Paul Bunyan Day," with lots of contests. One Saturday the Jimerson family drove up from Plaistow for the afternoon, along with all of Dad's family: Grandma Jim, Aunt Marian, Uncle Ced and Aunt Julie, with cousins David, Bob, and Doug.

The White Mountains began just north of Ossipee, but the foothills surrounding camp provided stunning views from rocky ledges overlooking Dan Hole Pond. On our first overnight camping trip our village of eight campers and two counselors hiked to the abandoned site of Canaan Village, near the base of Mount Shaw. Instead of setting up camp right away, Jim and Ed let us explore the woods, search for a small waterfall, and relax. Soon a downpour threatened to drown the campsite. The rain prevented us from setting up our small pup tents. We managed to raise a large tarp, but only two feet off the ground, where we huddled for warmth and to keep our soaked clothes from even more damage. We took turns standing over a small campfire holding a poncho to protect the fire while cooking spaghetti noodles and sauce. By the time supper was ready, it was dark. We were famished.

"Eeewww! This is the funniest tasting spaghetti ever!" someone said, while we huddled under the low tarp trying to eat.

"I don't care. I'm hungry enough to eat anything!" another boy said.

We all crowded under the tarp with our sleeping bags, sleeping soundly until dawn.

"What's for breakfast?" we said. "We're starving!"

Jim said, "Special treat: pancakes with apple butter."

Then Ed looked up from the food backpack. "Hey, Jim," he said. "Where's the apple butter? All I can find is a big jar of spaghetti sauce."

"Oh, gross!" we all cried out. "No wonder the spaghetti tasted funny last night."

On our last evening at camp, Dad, Paul, and Susie drove up to see the "high council" closing ceremonies in the outdoor council circle. Our village presented a skit giving our version of a Russian Lawrence Welk Show. Dad, Susie, and Paul stayed overnight. The next morning I said good-bye to everyone and we left for home. It was Susie's eighth birthday, August 28, 1963.

Dad drove to Plaistow to pick up the others. I had my first glimpse of the large white parish house where the family had been staying. Then we drove to the home of Reverend Don Johnson—another of Dad's seminary classmates—and his wife Merilee in Massachusetts. Mrs. Johnson entertained us and put us up for the night.

"Don isn't here," she explained. "He went to Washington for the Jobs and Freedom March in Washington."

We watched the evening news on television, which carried a brief report and film footage of the crowds engulfing the Mall, surrounding the Reflecting Pool in front of the Lincoln Memorial. After watching this, Dad shook his head and frowned. "Oh, man!" he said. "I wanted to be there so much. It would have been wonderful to be part of that. Part of history."

The film clips of Martin Luther King Jr.'s speech, with the refrain "I have a dream!" later became an iconic symbol of the civil rights movement. But on Susie's birthday, after she blew out the candles on her cake, we thought about the marchers in the nation's capital. We knew that the Birmingham campaign had made the March on Washington both necessary and possible. But it seemed bittersweet for Dad. Having played a valuable role behind the scenes in Birmingham, he felt left out of the celebration party.

18

September 15, 1963

The inspirational optimism of the March on Washington soon gave way to the harsh realities of Birmingham's racial climate. The negotiated settlement of the spring and summer mass demonstrations quickly proved only temporary. Project C and the children's crusade gained some small concessions in desegregation of public facilities. But generations of segregation would not end easily. By the time we returned home from New Hampshire, segregationists had begun preparations to undermine Birmingham's plans to integrate a few schools in early September 1963.

During the summer, before his working vacation in New Hampshire, Dad had assisted local chapters of the Alabama Council on Human Relations in preparing for school desegregation. The Huntsville chapter planned and carried out a successful week of meetings between white children and several of the black children planning to enter desegregated schools. The Birmingham Council arranged two similar meetings for black and white children to get acquainted before entering desegregated schools.

As early as the previous spring, the Mobile Council had held several programs to discuss peaceful desegregation of schools. As Dad reported: "The activities of the local council were helpful in creating interest in the white community in planning for desegregation of schools in September."

During the summer of 1963 the Alabama Council distributed material related to law enforcement to sheriffs and police chiefs across the state. The council also reprinted and distributed five thousand copies of the booklet "Can We Afford to Close Our Schools?" Through all of these measures, the ACHR sought to reduce racial fear and misunderstanding and to provide a hospitable environment for peaceful desegregation of public schools.

Dad had also continued his efforts to establish biracial committees to resolve tensions throughout Alabama. During demonstrations in Gadsden, reports of blacks beaten and assaulted by state troopers led prominent whites, including some elected officials, to have state troopers withdrawn. Dad made two trips to Gadsden during the summer to talk with elected officials, prominent white businessmen, ministers, and some of the black leaders. One white minister arranged for some biracial meetings, but the white power structure refused to be involved. Buses were desegregated, and several lunch-counter owners agreed to desegregate their facilities. The Muscle Shoals chapter also continued efforts to persuade elected officials in Florence, Sheffield, and Tuscumbia to establish biracial committees.

By the beginning of September, when we returned to Birmingham, school desegregation created renewed tensions in the city. Our schools in Homewood would remain segregated. But in Birmingham on September 4, two black students entered Graymont Elementary, despite rock-throwing white demonstrators led by members of the National States Rights Party and the Klan. Three more black students would integrate Ramsay and West End high schools in the next two days. In a last-ditch effort to prevent integration, Dr. George Fisher delivered petitions to Mayor Albert Boutwell demanding to close schools rather than desegregate them.

The next day, September 5, dynamite blasted attorney Arthur Shores's home. This sparked a riot, with black people throwing bricks, bottles, and rocks at police officers responding to the bombing. Shooting into the crowd, police gunfire killed twenty-year-old John Coley and injured twenty-one others. Three schools closed after this violence. It remained uncertain when they would reopen. After the bombing, Dad visited Arthur Shores, with whom he had worked on civil rights concerns, to express his concern and offer to help in any way he could.

On September 9 a firebomb rocked the home of black business leader A. G. Gaston. Again, Dad visited with Mr. and Mrs. Gaston after this attack. Fortunately the bombing did not injure anyone.

When the closed schools reopened that day, Governor George Wallace vowed his fight against school integration would continue. On September 10 more than 5,000 people jammed Dixie Speedway in Midfield for a night-time protest against desegregation of Birmingham schools. Plans to establish private schools accelerated. This effort to circumvent public school integration had become common in many southern communities. Meanwhile, as resistance mounted in Birmingham, on September 11 school segregation ended quietly in Mobile.

On Sunday morning, September 15, we attended the early morning service at Shades Valley Presbyterian Church. Dad sat with us kids while Mom sang in the choir, in the balcony behind us. After Sunday school, Dad drove us home, squeezed into the VW. Mom had to stay with the choir for the second service at eleven o'clock, so Dad would prepare lunch for everyone. We changed into comfortable play clothes as soon as we got home.

Before he started the charcoal grill on the back patio, below the kitchen and dining room windows, Dad turned on the radio. He wanted to get everything ready so we could eat when Mom got back from church. After soaking the charcoal with lighter fluid, Dad lit a match. The grill burst into a fireball. We could smell the burning lighter fluid.

"Oh goody!" Susie said. "Hamburgers and hotdogs!"

While the charcoal flamed red and orange, an announcer interrupted the music on the radio. Reports had come in that an explosion had blasted the Sixteenth Street Baptist Church, near downtown. This was the church where many of the civil rights mass meetings had been held during the protest marches in April and May. Authorities had not yet announced any details about possible casualties or damage.

By the time Mom came home from church, we knew that four children had been killed and others injured in the bombing. Dad and Mom kept an ear on the radio for any updates.

"Oh, Jim!" Mom exclaimed. "Not again! A bomb during the church service! Who could do such a thing?" All of us felt numb, in shock.

Mom told us how she heard the news: "I was singing in the choir up in the balcony, when Reverend Duncan came in for the second service. He announced that a terrible thing had happened, that a church down in Birmingham had been bombed. Details weren't available, but it was fairly certain that deaths were involved. Tears welled in my eyes. I thought of all the Negro community has been through—and now this!"

Still going through the motions of putting hamburgers and hot dogs on the grill, Dad said: "Oh, Mel, I had hoped it wouldn't come to this. How can we respond . . . ?" His voice faltered and he gave Mom a full bear-hug.

When she stopped sobbing for a moment, Mom said: "After that announcement, I don't know what happened in the service. Such tragic news! Reverend Duncan never once offered a prayer for the situation, but went on with his sermon as usual. I could hardly contain myself through the service. I just wanted to get back home. But I had to stay with the choir."

Every few minutes the radio blared a news update. New announcements about the number killed and injured. Every time the news came on, Mom or Dad would say: "Hush! Listen! Quiet!" Four black girls had been killed, another one blinded, and several others badly injured. Bodies and injured people had been pulled from the rubble. The bomb went off at the side of the church. The dead girls had been in the bathroom checking their hair in the mirror. No one knew who had been responsible. Some reports suggested that blacks had bombed the church to gain sympathy.

Instead of a joyous late-summer cookout on the rear patio, lunch became solemn. My parents were personal friends of Reverend John Cross, minister of the bombed church. They looked depressed, angry, confused. Even Susie and Paul looked sad and afraid. We fought back tears. I felt hollow inside. Just when things seemed to be getting better in Birmingham—.

As we finished eating, Dad said to Mom: "The ministers should be home from their church services. Time to call them. See if we can find some way to respond."

Then Dad began calling the white ministers he knew. The president of the Birmingham ministerial association said he didn't think there was anything he could do. Dad said: "Well, it seems like the least you could do as head of the ministerial association is to extend sympathy to the families, and go down to the funeral home to talk to them."

Later, the minister told Dad he called the police to see if it was safe for a white minister to go to the black community. He said he would have gone down if the police had told him it was safe. When Dad told us this story, he said: "What kind of a jerk . . . ? You call up the police and say, 'Hey, I'm a minister, and I want to know what my ministerial duties are.'"

Early that afternoon, Dad talked with several white ministers on the phone. He told them that as clergymen they should speak out about a church bombing in the community. They needed to condemn this kind of violence, to express sympathy and concern for the victims. In one form or another, each of the white ministers said that's really not my job, that's not my responsibility, that's something for the black people to deal with themselves. They refused to get involved.

Dad spent a lot of time on the telephone. Then he sat down next to me in the living room. "Randy, can you watch the kids for us? John Drew invited your mother and me to come over to his house to see what we can do."

"For how long?" I asked.

"I don't know. Probably all day."

"Where will you be?" I asked.

"At the home of Deenie and John Drew, downtown—on Dynamite Hill."

I asked, "Who are they?"

Dad explained: "John Drew is a very successful insurance agent, and a good friend of Gaston, the one black millionaire in Birmingham. John's a very gregarious, friendly, kind person. He's a friend of Dr. King. King stays in their home a lot of times, when he comes to town. John wasn't involved in demonstrations, but I'm sure he was involved in a lot of the planning for the demonstrations. Some of the negotiating sessions took place in the Drews' home."

"What's a die-mamite hill?" Susie asked. I hadn't seen her come into the room.

"Well, Susie," Dad began. He stopped to think. "It's a part of Birmingham where some Negroes live. So many houses and churches have been bombed there, that people started calling it Dynamite Hill. Mr. Drew's house has been dynamited, simply because he's a black man interested in civil rights. They've suffered a lot of harassment. The neighbors have been taking turns guarding their homes, because of all the bombings."

Dad told us that he had been to the Drews' home many times. "It's a good place to meet people and find out what's going on. That's why your mother and I are going there now."

"One of the interesting things about the Drews," Dad said, "is John's very dark-skinned, but his wife Deenie could pass for white. In Birmingham a white person can never say anything to Negroes about the shades of blackness. But Deenie talks about it freely. She looks white, and yet she has some Negro heritage—Negro blood. She says her father is white and her mother black. When traveling in the South she has to carry a card that states she is a Negro, so they won't be arrested for breaking the color line. But Deenie can go in the front door of restaurants, get some food, and take it out to her husband."

Mom came into the living room, holding her purse. She had washed the tear stains off her cheeks, put on fresh makeup and lipstick. She said: "If you're talking about the Drews, Deenie is just a very friendly, gracious person. The Drews have the self-confidence of moneyed people. But they don't act it. It doesn't go to their heads. They aren't elitist, even though they belong to the elite class of Negroes."

Dad had to get in the last word. "During the demonstrations, some black students said to Deenie, 'If you don't demonstrate and get arrested and go to jail with us, you're not one of us.' And she just said, 'Well, whatever you say,

I know my role and what I'm able to do. My role is to be a taxi driver for you people, and your nursemaid, and bring you home. But demonstrating is not my role.'" Dad laughed at this. "It's interesting how she knows exactly who she is and her role, and won't be intimidated by criticism or innuendos."

Mom said, "Randy, take care of the others. But don't be mean to them. No yelling or threats. I'll phone you when I can." Then they left.

For a Sunday afternoon it was strangely quiet. None of us had much energy for playing. Concentrating on homework became a lost cause. Ann played with Mark and changed his diaper when necessary. At thirteen months, Mark crawled everywhere, but was beginning to try walking. For me even listening to WSGN seemed uncomfortable. I wanted to listen to music, but I didn't want to hear any more news stories about the church bombing. The dead girls.

After a while I decided to try something I had always been curious about. In movies and TV action shows people often had to cling to a small branch or rock to avoid falling off a cliff. I wanted to see how hard it would be to pull oneself up, as the actors did easily.

I opened the rear dining-room window wide and looked down, one story below, to the concrete patio Dad had built in the corner where the garage jutted out from the walk-out basement's wall. On the garage side Dad had installed a basketball hoop for me to practice.

I straddled the window sill, then held on tight as I lowered myself from the window. Hanging from the window ledge, I tried to pull myself up. It was harder than it looked in the movies or TV. As I struggled, my arms grew tired and sore.

"Help!" I called out. "Paul! Ann! I can't get back up!"

Ann and Paul ran into the dining room, calling, "Randy? Where are you?"

"Here! Outside the window!"

Ann and Paul looked worried, but they each pulled at one of my arms. When my elbows got as high as the window sill, I was finally able to pull myself up. My stomach and arms were scraped. It hurt. But at least I was safe.

I thought about this all afternoon. What a stupid idea! I was supposed to be taking care of the other kids, not putting *myself* in danger. While my parents tried to deal with the church bombing crisis, I was acting foolish and irresponsible. I felt ashamed.

Mom called twice to tell us she would be staying longer. She asked me to make sure everyone had something to eat for supper. Ann helped me make sandwiches for Paul and Susie. We had potato chips, iced tea, and ice cream for dessert. Shortly after sunset, before the sky turned black, we heard a car pull up by the front curb.

Mom came in without Dad. She said, "I stayed as long as I could, but I didn't want to leave you children alone after dark. It was strange driving back from downtown. Most people were off the streets. The mayor had asked everyone to stay in. Everything looked so calm."

She checked on Mark, who slept soundly in his crib. The rest of us wanted to know what had happened at the Drews' house. Mom told us her story of the day's events:

When we arrived, John was alone, listening to the radio and watching TV, in great grief. He seemed glad to see us. Deenie had left a day or so before to drive Jeff, their only son, to New York to attend a military school. They wanted him to get away from the unbearable conditions here. John said that the parents whose children were killed were his friends. Three of the four girls killed that morning were personal friends of Jeff.

Soon the phone rang. Deenie said she heard the news on her car radio. She was calling from a rest area on the New Jersey Turnpike. We listened as John told her about Jeff's friends being killed.

The phone continued to ring all afternoon. People called to see what they could do, how to respond to the terrible news. Dr. Pitts, president of Miles College, arrived. Then a Negro high school principal came, and a well-known contractor. There were tears, there was silence, people began to come to the door, a white Catholic priest among them.

For most of the day I was the only woman there, since Deenie was traveling with Jeff. I don't think anyone asked, but I began to make coffee and refreshments for everyone. I acted as hostess for John.

Before long a group of men sat around the table in the rec room discussing the events and trying to decide what they could do. As these great, strong Negro men discussed whether to call President Kennedy and ask for federal troops, tears welled in their eyes. Urgent phone calls from John Drew and some of the other men tried to persuade Bobby Kennedy to send in the U.S. troops to protect the Negro community.

Things began sounding worse on the radio. A rally planned at a shopping center was held in spite of the turmoil. It should have been cancelled as everything else was, because it would only stir up things more. It was a group of States Righters (some actually Negroes), and their speaker was a so-called Baptist minister who was speaking against school integration. This was what had started the whole thing—cavalcades of cars protesting Negroes entering the white schools.

Then we heard of the shooting of a Negro boy on a bicycle by two white boys. I watched strong men with tears in their eyes as they talked of the dead girls and the turmoil. And I realized how hopeless their cause must seem. This was the last straw.

Later, your father left for a while. He said he wanted to see the bombed-out church for himself, and to see Reverend Cross if he could.

I quietly listened and mourned with the people all afternoon, but as dusk approached I felt I should come back to be with you kids. Your father returned before dark. He said someone could drive him back later.

I wanted to ask dozens of questions. But I felt too tired—too drained of energy—to put them into words. Ann, Paul, Susie, and I soon slouched off to bed. Mom stayed up, waiting for Dad.

Even though he had come home very late the night before, Dad prepared breakfast for us as usual. Ralston Purina this time, mixed with the last of the cream of wheat. We ate quietly, unlike most mornings buzzing with frantic preparations for going to school.

All day I could hardly pay attention to the teachers. I kept thinking about the girls killed in the church bombing, and the two boys shot to death the same day. Three of the four dead girls were my age, all of us born in April 1949. The other girl and one boy were younger. The boy shot by police was older than me. No one at school talked about the tragedy. Everyone went along as usual, except for me.

We learned that the four girls killed in the bombing of Sixteenth Street Baptist Church were Denise McNair, Carole Robertson, Cynthia Wesley, and Addie Mae Collins. Cynthia had been decapitated by the blast. Sarah Collins, Addie Mae's sister, had been blinded, but survived. Other church members suffered various degrees of injury. It was Youth Day. Children packed the church. As blacks gathered near the church to express their anger over the bombings, police wounded one black man and arrested nineteen others.

That evening Dad said he wanted to show us something. He brought a small cardboard box into the living room. He said that, after hearing about the bombing and talking with people about it, he wanted to see for himself. "Guess I'm just naturally curious," he said.

Police with rifles and helmets had blocked off Sixteenth Street next to the church. He could see a large hole in the back corner of the church, and rubble all over the street. Bricks and broken stone mixed with shattered pieces of concrete, mortar, and wood. Several cars had been damaged, and windows across the street were blown out. Most of the stained glass and other windows of the church were smashed by the explosion. Shards of glass and twisted lead from the windows littered the street. One large stained glass window showing Jesus remained intact except for a hole where Jesus's face had been. As though Jesus could not bear to see the scene of destruction.

Dad said: "I met the assistant pastor of the church. He gave me the addresses of the families who lost children. Everything was confusion near the church. When the cops weren't looking, I picked up some of the broken stained glass. I thought it would be a reminder of the violence and hatred. It might also be important evidence of the crime."

Carefully, as though raising the communion cup in church, Dad picked up the pieces of stained glass from the box. There were two large pieces, each about the size of book, and several smaller shards of glass. The large pieces included twisted lead holding together pieces of blue, yellow, and milky-white glass. I recognized at once the patterns typical of church stained glass windows. Not the fancy windows of wealthy white churches, but the simple colors and style of churches trying to add a hint of affordable elegance.

Seeing these shards of stained glass made the horrors of the church bombing real. Something we could see and hold in our hands. The desecrated house of worship—the young lives lost to this hate crime—became more than distant news from the radio and television. We knew it had really happened. We could see and touch the result—the evidence—of violence.

Mom picked up the larger fragment of stained glass pieces held together by lead, eerily twisted and broken. She said: "This shows what a twisted mind can do. The twisted lead and glass show what terrible things can happen when people get to thinking the wrong way."

The killing of four young girls did not mark the end of violence on September 15, 1963. Two black teenage boys were shot and killed that same afternoon.

An organization called West End Parents for Private Schools had been created to oppose integration at West End High and other Birmingham schools, by seeking to establish private schools for white children. They held a large rally that afternoon at the Dixie Speedway in Midfield, attracting two thousand supporters. Bobby Shelton and other Klansmen attended the rally, along with National States Rights Party members. Fiery speakers, including a Southern Baptist preacher, inflamed the crowd with denunciations of "niggers" and appeals to defend segregation at all costs. The anger displayed at this rally had built up during four months following the negotiated desegregation of public facilities in Birmingham that resulted from the spring demonstrations. But it also grew out of centuries of Negrophobia, racism, and white supremacy spawned by slavery and segregation.

Two sixteen-year-old white Eagle Scouts, Larry Joe Sims and Michael Lee Farley, left the rally and bought a forty-cent Confederate flag at the National States Rights Party headquarters nearby. They climbed on Farley's red motor scooter and drove into Sandusky, on the west side of Birmingham. When they saw two black teenagers on a bicycle, one riding on the handlebars, Larry Sims pulled out a pistol and fired twice.

Two bullets hit thirteen-year-old Virgil Ware, the son of an unemployed black coal miner, who fell from the handlebars. The bullets struck his cheek, pierced his lung, and sliced through his aorta. His older brother James pleaded, "Get up, Virge. You trimmin' me." Virgil only said, "I'm shot." Moments later he died.

During black protests over the church bombing, sixteen-year-old Johnnie Robinson threw rocks at a car displaying shoe-polished slogans such as "Nigger, go back to Africa." As he fled up a downtown alley, a police officer shot Robinson in the back. He was dead on arrival at the hospital. The officer killed Robinson for the alleged crime of throwing a rock. This display of excessive force against a black protestor did not even receive a reprimand from the Birmingham police force.

Within a few days my father visited the homes of each of the six victims of September 15. He wanted to express his sympathy and concern, to let the families know that at least one member of the white community cared about their losses and their suffering. Dad explained: "Deenie and John Drew were just amazed that I had taken the initiative to see the families. They hadn't thought about doing that, but with my ministerial background that just seemed logical."

One of Dad's favorite sayings declared that the role of religion was "to comfort the afflicted, and afflict the comfortable." He got this from theologian Reinhold Niebuhr, but it went back to Finley Peter Dunne, who wrote that this was the role of newspapers. This became one of Dad's guiding principles. He relished afflicting the comfortable, but his first instinct remained comforting the afflicted. Whether a car accident, a policeman's beating, or a church bombing, Dad responded as a Good Samaritan.

In response to the violence on Sunday, Mayor Albert Boutwell declared, "All of us are victims, and most of us are innocent victims." Local ministers called for a minute of silent prayer at noon the next day.

On Monday, September 16, Chuck Morgan—who had been my father's lawyer in the trial in Talladega a year before—spoke about the church bombing at the Young Men's Business Club luncheon held in the Redmont Hotel. At noon, church bells around Birmingham tolled in a public call to silent prayer for the victims. But the first carillon Morgan heard, from the Protective Life Building, played the segregationist anthem, "Dixie." At the luncheon meeting, Morgan spoke from the heart, addressing the prevailing question of the day: who was responsible for this tragedy?

Chuck Morgan said: "Four little girls were killed in Birmingham yesterday. A mad, remorseful, worried community asks 'Who did it? Who threw that bomb? Was it a Negro or a white?' The answer should be: 'We all did it.' Every last one of us is condemned for that crime and the bombing before it and the ones last month, last year, a decade ago."

He continued: "The 'who' is every little individual who talks about the 'nigger' and spreads the seeds of his hate to his neighbor and his son. The jokester, the crude oaf whose racial jokes rock the party with laughter. The 'who' is every governor who ever shouted for lawlessness and became a law violator." He indicted senators, representatives, courts, newspapers, "all the Christians and all their ministers," the mayor, police force, business community, and the "good people." The core problem in Birmingham, Morgan charged, remained that "no one accepts responsibility; everybody wants to blame somebody else."

Morgan concluded his remarks with condemnation of his hometown and its citizens: "What's it like living in Birmingham? No one ever has and no one will until this city becomes part of the United States. Birmingham is not a dying city. It is dead."

The response of public officials failed to meet the crisis. President John F. Kennedy did not send federal troops to protect the black community, as many black leaders had urged. Instead he called for restraint, and sent in a two-man team—Earl H. Blaik and Kenneth C. Royall—to try to ease racial tensions in Birmingham. Meanwhile, on September 20, Governor George Wallace made personal contributions of a hundred dollars to each of two groups seeking to form private schools for white pupils. His defiance continued.

The reaction to Chuck Morgan's September 16 speech—which the *New York Times* reported on September 17, and Morgan quickly prepared as a mimeographed statement—came from whites offended by his remarks. Throughout the South, public officials and newspaper editors condemned him and denied his allegations. Segregationists barraged him with hate calls and death threats.

Two weeks after the speech Morgan left Birmingham "for a rest." When he did return he turned over his law practice, furniture, and books to five other lawyers, put up a for-sale sign, and let his young son say good-bye to his friends. As he wrote several months later: "There was no way for us to remain in the city of which I had been a part yet from which I had grown apart."

For denouncing Birmingham's culture of violence, the ambitious young attorney—who had once held aspirations to run for political office, hoping to be governor someday—had been forced to leave his home community. Charles Morgan Jr. moved to Atlanta and, later, to Washington, D.C., becoming a prominent attorney with the American Civil Liberties Union. Merely speaking out against violence was enough to get one ostracized from Birmingham.

19

Four Funerals

In the aftermath of the bombing, reporters from all over the country converged upon Birmingham for the funerals of the young victims. National and international attention focused on the four young girls brutally killed in the Sixteenth Street Baptist Church bombing. The loss of innocent young lives, the images of crisp white dresses and new patent leather shoes violated by the blast, evoked both pathos and horror. How could senseless violence desecrate a house of worship? Who could place dynamite where it would obliterate unsuspecting children? After forty-seven bombings in Birmingham since 1947, these four girls became the first fatalities. Previous explosions had destroyed homes, businesses, and churches. The people targeted had been injured but not killed. Almost lost in the press coverage and national outpourings of grief and recrimination, the two young boys killed that same Sunday became forgotten footnotes to the central tragedy of September 15, 1963.

After visiting the families of all six victims, Dad attended all four funerals. He took part in the funeral services for Carole Robertson, Johnnie Robinson, and Virgil Ware—the only white person to do so.

The Robertson family resisted Martin Luther King's appeal for a single funeral service for the four girls killed in the church blast. Alpha Robertson said: "We realize Carole lost her life because of the movement, but we feel her loss was personal to us." On Tuesday afternoon, September 17, Fred Shuttlesworth joined Reverend John Cross of Sixteenth Street Baptist Church in leading Carole Robertson's funeral.

As Dad noted the next day: "An orderly, restrained crowd of some 2,000 Negroes and more than 100 whites filled the St. John's A.M.E. Church and lined the sidewalks outside yesterday to pay tribute to one of the four Negro children killed in Sunday's bombing of a Negro church."

At the same time, Dad reported:

The leader of a small militant white racist group which has stirred up much of Birmingham's school integration trouble says Sunday's bombing of a Negro church here is 'wrecking the segregationist cause.' Edward R. Fields said he expected to be indicted, along with other members of the National States Rights Party who led demonstrations around the city's three integrated schools, and charged he was the victim of 'a frame up by the Kennedys.' Birmingham police disclosed that two white teen-agers charged with shooting a Negro boy to death were traced as a result of their participation in school demonstrations fostered by the National States Right Party. Merchants are concerned with crises. Racial unrest and violence cause sales to decline.

The following day, September 18, Martin Luther King Jr. led the funeral service for the other three victims of the church bombing. My parents both attended this funeral. As Dad reported: "Mourning three bombing victims, more than 6,000 Negroes jammed Sixth Avenue Baptist Church Wednesday for the combined funerals of the three young girls."

During the funeral service, Dad's friend Reverend Joseph Ellwanger—leader of the Birmingham chapter of the Alabama Council—read the Scripture and prayed that the Kingdom of God would come to Birmingham. In his sermon, Dr. King called the dead girls "unoffending, innocent, beautiful children of God." He declared: "They have something to say to every minister of the Gospel who has remained silent behind the sanctuary of the stained glass windows." The girls were "heroines of a modern crusade."

Mom told us about the funeral for the three girls, Denise, Cynthia, and Addie Mae. "I went into the service and the place was packed," she said. "I sat down and I felt kind of lost, because the church was huge and I was just one little person sitting there. Right away Jim was called out to talk to one of the important NBC newsmen. And I was annoyed because I had to sit there all by myself among strangers. I didn't know when he was going to come back. I didn't know what was going to happen. And I had a fear that somebody might bomb that church where we were. So I sat there a long time, and finally he slipped into the seat and sat down and the service began."

"I really didn't know what was going on," Mom said. "It seemed confusing, and I felt so helpless and sad." She turned to Dad and asked, "Who preached that sermon?"

Dad said, "Martin Luther King."

Mom replied, "I didn't even know that. I've never seen him, so I don't know what he looks like. The newspaper never shows his picture."

"Not here in Birmingham," Dad said. "He's probably recognized every-where else but here."

Mom said: "Well, it was almost a blur to me. But I realized as we went out of the church that it was a very important time and I was really fortunate to have been there." She thought for a moment and added: "As we left, Governor Wallace had state troopers in uniform taking pictures of the whites who were there."

Many of the white people attending the funeral service were Alabama Council members. Marge Manderson, a Southern Regional Council staff member from Atlanta, represented my father's employing organization. She visited Dr. Pitts and Chuck Morgan to give them regards from the SRC staff. Shortly after, she met Myrtice Woods, Dad's secretary, who stopped by Morgan's office to pick up copies of his speech. They decided to attend the funeral together. In an interoffice memo to Leslie Dunbar, Vernon Jordan, and Paul Anthony, the next day, she reported:

Myrtice and I were unable to get inside the church, and stood outside. I met a few people from Birmingham, about 9 or 10 of them white. They were all ACHR members or people who had been involved in interracial activity of some kind before. Despite what the papers said about several hundred white people attending, I didn't see but about 25 or so in all, some of them from out of town. If any city officials or dignitaries were there, I heard no mention of the fact. Even the white ACHR members seemed to stand apart, huddled together, poor things.

Incidentally, during the service we could hear chimes downtown playing the first phrase of "Dixie," which they do every day.

As Myrtice, who is a Negro, and I went from place to place in the city together, I saw nothing—in attendance at the funeral, in the attitudes of people we encountered on the street, outside the church, in traffic, parking lot attendants, etc.—which would indicate the least degree of change of heart from white Birminghamians. They all seemed hostile.

In one of the Negro families, the daughter killed was an only child. Local papers, radio-TV stations have said nothing about any of the Negroes injured in the dynamiting. They do report, on every newscast, on the condition of a white youth hit by a brick or rock.

I wonder if the Wares and the Robinsons aren't being overlooked in expressions of sympathy. We called on the Ware family in Sandusky yesterday evening. They are quite poor. At least four sons and one daughter remain in the family, ranging from about six to sixteen. They seemed touched by two letters they had received, apparently the only two written communications, one from a lady in California, one from a Baptist women's organization (outside the South, I think). They brought them out and showed them to us. Virgil Ware's funeral will be Sunday.

Before the young boy's funeral, Dad visited the Wares once or twice. The family asked him to participate in the funeral service, one week after the shooting, at a Baptist church in Sandusky. Dad felt honored by this request. On the same day, September 22, Dad also took part in the funeral for the other murdered boy, Johnnie Robinson, held at New Pilgrim Baptist Church.

The next day Mary McGrory discussed the aftermath of the Birmingham church bombing, and mentioned my father, in her *Washington Evening Star* column, dated September 23, 1963:

> The President's two-man truce team is coming too late to hear the most vehement expressions of the Negro community. They should have been at the funerals of the victims. . . . Kenneth Royall and Earl H. Blaik would have heard groans at Johnnie Robinson's funeral more eloquent than any words about how the Negroes in Birmingham really feel. . . .
>
> Earlier yesterday, they could have gone up to a grubby hilltop in outlying Sandusky, overlooking Birmingham's belching steel mills. There in a tumbledown Baptist church, they were mourning Virgil Ware, 13, who was shot as he rode the handlebars of a bicycle last Sunday after the bombing. They could have found the church with no trouble. They only had to follow the line of State troopers' cars with their shotguns hanging out the windows.
>
> They would have been the only representatives of their race at the ceremonies, save for the Rev. Norman Jimerson. Mr. Jimerson, an ordained Baptist preacher, has been denied membership in Birmingham's Baptist Church because of his association with the Alabama Council on Human Relations, a group that holds the view, preposterous by local standards, that Virgil Ware was just as valuable as the two white boys who are charged with his murder.
>
> The families of the boys, Mr. Royall and Col. Blaik could easily have learned, have expressed no regret to the family of Virgil Ware, whose father is an unemployed coal miner and whose mother is a maid. . . . They would have heard at Johnnie's funeral the mournful hope expressed that "this would be the last in this bitter drama of evil." Outside they would have heard the low-voiced prophecy that more bombings are coming.

In the angry laments of the Negroes, the President's truce team would have heard the true story of Birmingham, a city that would rather die than desegregate.

Our family's involvement with the Ware family did not end with Virgil's funeral. Dad visited their home several times. One cold overcast day our whole family drove to the impoverished neighborhood on the northwest edge of Birmingham.

Finding the house proved difficult. Dad drove up a steep hill on an unpaved, very rough road. The Ware family lived in a shanty on a gravel road lined with slag from the nearby steel mills. Black coal dust covered everything in sight. No grass grew in the front yard. Sickly looking dogs sniffed at us and wandered away.

As we sat in the living room on a cold day we could feel drafts all about us. Gray light showed through holes in the walls. It was dark and dingy with a single light hanging from the ceiling. The older son, James, stood in the kitchen washing dishes by hand. Mrs. Ware, a heavy woman with five children, recounted the events of Virgil's death. She said she knew her boys had not thrown rocks at the white boys, as they had been accused. They were merely trying to pick up a second bicycle for their paper route.

The father was a yard man unable to get work in the winter. When he could he worked in the white community, if anybody had leaves to rake or grass to mow. He had lost his job as a coal miner for the Tennessee Coal and Iron steel mills. Virgil's mother, an obese but gentle woman, worked when she could as a maid. She spoke of the dead boy with tears in her eyes. We talked with her and let the family know there were people concerned with the loss of their son. Mrs. Ware thanked us over and over for coming to visit.

The Ware family literally didn't have enough food to eat, and they had never heard of the food stamp program. You had to pay two dollars to get enrolled in the program, and it was a long time since they had seen two dollars. My parents gave them the two dollars so they could start getting some assistance. Besides food, Mrs. Ware told us, their biggest need was for coal to keep warm. Dad offered to help them find financial support.

While driving home, Dad and Mom pointed out the corner on a lonely road where the two white teenagers had shot Virgil Ware. We stared out the car windows as we passed. We didn't say a word.

For several years, even after we moved away from Birmingham, my parents sent the Wares money when they could. Dad didn't have a large salary, but he wanted to do something to help. Mom kept the poorly spelled letters that Mrs. Ware sent asking for money.

That was my first time of seeing firsthand the impoverished conditions in which many black people lived. The visit to the Ware home in Sandusky made a lasting impression on each of us. Even at eight and nine years old, Susie and Paul found it eye-opening. As Paul remembers now, almost fifty years later: "I can still picture the dirt front yard, the ramshackle house, the large black woman with a long skirt, and the little black faces peering from behind it. Whatever combination of emotions I was feeling—perhaps fear, alienation, curiosity—that visit made an indelible impression on my mind. I realized that there were two Americas: one white, comfortable, middle class; and one poor and black. It was like visiting a strange planet."

On September 18, three days after Virgil Ware's death, as Dad reported: "First-degree murder charges have been placed against two sixteen-year-old white youths charged with the fatal shooting of a thirteen-year-old Negro boy Sunday."

In her September 21 column reporting on the preliminary hearing for Larry Joe Sims and Michael Lee Farley, Mary McGrory wrote: "The two Scouts did not look like killers. They both appeared—as they sat pale and hangdog, handcuffed together on a bench—merely young for their years." The defense attorney referred to the shooting only as "this unfortunate accident." He could not even remember the victim's name and gave up trying, saying "this colored boy." Seeking sympathy for his clients, McGrory wrote, he said they had lost their appetites and couldn't sleep, and referred to the killers as "two raw, grieved, untutored boys who have had this unfortunate thing come into their lives at their age." According to McGrory, he seemed to suggest that "Virgil Ware was not a victim of white violence but, somehow by being colored, its agent."

The trial of Sims and Farley opened on January 14, 1964. Dad reported: "In Birmingham testimony will begin this morning in the murder trial of a sixteen-year-old former Phillips High honor student, Larry Joe Sims, who is charged in the fatal shooting of a young Negro boy here last fall. Young Sims and another youth, Michael Lee Farley, also sixteen, are charged in the slaying of thirteen-year-old Virgil Ware, who was shot September 15, 1963, as he rode on the handlebars of his brother's bicycle on a lonely stretch of the Docena-Sandusky road."

Having met Virgil Ware's mother and family, my mother decided to show them that some white people truly did care about their loss. She would attend the trial of the two white teenagers accused of the murder. On the back of mimeographed copies of our family Christmas letter for 1963, she wrote about her experience:

> On a Thursday morning I sat in on the trial of Larry Joe Sims, who had shot Virgil Ware. I sat on the Negro side of the court room and spoke with Mrs. Ware. People looked askance at a white person who dared to sit with colored people. When a white woman came forward to sit beside me, I must say I was nervous. Then I learned that, although the choir director from her church was an uncle of the Sims boy and had asked her to come, she had much sympathy for the Negro cause and had been working, against her husband's wishes, for years with an integrated group of women.
>
> That part of the trial that I observed had character witnesses to verify that Larry Joe Sims was a fine boy from a very fine family. Along with a Boy Scout representative (he was an Eagle Scout) and teachers, there appeared on the stand a Baptist minister, now doing denominational work in the area. He said that the boy was a regular attendant at Sunday school. (Doesn't this speak well for what the Sunday school teaches!)
>
> When I had talked earlier to a reporter who was in court shortly after the two boys were apprehended, she was appalled that when she asked if there had been any move on the part of the family of the guilty to express sympathy to the Ware family, the answer was, 'No, the NAACP might misconstrue what we were doing.' Yet they continually passed in the halls of the courthouse.

Later my mother added some details in a speech to a church women's group in Elmira, New York, where she lived from 1967 to 1970:

> I attended a half day's session of the trial of the white boys who were involved. I felt rather conspicuous sitting on the Negro side of the courtroom. I could see the attorneys looking at me. I feared that they might say something to me, that I might be questioned. But no one bothered me. I talked briefly with Mrs. Ware during a break. But the words I heard coming from the stand broke my heart, for here was a white boy, brought up in a Baptist Sunday

school, an Eagle Scout, an honor student, being defended by a teacher, a minister, and a Scout leader as a fine boy. Yet he had deliberately killed another human being!

As usual in cases like this the sentence was light—seven months' probation and the judge added that if this were to interfere later with his college education that it would be suspended. On the other hand a Negro boy who threw a rock at a white motorcyclist (injuring him only) was held under a $100,000 bond. This was Alabama justice!

We have kept in touch with the Ware family through the years. She writes that she has heart trouble now and of course, as the problem always was, her husband can find employment as a yard man only in the summer. Winters are hard, and they find it difficult to keep clothed and fed, as well as warm.

The legal responses to the September 15, 1963, killing of six black children failed to secure justice until many years later. The murderers of Virgil Ware went free with only a suspended sentence, even though they confessed to shooting in the direction of two black teenagers riding a bicycle. The judge who suspended Larry Joe Sims's sentence commented on the defendant's fine background, and only admonished him, "Don't ever have another lapse where you act before you think." If even a suspended sentence would hamper his admission to college, the judge said he would consider lifting this mild probation.

The police officer who shot Johnnie Robinson was never charged or even suspended. In June 1964, as my father reported: "A thirty-six-year-old Ku Klux Klansman, the last of three men charged with illegal possession of dynamite during an investigation of last year's racial bombings, went free in Circuit Court Monday in Birmingham." Shoddy police work, half-hearted investigations, and a long series of legal maneuverings delayed justice for many years.

More than a decade later, William J. Baxley, who in 1970 defeated MacDonald Gallion in a race for attorney general of Alabama, reopened investigations into the Sixteenth Street Church bombing. In 1977, suspect Robert Chambliss went on trial for the bombing. Defended by former Birmingham mayor Art Hanes, Chambliss was found guilty of murder. He died in prison in October 1985. In May 2000, two more suspected conspirators in the church bombing were arrested: Bobby Frank Cherry and Thomas Blanton Jr. Other suspects had already died by then. Following his conviction on four counts of murder in 2002, Cherry died in Kilby Prison in November

2004. Convicted in 2001, Tommy Blanton remains in prison in Springville, Alabama. All of these bombing conspirators had been active Klansmen.

Justice for four young victims—Addie Mae Collins, Denise McNair, Carole Robertson, and Cynthia Wesley—moved slowly in Alabama. But justice finally did prevail.

20

How Many Deaths Will It Take?

In the immediate aftermath of the bombing of Sixteenth Street Baptist Church and the murders of Virgil Ware and Johnnie Robinson, the beginning of a new school year blurred past me. Ninth grade at Homewood Junior High, with not even the hint of integration. I was there but I wasn't there. My school now included seventh graders, so Ann joined me on the school bus or in Dad's VW every morning.

The junior-high counselor recommended that those of us planning to go to college should start language classes. We had two choices. The fast-track students picked Latin. Others, less ambitious, took Spanish, considered less difficult.

I struggled through the inverted grammar of Latin, with a verb at the end of each sentence and "objects" preceding the action words. It sounded funny when translated back into English in the same order. We learned verb conjugations, which made me conscious for the first time of the eccentricities of English verb tenses and the large number of irregular verbs in my native language. The teacher emphasized the Latin roots of many English words. The one that caught hold in my memory—perhaps the only specific thing I did remember from first-year Latin—was that "equestrian" came from the Latin root "equus," meaning horse. I wondered: Why not just say "horse rider"?

The school counselor also recommended taking biology, normally a tenth-grade subject, in ninth grade. This would give me some sort of advantage in high school, so I could take an extra, advanced, science class. I had already started algebra in eighth grade, so I could get to calculus in high school. So I signed up for biology, with the other college-prep kids.

I remember two things about biology class. First, one of the girls had to inject herself with insulin periodically because she had diabetes. It sounded awful. Glad I don't have diabetes, I thought.

Second, we had to design and carry out a major experiment in biology. I had no idea what to do. When I complained to Mom and Dad, Dad said he'd talk to a friend of his who was a biologist. "Abe Siegel is a member of the Alabama Council," Dad told me. "He was a C.O. during the war."

"What's that mean?" I asked.

"C.O. means conscientious objector," Dad said. "He refused to fight, even against Hitler, because of his moral values."

I said: "You mean he was a coward?"

"That's what a lot of people think. But sometimes it takes more courage to stand up for what you believe than even risking your life in battle." Dad rubbed his chin, thinking. "I didn't know anything about that when I went into the Army. Now, I think I would be a C.O. rather than get in a position to kill anyone."

So one afternoon I took the bus down to the University of Alabama Medical Center, just over Red Mountain on the way into Birmingham, near the hospital where I had visited Mike Ham after a bullet collapsed his lung in seventh grade. Dr. Siegel suggested an experiment that he called "Sugar Fermentation by Yeast and Bacteria." He loaned me a set of test tubes, some yeast and bacteria cultures, and explained how to conduct the experiment. All I had to do was follow his instructions. Easy-peasy, I thought.

The biology teacher let me and others set up experiments in the classroom. I grouped my test tubes on part of the windowsill that ran the length of the back wall, facing north with no direct sun. After several weeks of measuring things ("collecting data"), I planned to compile the final results of my experiment the day before our papers were due. But when I entered biology class that day, I couldn't find any of my test tubes. I asked the teacher. She said the cleaning lady must have thrown them out the night before. So I didn't have to write up my results, but I still passed.

From algebra I moved to geometry in ninth grade. Dad had been able to help me with algebra homework, but now Mom usually had to answer questions. I told Gregg Beasley: "If I have to take geometry, it's nice to have a mother with an architecture degree."

Social studies class began with Alabama history in the fall, and then civics for second semester. I enjoyed reading about the early Indian tribes—Creeks, Chickasaws, and Choctaws—who had given names to many of the rivers, creeks, towns, and landmarks in the state.

But when we got to the Civil War (always called War Between the States, or War for Southern Independence), the textbook presented a pro-Confederate interpretation of history. Reading about Reconstruction, I grew more and more angry. According to the Alabama history text, the saviors of the South, protecting the state from evil and sinister Yankees, carpetbaggers, and scalawags (white southerners who sided with the hated conquerors and ruling despots from the North) were the mounted knights of the Ku Klux Klan. I couldn't believe that this was the official interpretation sanctioned by the State of Alabama. Well, I could believe it, but I didn't like it. But I bit my tongue and didn't complain to the teacher.

One day the buzzing of the boys in ninth grade signaled something special. Word spread that we would watch "The Film Strip" today. I didn't know what that meant, but some of the guys were winking slyly at each other, grinning, whispering—even giggling, which only girls did! The teachers led boys and girls to separate large rooms. "The Film Strip" provided what passed for sex education in 1963 Alabama: clinical, technical, not too explicit, just enough to be confusing.

"I already knew all that stuff," one boy boasted.

"Yeah, nothing new here," another said.

Someone else chimed in: "Pictures were kinda cool, but they need real *photos*—movies!—of people 'doing it.'"

I didn't say anything. I felt embarrassed. These were things you weren't supposed to talk about. Maybe not even think about. Yet I wanted someone to explain this "birds and bees" stuff, without having to admit I didn't already know it all.

The year before, in the changing room at the Homewood swimming pool, Dad watched me change into my swimsuit.

"Randy, you're what—thirteen—now?" Dad said. "Pretty soon you'll start growing hair under your arms, in your crotch, and on your face. That's a sign you're getting to be a man."

That was about it for "The Talk"—parental education about maturation and sexuality. I waited for more, but that was all. And I didn't dare ask questions, or show any interest. After all, I was a former leader of the fourth-grade "he-man woman haters club" in Hopewell. You could get kicked out for even talking to a girl. Before long I was the only club member.

Only recently had I admitted to myself that I found girls interesting or attractive. I wished I could get to know some of the pretty girls in school, but braces made me self-conscious. Besides, I had always been shy. Mom said it started when I was three and the ladies in church, where my father was minister, would crowd around and talk about me.

More than anything else, though, I realized that I did not fit in here in Alabama. I could not imagine liking any girl prejudiced against black people or who wanted to maintain segregation. How would I be able to find out about a girl's political or racial views? Her moral values on social issues? I couldn't imagine asking such things.

I wasn't the only Jimerson thinking about these matters.

Mom said that one day, after two and a half years in Birmingham, eight-year-old Susie asked her a similar question. Out of a clear, blue sky, Susie said, "What if I marry the wrong person?"

Having no idea of what she was thinking, Mom said, "What do you mean?"

Susie replied, "I mean, what if I marry someone who doesn't like Negroes?"

Later, beaming proudly, Mom told us: "Evidently she has some understanding of what we're trying to do here."

In seventh grade at Homewood Junior High, Ann especially enjoyed art class. Miss Lemon taught them how to work with glass. They melted broken pieces of a Coke bottle or another type of glass in the kiln to soften the edges and flatten them out. Then they arranged the pieces as tiles to make a mosaic coffee-table top.

Ann asked Mom if she could take a few shards of the stained glass from the Sixteenth Street Baptist Church to create a mosaic. There were a dozen or so small fragments, in addition to the larger pieces. Ann put a few of the glass fragments into the kiln with other kids' projects. The glass retained its shape and color—just "softened" around the sharp, broken edges.

Ann handled the shards of stained glass carefully, and spoke about them with her art teacher in hushed tones. Ann recognized that these were sacred and symbolic objects, and felt chills when she thought about the four dead girls. Miss Lemon responded respectfully. Even if her classmates didn't appreciate the significance of the small pieces of glass, to Ann these were precious objects.

She imagined several different ways to incorporate the stained glass pieces into a larger and meaningful project. But she never did turn them into an artwork. She just held onto the shards of glass, picking them up now and then over the years to feel their meaning.

We had celebrated Mark's first birthday in the summer. Mom and Dad wanted to move his crib out of their bedroom. They suggested having me move to the den, so Mark could share the middle bedroom with Paul. That gave me a private room, but it was small and only a louvered door separated it from the living room. The den had once been a screened porch, which a previous owner had closed in to make an extra room.

The biggest disadvantage of the den soon became apparent—cockroaches. Alabama cockroaches were to northern cockroaches what a full-sized Bengal tiger was to a newborn kitten: sinister two-inch terrorists, threatening to spread disease and spine-chilling terror. Not to me, of course; I was a fourteen-year-old boy, not afraid of any bug. Sleeping in a converted screen porch meant constant swatting at these giant cockroaches, being careful where I stepped, and waiting a few seconds before entering my bedroom after turning on the ceiling light.

One night, as I was drifting off to sleep, I felt something fall onto my face. Cockroach! I jumped straight up out of bed. It felt like the cartoons: Bugs Bunny jumping up, straight as a board, when scared.

But cockroaches weren't the only things keeping me awake. I began having almost constant headaches, and it often took an hour or more to fall asleep at night.

"My head feels like it's in a vise and someone keeps tightening it," I complained to Mom.

"Where does it hurt?"

I put my hands over the back of my head. "Here—all over. . . ."

Mom said: "I'm so sorry. It must be all the stress and tension we've been under." She gave me two aspirins and a sad smile. "Try to think of something quiet and happy."

So I tried to think about playing baseball, or hiking in the mountains at Camp Merrowvista, or canoeing on Dan Hole Pond. Sometimes it helped.

Before long I created names for the various headaches: the vise, the jackhammer, the bouncing ball, the big throb. I turned coming up with new terms into a game. But it still hurt. The constant tension of being an outsider in Alabama had created almost unbearable stress.

Ever since I was nine or ten in Hopewell, I had enjoyed listening to pop music on the radio. I moved from the Everly Brothers, Johnnie Mathis, and Paul Anka into folk music: the Kingston Trio, Pete Seeger, and Joan Baez. In 1963 Peter, Paul and Mary introduced Bob Dylan's "Blowin' in the Wind," which I adopted as a favorite. Its message of peace, justice, and brotherhood seemed to confirm our family's commitment to civil rights. But when the Homewood Junior High student body sang it during an all-school assembly in the gym, I wondered how many of the kids around me understood its meaning: "How many years can some people exist / Before they're allowed to be free? . . ." Even the die-hard segregationists in the gym sang along. "Yes, 'n' how many deaths will it take till he knows / That too many people have died?" Ironic, I thought.

Mom had given me an old tube radio from her college days, which I kept tuned to 610, listening to "The Good Guys" of WSGN. I got hooked on rock 'n roll and Motown. I didn't start buying records until 1963, however, after turning in enough S&H Green Stamps "books" to get a portable hi-fi. My first purchase, at a Homewood record store, showed my still-eclectic music taste: Jan and Dean's "Drag City," almost copied from their earlier beach-scene song "Surf City"; and the Village Stompers' "Washington Square," a Dixieland instrumental named for a New York City landmark.

After spending time with cousins Marilyn and Barb Poister in Beaver Falls, Ann came back excited about a thirteen-year-old blind singer, "Little Stevie Wonder." His hit song "Fingertips"—featuring soaring harmonica solos and call-and-response lyrics—finally came to Birmingham.

During the fall of 1963, an electrifying new song began getting nearly constant radio time: "I Want to Hold Your Hand," by a new British band called the Beatles. From the first harmonized lyrics and crisp guitar notes, I knew this was something totally different.

Ann heard "I Want to Hold Your Hand" at a junior-high sock-hop dance. Soon, she said, "Everyone in seventh grade is Beatles crazy!"

The radio and TV news began featuring stories about "Beatlemania." Adults in England and the United States expressed shock at their long "mop-top" hairstyles. Teeny-boppers screamed so loud at Beatles concerts that no one could hear the music. Not since Ed Sullivan refused to show Elvis Presley's gyrating hips had popular music seemed so dangerous.

In January, while Tony and I were hanging out at High-Kel Drugs, we saw the album cover for their first major-label U.S. release, "Meet the Beatles!"

Even in a half-lighted photo, the faces of John, Paul, George, and Ringo—framed by thick bangs and hair covering their ears—looked daring and rebellious. I bought the album and played it until the grooves wore thin.

When the Beatles first came to the United States for a concert tour in February 1964, I worried that I wouldn't be able to see their appearance on the Ed Sullivan Show. Our family had taken advantage of a school break to travel to Vicksburg, Mississippi. I enjoyed visiting the battlefield where General Grant had besieged the last major Confederate stronghold on the Mississippi River in 1863. Dad drove us over the long bridge so we could say we had been to Louisiana. But we got back to the motel in time for the Sullivan program, and Mom and Dad let us watch the Beatles perform. They sang some of my favorites songs: "All My Loving," "Till There Was You," and "She Loves You," in the first half of the program, and at the end of the show, "I Saw Her Standing There" and "I Want To Hold Your Hand." Even just seeing the band on television seemed exciting. Music wasn't the same after that.

In the months following the bombing of Sixteenth Street Baptist Church, Dad conferred with Reverend John Cross and members of his church several times concerning various funds established to aid the church and the families of the victims. He also spoke about the Sixteenth Street Memorial Fund, established to aid the families of victims, with Bishop George Murray, one of the racially moderate religious leaders Dr. King had criticized in his "Letter from Birmingham Jail." He continued to visit the families himself, including the family of John Coley, who was killed by a policeman the night of the second bombing of Arthur Shores's home.

But Dad seemed less hopeful and optimistic than usual. He talked with us less often about his work, about the people he met. The racial climate in Birmingham and the rest of Alabama continued to deteriorate. Governor Wallace repeatedly interfered with court-ordered desegregation of public schools in Mobile, Birmingham, and Tuskegee. In late September state troopers and local police jailed 156 black protestors in Selma, a city Dad called one of the fiercest centers of anti-black and anti-integration resistance. Only ten days after the church bombing, Dad reported to Southern Regional Council headquarters: "Birmingham police are investigating two explosions believed to have been designed to commit wholesale slaughter in a Southside Negro area early yesterday."

Throughout September, October, and November, Dad conferred with Birmingham city officials about the importance of stopping police brutality. It must have seemed a hopeless cause, but he kept trying to change the mindset of public authorities. One potential source of change appeared with the city's creation of a biracial committee to seek solutions to racial problems. At the beginning of October, Dad wrote to Bishop C. C. J. Carpenter and other members of the Group Relations Committee, which he called the most important committee in Birmingham. He suggested several steps for the committee to consider pursuing, including: assuring impartial, fair, and firm law enforcement; hiring black policemen; and eliminating police brutality. The latter, he stated, "is by far the most important insurance against riots and breakdown of law and order." He also urged committee members to shun all advice that "Negroes must be taught patience"; or calls for the committee to "move slowly," "don't rock the boat," "don't antagonize the segregationists," or "don't go ahead of the people." He certainly must have been aware that Bishop Carpenter had been one of the white religious leaders whom Dr. King had accused of encouraging these very attitudes.

Dad also urged restraint to one city-hall official, who had expressed hostility toward Dr. King and other black leaders who criticized the city's slow progress in desegregation. Dad wrote: "I am going to preach a sermon in one sentence: 'Whenever one person allows some other individual's words or actions to create in him hatred, he has allowed the individual to destroy him.'" It was advice I had often heard from my father.

Alabama's strict segregation laws and customs limited the opportunities that even committed civil rights activists found for interracial social activities. Our parents attended integrated parties and informal social occasions, but since Mom and Dad didn't drink—a legacy of strict Baptist upbringings—they didn't always feel comfortable in such settings. They went because they wanted the interracial connections, but not as often as they might otherwise have done. In any case, children weren't invited.

Since we lived in a segregated neighborhood and attended all-white schools and churches, we didn't even know very many blacks. A few times Mom hired a black woman to clean the house. But she spent so much time straightening up and cleaning beforehand that there wasn't much left to do for the cleaning woman. The purpose seemed more about providing a job for someone in need of work. Mom did enjoy having someone to prepare lunch, since cooking never appealed much to her. She tried to insist that the black maid join us at the dining-room table, but she replied, "No, ma'am. Thank you, but I feel more comfortable here in the kitchen." By the second or third visit, however, Mom convinced her to join the family. It seemed awkward at first, but Mom had made a statement for equality and integration, in her own quiet way.

Several times our family visited Miles College for music performances, plays, or Alabama Council meetings. On one memorable occasion, President Lucius Pitts invited us for dinner. We walked up to the president's home, a Georgian-style two-story house with tall narrow posts supporting a high porch roof across the wide front. Susie's eyes grew wide, and her mouth dropped open. "What a big house!" she said.

Inviting aromas greeted us from the kitchen. Dr. Pitts and his wife shook hands with us and introduced their four children. We gathered around the dinner table, enjoying a good meal. We kids finished quickly and went upstairs to play on the second floor. At our home, playing board games provided a good time to relax. We thought we knew most of the popular board games, but the Pitts children introduced us to *Sorry!* For weeks after, Susie lobbied to get that game for our own family. The fact that this dinner made a big impression on us showed how unusual it was to be with people of another race in a social setting.

Another meal that we remember vividly became known as the fish-sticks dinner for a millionaire. We laughed every time we told the story, but at the time it wasn't very funny for mother. "That story was terrible," Mom said years later. "That guy that was a millionaire who came and had fish sticks!"

Dad often invited journalists, ministers, and other white visitors to Birmingham out to our house for dinner. (Having black people visit our white neighborhood would have been dangerous to them and to our family.) Since Mom didn't enjoy cooking, the added stress sometimes bothered her. Late one afternoon, Dad phoned and asked Mom if he could bring over a man from New York. "All right," Mom said. "But we're just having fish sticks." For a family with five children and a limited budget, taking a package of frozen breaded fish strips out of the freezer saved both time and money. Mom heated them in the oven and served French fries on the side.

Dad said not to worry about changing dinner plans. He knew it was already too late for any new preparation. When Dad drove up in his battered VW, he introduced his guest by name, but only said that he lived in New York

City. He was short and Jewish. The visitor said he heard about what Dad was doing in the civil rights movement and wanted to meet him. Mom apologized for serving only fish sticks and fries. She said she would have made something nicer if she had known he was coming. But he said it was fine; he didn't mind. He was just glad to meet Dad and our family.

As Mom retold the story for us years after, she said how embarrassed she had been. "I didn't know he was a *millionaire* until afterwards," she told us. "I felt so bad. I thought, 'Oh the poor guy, having *fish sticks!*'"

After school a few days before Halloween, Mom asked if I wanted to go downtown with her to hear Governor Wallace speak. The idea of listening to Wallace made hairs stand up on my arms, but I also felt curious. Mom never said whether this was Dad's idea or hers, but she did tell him all about the event later.

Mom drove downtown and parked near City Auditorium. We walked through one of the glass doors in a wide row of entrances to the modern new building. Our seats were on the left side of the seating tier that made a horseshoe slightly raised above the main floor. People talked excitedly while waiting for the governor. Our seats faced directly across the auditorium. On the stage far to our left, I could see the Alabama state flag and the Confederate battle flag, along with an American flag.

A band at the front struck up a marching song, and the rear doors on the main floor opened. A short man with dark hair strode up the center aisle, followed by several other men in suits. I thought that Governor Wallace looked different in person from when I had seen him on television. But this man turned out to be a warm-up speaker, who riled up the audience before introducing the governor of the "great state of Alabama." The band burst into a stirring rendition of "Dixie."

Wallace's grand entrance outdid the previous speaker's march to the platform. He strutted up the center aisle, jaw jutting out, looking every bit as defiant as when he confronted federal marshals trying to integrate the University of Alabama. The audience stood en masse and applauded loudly, with shrill whistles and Rebel yells (once designed to terrify the Yankees during battle, now accompanying many segregationist rallies). Everyone stood except Mom and me. I put my hands under my thighs for the entire speech—a silent show of disapproval, which I hoped no one would notice. I didn't want trouble.

I hardly heard what Wallace said, but the audience cheered robustly and frequently interrupted with applause. I looked around in amazement. Afterwards, I could remember only the spectacle, the roaring crowd, the ice water running down my spine. Later, in a report to Paul Anthony in Atlanta, Dad wrote: "October 29: Wallace speaks at City Auditorium in Birmingham in support of private schools, and charges U.S. District Attorney Macon Weaver with responsibility to prosecute the 'communists' who 'organized' the demonstrations in Birmingham in Spring of '63."

At Homewood Junior High School, ninth graders had the late lunch period. Ann and the other seventh graders had already eaten and started a new class period by the time I got to the cafeteria, shortly after noon. One Friday as I almost finished my lunch, Principal Joseph Prickett spoke over the loudspeaker system. The school usually didn't have announcements during lunch, so this surprised me. I heard the principal saying he just heard a news report that President Kennedy had been shot. He didn't know how serious the president's injuries might be, but he thought we should know that the president had been shot in Dallas, Texas.

A moment of stunned silence. Then I heard a great cheering from the students in the cafeteria, rippling along the outside covered walkways, and echoing in the classrooms. It sounded like the jubilation when our football team won a big game. I couldn't believe the news. Almost as bad as President Kennedy being shot, it seemed, was the fact that students cheered the news. It completely astonished me. I was so upset, I covered my face with my hands and put my head down on the lunch table. I probably was sobbing, but I'm not sure.

John Calhoun, one of my classmates from Alabama history, came up on the other side of the table and said, "Hey, what's the matter? What're you looking so sad for? *Kennedy's* been shot!"

I looked up. I didn't know how to respond. Finally, I said: "I wouldn't be happy if *anyone* had been shot—even George Wallace."

"Of course not! He's a *good* guy." What he meant, I knew, was "He's on *our* side. He's in favor of segregation." John walked away, joining the other cheering students.

I realized that, for many of my classmates, this was welcome news. A few months before, President Kennedy had spoken in support of civil rights legislation, calling civil rights a moral issue for our country. Many people in the South saw Kennedy as being an enemy, someone to ridicule, hate, and despise.

The bell rang for the next class period, and I stumbled towards my classroom in a daze. Students still chattered excitedly about the news. Principal Pritchett made another announcement. This time he said that President Kennedy was dead. Lyndon Johnson was the new president. More cheering rang out. But I could see a few girls with tears in their eyes.

The teacher—herself an outspoken opponent of integration—nonetheless looked sad and angry. She said that anyone who cheered for the killing of a president should be ashamed of himself. Even if you disagreed with the president and his values, his beliefs, this was a tragedy for the country.

Within an hour the principal announced that school was canceled. Buses would take us home, or our parents could pick us up. I found Ann waiting in front of the school, red-eyed. Soon mother drove up in the station wagon, with Mark in his baby seat—supported by two curved aluminum bars that hooked over the front seatback—and Paul and Susie in the back seat.

"They were cheering, Mom!" I said, as we drove home. "What will happen now?"

Ann said: "After the announcement an older boy came running up the sidewalk by our outside door. I saw his face in our doorway, cheering that Kennedy was shot. It was awful! But no one in my class cheered."

Paul said: "Three kids in *my* class cheered. How could they do that? Isn't that *wrong*?"

"Yes, Paul, that is very wrong," Mom said. "I'm sure they don't know any better. They probably heard that Kennedy was bad, and they thought that bad people deserved to die. . . . What a tragedy!"

Susie said: "When I grow up I'm going to vote for President Kennedy. He's so handsome."

All weekend Mom sat glued to our small black-and-white television set. We each joined her to watch parts of the nonstop coverage of the president's assassination and funeral. From the time we got home from school, and for the remainder of the weekend, almost nothing else was on television. When police arrested Lee Harvey Oswald, suspected as the murderer, we saw him being led from a movie theater in handcuffs. There were stories about President Kennedy's life, his years as president, his family. Interviews with journalists, political figures—almost anyone who had known him—presented somber, grief-laden tributes. The next four days were filled with confusion, terror, shock, and grief.

On Sunday we saw Lee Harvey Oswald being led out of the Dallas jail. Sheriffs in Stetson hats led him towards a car, parked in a large garage. Suddenly there was confusion, people pushing around Oswald, who doubled up in pain. Bewildered news announcers said that someone had shot Oswald. Before long we heard that Oswald had died.

On the same day, NBC carried a rebroadcast of a British television program—a political satire show called *That Was the Week That Was.* TW3, as the show was called, had carried the day before a twenty-minute tribute to our slain president, instead of its usual biting satire. This reminded us of the popular record album *The First Family,* a gentle spoof of JFK and his extended family, which had been released a year earlier. We had all laughed along with the album's jokes about JFK's rocking chair, his Boston accent, PT-109, and other topics. But now the jokes no longer seemed funny.

School was cancelled on Monday, a national day of mourning. We watched the heart-wrenching televised coverage of President Kennedy's funeral. I remember vivid images: the flag-draped casket being carried to a military caisson; a horse with high-topped boots backwards in the stirrups; Little John-John—whom we had seen in photos romping on the White House lawn or hiding under the Oval Office desk—bravely saluting; Jackie Kennedy tall, composed, and grief-stricken behind a black veil; the burial at Arlington National Cemetery.

Following President Kennedy's assassination, my father wrote to Paul Anthony, on November 27, 1963: "Mr. Clancy Lake, chief of the news bureau at WAPI-TV, gave an excellent editorial condemning the action of those students in public schools in Birmingham that cheered when informed of the death of President John F. Kennedy. He said that, unless we make an effort to attack bigotry and hatred that the students evidently learned at home, we should call for the pallbearers of Birmingham."

Later, Mom bought us each a copy of *The Torch Is Passed,* a hundred-page book of photographs, compiled by the Associated Press. She wanted us to have a memento commemorating the tragic death of a young president.

In the years since, Americans of my generation and my parents' generation could always remember what they were doing when they heard the news of President Kennedy's assassination. Most accounts describe the grief and sadness that overwhelmed them, their friends, their community. I share those sentiments. But what always haunts me is the sound of junior high-school students cheering.

How many deaths will it take?

❖

The Jimerson family Christmas letter for 1963, written shortly after Kennedy's death, discussed both family activities and concerns about the racial situation in Birmingham, but did not mention the assassination. Once again, Mom put a hopeful spin on a tragic year:

Christmas, 1963

Dear Friends,

As we listen to Randy rehearsing Christmas music in preparation for the Junior High Concert, as we watch Ann designing cards for Art class, as Paul intermittently sits down at the piano to pick out Christmas carols and Susan claims she can't wait until Christmas, and as all of us point out things of beauty to Mark, our dear baby—now sixteen months old—the Jimerson family realizes again that the loveliest season of the year is here.

Unfortunately Birmingham has become synonymous with violence, but as we write this letter, new hope fills our hearts for the future of the city. At present Jim is announcing an essay contest for all Alabama high school students, the subject, "Human Rights—The American Dream." This was prompted by the knowledge that December 10–17 has been proclaimed Human Rights Week. He has high hopes that this may cause some real seeking for truth on the part of those who enter.

This past August we had a wonderful vacation in New England. Ann and Randy enjoyed Camp Merrowvista near Ossipee, New Hampshire and the rest of us stayed in the Baptist parsonage at Plaistow. It was so good to see many of you and to revisit our former homes. We are especially grateful to the Woods for sharing their home with us that month. Otherwise it would have been impossible to have had such a long vacation.

Our return to Birmingham was marred by the awful bombing on September 15. Jim and I attended the first funeral; he attended the one for the other three girls; and he had a part in the service for one of the two young Negro boys shot that same afternoon. Since then we have met his family, who find it difficult to keep warm and to provide food enough for the other children.

Another eventful year has made all of us aware of the need of the Savior whose birth we celebrate. May this Christmas season bring us closer to the living Christ.

Sincerely,
Melva—and Jim

21

Nigger-lover

In the first few weeks following the assassination of President Kennedy, my father wrote at least two letters to the new president. In the first letter, he urged President Lyndon Johnson to honor the slain president's memory by pushing the Civil Rights Act through Congress. Kennedy had supported such legislation, and Dad and other civil rights activists thought this would be an opportune moment to garner public support in his memory.

The other letter to President Johnson protested news reports that Mac-Donald Gallion, the former attorney general of Alabama who had requested the Talladega injunction in 1962, had been nominated for a position with the Interstate Commerce Commission. Dad wrote to President Johnson: "People who believe in the Constitution of the United States, and who reject the theory that Alabama is a sovereign state will be most distressed if Gallion is rewarded for his efforts to circumvent United States Federal Court orders." He warned that voters would not accept giving "political rewards to people who have acted contrary to the best interest of the United States." To ensure greater notice of his letter, Dad sent copies to Attorney General Robert Kennedy, Assistant Attorney General Burke Marshall, Lee White (presidential advisor on civil rights), and LBJ advisor Bill Moyers.

In his annual report for 1963, Dad provided a clear statement of the goals and methods of his organization, summarizing things he had been saying for the past two and a half years:

> The Alabama Council on Human Relations is the only state-wide bi-racial organization interested in promoting better race relations. . . . It is carrying out the very essential task of promoting a calm deliberate search for local solutions arrived at by local people to resolve tensions in the area of human relations. We are carrying out effective work in bringing together civic, religious, and business leaders to promote understanding, goodwill and mutual

respect among the various groups in our State. We continue our efforts to replace emotion with reason, intolerance with brotherhood, and fear with understanding and mutual respect.

He then pointed out that "the most effective work of the Council would be destroyed if these efforts were known." The political futures of city and state officials who had relied on Dad's assistance "would be in jeopardy" if this became public knowledge. Dad therefore had to work behind the scenes, without public credit or recognition.

In his report he stated that the essay contest that Mom had mentioned in our 1963 Christmas letter had drawn public condemnation from segregationist forces. On December 11, 1963, the Alabama Council placed a large ad in the *Birmingham News*. It announced an "ESSAY CONTEST for High School Students in Alabama," with prizes up to a hundred dollars for the best five-hundred-word essay on the topic "Human Rights . . . The American Dream." Essays would be judged on "originality, grasp of subject, neatness, and grammar." The contest was announced "In observance of Human Rights Week, proclaimed by President Lyndon B. Johnson, December 10–17."

The news services in Birmingham did not carry the president's proclamation on Human Rights Week, Dad stated in his annual report. To rectify this neglect, he sent copies of the proclamation to every newspaper, radio and TV station in the state, and to the mayors of fifteen cities. A second appeal to the mayors to declare December 15 as Human Rights Day resulted in at least one city officially making such a proclamation.

In response to this Alabama Council initiative, the segregationist *Cahaba Valley News,* on December 18, 1963, carried a front-page article entitled "Parents Combat Essay Contest as Contamination of Children." The article stated that "many parents and civic groups of Jefferson County and throughout Alabama" objected to the essay contest announcement because of "the identity of the organization sponsoring the contest and its executive director."

The article repeated earlier allegations that the Alabama Council included "communists or known associates of communist front organizations." It stated that "'Rev.' Jimerson came to Birmingham in 1960 [actually, 1961] from . . . Hopewell, Va.," and falsely claimed: "It was in Hopewell that the organized sit-ins and mass demonstrations had their beginning." The paper then linked my father to "'Rev.' Wyatt Tee Walker," "Charles 'Chuck' Morgan . . . who 'Saw Birmingham Die' in a recent magazine article," Martin Luther King, Fred Shuttlesworth, and other dangerous people such as suspected communists James Dombrowski, Carl and Ann Braden. After other slurs against both my parents, the article concluded: "These, the information provided to the school principals points out, are the powers that are attempting to entice high school students with the essay 'contest.'" Opponents of integration portrayed even this seemingly innocuous essay contest as a dangerous communist plot.

Unable to take an active role in Dad's civil rights efforts until now, Mom began to state her convictions publicly. She started by writing a letter to the newspaper, and then submitted an article for a national magazine.

My mother's letter to the *Birmingham News* appeared on January 1, 1964, under the heading "Is This Freedom?" She wrote:

> Living in Birmingham is a nightmare for those who care about the basic human rights of all people. Either they suffer inside because they have kept silent, not wanting to subject their families to threats and intimidations, or they have freely spoken, that expression of their dream of a better world only leading to the nightmare of threatening and obscene phone calls at any hour of night or day.
>
> Is this what we call freedom? Freedom to bother and curse people who are concerned for others?
>
> Is this real democracy? Democracy that lets a hoodlum element attempt to "run" the city and state?
>
> It's about time (actually it's 'way past time) that emotionally stable, concerned, fearless people come forth and be counted. We have but one lifetime in which to do those things that really mean something—that will help make the world a better place to live. Who knows just how soon that opportunity will be gone?
>
> Melva B. Jimerson
> 1905 Saulter Road

My mother must have known that she would receive hate mail in response to this public statement. She saved one anonymous letter:

> If negroes get the so-called freedom they want our children will be in danger. When negroes make up 10% in a school they "run things." They carry

razors, knifes and etc. The teachers fear them. I am not just telling you these things I know it to be a fact.

Do you remember reading several years ago about a young white girl who let a negro student kiss her and then a day or so later the same negro and his negro friends raped her right outside of the school in broad daylight? No white boys would have did such a horrible thing.

I want "freedom" for my children. Freedom to always go to an all white school, freedom to always live in an all white neighborhood, freedom to always go to an all white church, and freedom to always have recreational and social events where negroes are prohibited.

The "hoodlum element" is *forced integration*.

. . . I believe the communists had Kennedy killed because his usefulness was gone. Communists don't treat negroes equal why do they want us to? Think!

The only other response to her letter that Mom kept provided encouragement and support in a brief typed message:

I want to tell you how very much I enjoyed your letter in the News. I am an Alabama white man. Born here, raised here. I know that Gov. Wallace does not speak for good white Alabamians. But, as you say, we have not spoken for ourselves. The election of Wallace was the triumph of ignorance over knowledge. I hope you will write more letters. How about one to our paper, The Dothan Eagle. Meanwhile, my very best wishes to you and yours. A friend,

[signed] M.G. Marsh

Clearly, Mom had been deeply engaged alongside Dad in the civil rights struggles in Alabama. She could not leave her five young children to participate in movement activities—other than an occasional Alabama Council or women's support group meeting—but she wanted to contribute. Writing provided one such outlet, which a mother and housewife could seize.

Mom knew that some women's magazines wanted articles on public issues, from a woman's perspective. Early in 1964 she decided to enter a contest sponsored by *Redbook* magazine. The article she prepared came from deep feelings of concern for civil rights and her own religious convictions. The title she chose was "Immunizing Children against Prejudice." Her essay did not win and was never published. But it provides insights into her own values and beliefs. A few excerpts are enough to reveal her thoughts.

The essay begins with a story about the Eagle Scout who received only a seven-month suspended sentence. During the trial, she writes, "I realized what horrible things prejudice in a society can do." Then she states:

> As a mother of five young children, I am deeply concerned that this soul-destructive force called prejudice does not endanger their spiritual lives. When all around them—their peers, their teachers, and prominent politicians—are showing deep-rooted bigotry, how can such a feat be accomplished? . . . How do you instill into a child the belief in the dignity and worth of all people? How do you make him realize that color of skin has nothing to do with the matters of the heart?
>
> I believe, first of all, that regular daily worship is a must. . . .
>
> We can invite people of all nationalities and races into our homes as guests, so that our young children will be exposed to people and situations that reveal the humanity of everyone. Very often there are foreign exchange students or men in military service stationed nearby. . . . Our family has been more fortunate than most in this regard, since we have had the opportunity to entertain reporters and writers from many countries, as well as a few foreign dignitaries. The children have been thrilled to have our guests speak, yes, and even sing in their native tongues. Our one little girl has to sit beside the guest at the dinner table regardless of who it is. . . .
>
> We can encourage the reading of books by and about people of other races, the study of accomplishments of people with skins unlike ours or with differing ethnic backgrounds. . . .
>
> To share real Christian worship together in the house of God should not have to be mentioned, let alone emphasized. . . . I remember in a small town in Virginia one evening when several couples, Negro and white, worshipped together in the home of one family, because the pastor of the church where the World Day of Prayer service was being held, was afraid it would not be acceptable to bring the Negroes, stationed at a nearby army base, into a "white" church. How unforgivable that we should have "white" churches! . . .
>
> A child or an adult is not complete—has not really lived—until he has learned to know and appreciate individuals of other races and nationalities. . . .
>
> Until we can learn to think of people as individuals and be completely color-blind; until we realize that not one of us can help what he was born; until we know that an individual must be understood, not underrated—and instill this into our children, we shall continue to raise future citizens full of bigotry, who as adults will do no better than we in making this one great world under God.

Such a desire to achieve a "world under God" also had a darker side: the American obsession with stopping "communist aggression." One tactic of segregationists had been to denounce anyone supporting integration, equality, justice, or peace as a communist. As a ninth grader, I wanted to demonstrate that such allegations were untrue. I might be a "damn Yankee," but I was not a communist. When a petition opposing communism circulated at Homewood Junior High, I saw that it did not target civil rights workers or other reformers. Communism seemed wrong to me, as a broad ideological/political movement. So I boldly signed my name—at the top of the list of signatures.

The petition went to the office of U.S. Senator Lister Hill of Alabama, one of the southern Democrats opposing integration. When his office staff sent back to the school a standard response letter, signed by Hill himself, they addressed the letter to me. Now if anyone accused me of being a communist, I could produce evidence that I opposed communism.

News about the growing communist menace in Southeast Asia began to reach public consciousness in 1963. I saw a newspaper photo of a Buddhist monk setting himself on fire to protest the corrupt government in South Vietnam, and heard about the coup against the government leaders only weeks before the assassination of President Kennedy. The United States seemed prepared to increase its engagement in the warfare in Vietnam. For a brief time in ninth grade, I worried that it would end before I was old enough to fight. I wanted to live out my childhood John Wayne fantasies, to show my patriotism, to prove my opposition to communism. (By the time I turned eighteen, however, I registered for the draft as a conscientious objector.)

❖

By early 1964 the major crises in Birmingham had given way to uneasy calm. President Kennedy's assassination brought an emotional closure to "the year of Birmingham," as people would refer to the months of marches, sit-ins, police dogs, fire hoses, and bombings. National attention shifted to other topics. In the aftermath of the assassination, the onset of Beatlemania brought welcome relief. After the grief of a president's assassination, Americans at last could "twist and shout" their cares away.

For the Alabama Council on Human Relations, 1964 turned attention back to ongoing problems besieging the state and its largest city. Dr. Lucius Pitts served now as the council's first black president, making it a more truly biracial organization. In his quarterly report for January to March 1964, my father stated that the Alabama Council's annual meeting on February 1 had been "a splendid success." Dad wrote: "The members seemed to have gone away with a renewed spirit." The membership committee began an intensive drive for members, and Dad concluded optimistically: "I am confident that this is going to be an excellent year for the Alabama Council on Human Relations."

Between April and June, Dad stated in his next quarterly report, civil rights problems continued to plague the state: A cross was burned outside the suburban home of a white family who had entertained a black guest. In Hartselle, police had to take special precautions to protect noted author William Bradford Huie, "whose life and home were threatened after he publicly criticized Gov. Wallace," Dad reported. Two Birmingham police officers were questioned in connection with the alleged beating of an Eastside black man.

Dad continued to send information about racial problems to the U.S. Commission on Civil Rights. In early May he wrote to Samuel Simmons of the commission, informing him that Reverend C. Herbert Oliver, leader of the Inter-Citizens Committee in Birmingham, had discontinued preparing reports on police brutality because he could not find cases for the past several months. "However," Dad wrote, "I know of at least one person severely beaten by officers in Birmingham not reported by him." He then offered to conduct any research needed by the commission.

As the Civil Rights Bill—first proposed by President Kennedy in June 1963—slowly moved through Congress, under President Johnson's prodding, the southern backlash had already begun. Dad reported that on April 9 (my fifteenth birthday), "The Alabama Legislature's Commission to Preserve the Peace, comparing the pending Civil Rights Bill to the Communist Party Manifesto, has charged no other proposed legislation ever 'presented so bold an attempt at creating a Federal dictatorship.'" On May 27 the Birmingham Council on Human Relations sponsored a debate on the Civil Rights Bill, by then under consideration by the U.S. Senate. Speakers, both pro and con, agreed that the bill "will not speed up desegregation of schools."

By June 5, Dad could report very good news: "Members of Sixteenth Street Baptist Church went back to their church home yesterday. For the first time since the September 15th bomb blast that shattered part of the sanctuary and Sunday School rooms and killed four little girls, the congregation worshipped in their rebuilt church." This sign of healing offered hope to those concerned about civil rights.

For the second year in a row, in 1964 the Alabama Council hosted a student intern from Kalamazoo College. Jeanne Tiller, whose parents Dad and Mom knew through the American Baptist Churches, followed Mike Morden's footsteps, but made her own impressions. For one research project, she contacted the Southern Regional Council office in Atlanta to ask about comparative studies of progress in integration. In response, Mrs. Montez Albright said she could only provide a list of known desegregation steps in Alabama cities. Her list for Birmingham included ten lunch counters, four restaurants, one elementary school, two high schools, and the University of Alabama Extension Center, but no hotels, motels, or theaters. Desegregated municipal facilities included the Birmingham Zoo, Botanical Gardens, State Fairgrounds, Kiddieland amusement park (mentioned by Dr. King in his "Letter from Birmingham Jail"), the museum, and drinking fountains in City Hall. The report also included listings for six other cities and two counties in Alabama.

Jeanne passionately advocated racial equality and social justice. She also "ran hard," as Ann later recalled. A little too hard, it turns out. Against Dad's express instructions, Jeanne drove our VW bug through the city with a black man in the car, a reckless act that could have landed both of them dead in a ditch someplace. Dad was out of town when Mom got the call from a council member that Jeanne had been spotted. They whisked her out of town on the first flight north. This presented an important lesson for Ann: Jeanne's recklessness could have proven fatal.

In remembering these events, Ann later said: "Another lesson I took away from this came straight from Mom, who had packed up Jeanne's clothing and belongings and shipped them out after her flight: 'For heaven's sake, Ann, if you ever live on your own, I hope you do a better job of keeping the necks of your dresses clean.' Jeanne's shifts were apparently pretty grimy."

❖

After almost three years of working anonymously out of public sight, my father's efforts on behalf of the civil rights movement began to attract favorable notice. The Andover Newton Theological School published a new admissions booklet, featuring an article entitled "Alumni Lead the Quiet Revolution" depicting several alumni "at work wherever Christian leadership is most needed":

Consider Norman Jimerson, '53, executive director of the Alabama Council on Human Relations. Headquarters—Birmingham, a city that has earned infamy in two years by beating up Freedom Riders and jailing hundreds of school children. Norman's mission is to open up channels of communication between Negroes and whites and to help people accept the inevitability of social change. As a result of his quiet work on behalf of non-violence, he has received six death threats on his life in eighteen months. He explains, "As long as they're anonymous, you just hope they don't mean it."

In April 1964 the *Christian Science Monitor,* one of the leading national opinion newspapers, discussed my father's work with the Alabama Council in two articles written by Robert Colby Nelson. The first article focused on the racial climate in Birmingham:

"Most Negroes and some of the white people of Birmingham," says the Rev. Mr. Jimerson, an American Baptist pastor, "feel that the white power structure here learned very, very little as a result of the demonstrations last April and May. It is fair to say in balance, however, that now there is at least the Community Affairs Committee and its subcommittees, which provide the organizational structure for carrying out interracial negotiations.". . .

The Rev. Mr. Jimerson fully expects demonstrations in Birmingham in the weeks and months ahead.

In his second article, Nelson focused on my father and his colleague, Reverend Duncan Gray, president of the Mississippi Council on Human Relations, regarding their efforts to "help provide a neutral middle ground on which interracial conflict may be resolved." Nelson wrote: "Two soft-spoken young clergymen carry on what may be two of the most unsung and fragile missions in the South." The article quotes my father extensively.

The most prominent attention Dad received came from his former attorney, Charles Morgan Jr., who published his memoir about Alabama in April 1964. Entitled *A Time to Speak,* Morgan's book told "the story of a young American lawyer's struggle for his city—and himself." It included separate chapters for various legal cases or clients, including Bob Hughes and Bob Zellner. One chapter described the reaction to Morgan's September 16, 1963, speech following the Sixteenth Street Baptist Church bombing.

The chapter about my father's trial in Talladega carried the title "Blessed the Peacemaker." Morgan described Dad as "a young, intense Baptist minister." He briefly recounted the real estate agent's refusal to sell a house to Dad, the churches that asked us not to return, and the Talladega injunction and trial. My father's experiences reflected "the community's essential moral problem—not the inaction of 'extremists' who attack, but the inaction of 'moderates' who abstain." Morgan commented: "Like a modern-day Job, Jimerson seemed to take from his ordeals an increased strength and faith in the Christian peace-making aims of the Alabama council." Morgan concluded:

> Here then was the classic case of the man-in-the-middle, fair game for both sides. But the Negro side merely ignored Norman Jimerson. The white side regarded him as an apostate to the Caucasian faith and dealt with him as societies have dealt with apostates. He was cast out, to be shunned at best, pilloried at worst. . . .
>
> In Norman Jimerson I saw a human being, a good but a misunderstood human being, lose his social moorings. He was not merely cut adrift from the white society of the community, but neither did he have any place in the Negro society for whose cause he had sacrificed himself.

Dad ordered copies of this book for each of the five children, and sent them to Chuck Morgan to autograph. He wanted us to have this slim book—with the twelve-page chapter about his work in Alabama—as a memento of the difficult experiences we were living through. Chuck Morgan inscribed a personal message for each of us, signed and dated May 26, 1964.

Dad also sent a copy of Morgan's book to Bob and Dottie Hughes in Salisbury, Southern Rhodesia. Dottie wrote an aerogram letter to thank Dad for the book. She commented: "So often have I felt the difficulty of your own situation there in Birmingham and have prayed for strength and guidance for you. Your struggles have been so much more trying than our own were, I think, in that you arrived when the Council was already under fire. Birmingham itself has erupted around you, and your children are old enough to experience some of the rejection and isolation. . . . We do pray that the confidence and assurance which only God can give will be yours in all that you undertake."

Meanwhile, Dad sent Morgan a letter stating his worry that Governor Wallace would block the Alabama Council's tax exempt status. "Wallace sure does strut like big stuff, as does everyone with a big goon squad clearing his path," Dad wrote. "Sure am glad you got out while things were good. Seriously, the general situation does look darker than when I came to Alabama, although I'm not getting much abuse now."

Chuck Morgan's memoir, along with the few news stories that discussed his work with the Alabama Council, provided the kind of recognition that Dad had hoped to receive—a small measure of thanks, an acknowledgment of his sacrifices and commitment on behalf of social justice and civil rights.

At the same time, Dad seemed to feel guilty for wanting such public notice. One of his favorite jokes seemed personal, self-mocking: "Did you hear about the man who received a pin from the local Rotary Club as the most humble man in town? They took it back a few days later, when someone saw him wearing it in public!"

For me, three events during spring 1964 stand out in my memory: a car, a party, and a confrontation, not necessarily in order of importance.

A car: Tony and I always enjoyed checking out cars on the streets and parking lots in Homewood. We could identify the year and model of almost every car we saw. One evening Tony and his brother-in-law invited me to join them for a special event. The new Ford Mustang had just arrived in a downtown Ford showroom. We drove over Red Mountain and ogled the Mustang on display.

"It's the best new car since the '55 Corvette!" Tony said.

"Almost as nice as the '57 T-Bird," I replied.

A party: I rarely attended parties during junior high. I didn't have many friends, and they weren't the kind to attend school dances or throw parties at home. But Dad asked me if I would go to a special party that some of the civil rights supporters had planned. It would include both black and white teenagers, in an effort to demonstrate the benefits of biracial social activities. Such parties—for both teens and adults—also sought to enhance racial understanding and tolerance. All the things Dad had been working to achieve.

I felt nervous as Dad drove me downtown to the home of a black family with children my age. There were about thirty or forty teenagers, about three-quarters black and one-quarter white. Many of the kids seemed to know each other, usually within respective racial groups. People walked through the house eating snack foods and drinking soda pop, talking in small groups, laughing, having a good time. Music played loudly. Most of it I recognized as Motown or soul, with some white groups as well.

One song I had never heard before grabbed me with its upbeat tune and energy. For weeks I couldn't get it out of my mind. It was a new release by The Temptations, one of the great Motown groups. Later, every time I heard "The Girl's Alright with Me" on the radio it reminded me of my small role in integrating this private party for black and white teenagers in Birmingham.

A confrontation: This requires some background. After learning about the "heroism" of the Ku Klux Klan in Alabama history class in the fall, I gained a new education in civics during second semester. Civics class focused on the study of government, political issues, and citizenship. We had to prepare book reports, make panel group presentations, and debate topics selected by the teacher, a middle-aged heavy-set woman with glasses and a strong segregationist mindset.

For one debate on capital punishment, Dad urged me to read his worn paperback copy of *Cell 2455, Death Row,* by Caryl Chessman—one of the rare books that I knew Dad actually read. Usually he learned just enough about a book to cite it in conversation; it was difficult for him to sit still long enough to read a book. Having spent more than a third of his life behind bars, Chessman produced a searing indictment of the criminal justice system. Dad discussed with me the reasons he opposed capital punishment, as I took an unpopular position in the ninth-grade civics debate.

A more memorable confrontation occurred, however, when the civics teacher assigned me to a panel discussion about FBI director J. Edgar Hoover's polemic *Masters of Deceit: The Story of Communism in America and How to Fight It.* The book began: "EVERY CITIZEN has a duty to learn more about the menace that threatens his future, his home, his children, the peace of the world—and that is why I have written this book." It seemed to give a logical explanation of how communists used deceptive practices and arguments to gain adherents to their anti-American agenda.

I talked to Dad about this. He compared Hoover's arguments to those of Senator Joseph McCarthy, who led the anti-communist witch hunts of the early 1950s.

"I got into a lot of trouble in Hudson, when I spoke out against McCarthy," Dad said. "He was lying and stirring up fear, but a lot of people swallowed it."

He said that in his experience Hoover and the FBI opposed integration and sought to maintain the status quo. "They say they can't get involved in segregation because that would disrupt their good relationship with the local police on interstate theft of cars and that kind of stuff. Plus, of course, Hoover is such a strong anti-communist, and that includes anti-integration and anti-human rights."

I asked: "But isn't Bobby Kennedy trying to stop Hoover, so they can support civil rights?"

"Hoover opposes any gestures towards integration," Dad said. "But the Kennedys have been playing a political game. They only got involved when it was absolutely essential for their own political future. For political expediency."

A scowl crept across Dad's face. "The local FBI agents have been keeping me under surveillance," he said. Then he grinned his I'm-smarter-than-you grin. "But I decided it's better to be friendly and open and above-board with them, and show I have no fears in what they were doing."

"Why would the FBI do that?"

"Well, I'm sure it's because I'm working for human rights. That makes me a suspect."

As I read *Masters of Deceit* I became more and more angry about Hoover's attempts to scare people. He claimed that the Communist Party stirred up people by making false claims about "'victims' of 'framed evidence,' 'lynch justice,' 'Gestapo brutality,' 'academic witchhunts.'" But I knew this wasn't true. Most of the people defending such victims were not communists.

Hoover wrote: "The Party searches American life for agitational points: the eviction of a family, the arrest of a Negro, a proposed rise in transit fares, a bill to increase taxes, a miscarriage of justice, the underpayment of a worker, the dismissal of a teacher, a shooting by law-enforcement officers." Again, I argued to myself, these were reckless lies or half-truths.

On the morning of our panel discussion, I told Mom I felt sick and couldn't go to school. But she told me I couldn't stay home just to avoid a difficult situation. "You have to face up to it, Randy."

Four of us on the panel took turns talking about *Masters of Deceit*. We sat in a row at the front of the class, our desks turned to face the other students. I sat on the far left, with the teacher at her desk near the window at my far right. One of the other panel members, John Calhoun, had earlier asked me why I wasn't cheering when President Kennedy was shot. When it was my turn I just tried to report what Hoover had written, without saying whether I agreed with it.

When his turn came, John Calhoun strongly endorsed Hoover's anti-communist attacks. He said that the book showed how communists used agitation about issues concerning women, veterans, racial and nationality groups, farmers, and trade unions to get people upset with the government. This trapped people into supporting the Communist Party. John said: "It's clear from Hoover's book that anyone involved in human relations or civil rights work is a communist. And the nigra organizations like NAACP and CORE and the Black Muslims are all communists."

Following our presentations, the teacher asked if there were any questions for the panel members. After a couple of questions from the class, I leaned over and raised my hand. "I want to ask John a question: What evidence do you have that all of these civil rights groups are communists? Because from what I can see, most of them are led by Christian ministers."

Immediately the room buzzed with surprise, confusion, and anger. The teacher turned red in the face and spluttered, "You're all wet! You don't know what you're talking about!" She was practically screaming at me. John's pale face turned purple. He was yelling but I couldn't hear what he said. Other students turned to talk to each other. I didn't know what to do. I sat still and watched.

When things began to quiet down, Gregg Beasley raised his hand. Gregg was the smartest kid in the class. He said, "Actually, the Black Muslims are not communists. They want separation from whites, not integration." Gregg briefly explained the main ideas of the Black Muslims. He was the only other person in the class who said anything at all that contradicted Hoover's book and the segregationist views that John expressed. Within another minute or two the bell rang to end class.

I walked to my next class, geometry, in a daze. I didn't want to look at anyone in the halls. As I sat down, one boy who had been in civics class walked to my desk and loomed over me. He asked: "Are you really a nigger-lover?"

I didn't know what to say. I couldn't say "yes" or "no" to such a question. Should I object to his use of the word "nigger"? Should I try to explain why I opposed discrimination? How could I respond?

I paused for a moment or two, and as the bell rang to begin class, I finally said, "I try to love *everyone*. I think that's what we should do." That's the only answer I could give to his question.

I couldn't pay attention to anything during geometry class. I hoped the teacher wouldn't call on me. I wondered: Why did he ask that question? Was he trying to pick a fight? Or did he, perhaps, really want to know what I thought? Was he curious about talking to someone with different ideas from his own? I couldn't ask such questions. I would never find out.

22

Leaving Alabama

The pressure and harassment of working for civil rights in Alabama had become overwhelming for my father. He knew he needed to leave before he succumbed to stress. Moving back north would solve another problem. Mom had always regretted being so far from her family in Pennsylvania, and would welcome moving closer. Another consideration arose from the economic difficulties of caring for a family with five young children on the low salary that the Alabama Council on Human Relations could afford. With his oldest son only a few years away from college, Dad knew he couldn't afford tuition and related costs.

Dad didn't tell us children, but he had already put out feelers for new positions before the Birmingham crises of 1963. In March 1963 he had written several letters inquiring about jobs in the north. In one letter he wrote that he hoped to find a position as a church minister—perhaps in "a changing neighborhood with a high crime rate" (I wonder if he ever mentioned this to my mother?). Other letters asked about working in race relations or juvenile delinquency. Some letters conveyed a sense of urgency: "I am interested in getting my family out of this climate by summer."

Nothing came of this round of inquiries, but by early 1964 Dad began a job search in earnest. This time he did tell us about his plans. It didn't surprise me. I hadn't lived any one place for more than three and a half years, so it seemed only natural for Dad to plan another move. I was ready to leave.

As he secretly considered leaving Alabama (only the family knew), my father received a welcome letter of support from Marjorie (Mrs. Moreland G.) Smith of Montgomery: "At the April 18th meeting of the Board of the Alabama Council on Human Relations, the members were unanimous in their praise of your very fine work since you came to Alabama. Against the odds of a limited budget and a hostile climate of opinion, you have moved steadily and constructively forward on behalf of interracial understanding."

The same board meeting also approved Dad's request for authorization to attend the American Baptist Convention in Atlantic City. He would combine this with a visit to New York after the convention to seek funds for the council. In addition to obtaining support for the Alabama Council, Dad also used the Baptist conference to renew connections and inquire about job opportunities.

Guest speakers at the convention included Dr. Martin Luther King Jr. and Senator Hubert Humphrey of Minnesota. The American Baptist magazine *Crossroads* later published a photograph of Dr. King and his wife Coretta Scott King talking with Senator Humphrey at the convention. The caption read: "Dr. and Mrs. King at Atlantic City in 1964 are surrounded by admirers including then vice-presidential hopeful Sen. Hubert Humphrey." Besides the three people named, the only face visible is my father's. He is standing right behind the dignitaries, tight-lipped and waiting for a chance to speak with them.

When Dad returned from the convention, he didn't know about the photograph. But he told us excitedly about meeting Humphrey. "I wanted to ask him about possible jobs in the poverty program or some other federal agency," Dad said. "So I followed him. When he got into the front seat of a taxi, I pushed my way into the back seat." He looked around to be sure we were paying attention. "But while I was getting into the cab, my knee bumped the back of Humphrey's head. Not hard, but it's not the kind of impression I wanted to make."

"What did he say?" Mom asked.

"Was he mad?" Ann asked.

"No. I apologized. But I finally did get a chance to talk with him," Dad said. "He didn't know of any job available, but said I should send him a résumé."

From March until July, Dad continued to send out letters asking about employment opportunities and applying for positions. The American Baptist Ministerial Board in Valley Forge, Pennsylvania, sent his dossier to their state offices in New England, the mid-Atlantic states, and Ohio. Dad applied for both church positions and campus ministry, as well as positions with the U.S. Commission on Civil Rights and the Fair Employment Practice Committee in Youngstown, Ohio.

Now that I knew Dad was looking for another job, I felt relieved. It would be good to get rid of the nearly constant stress headaches, to find a place where I could feel more at home. Dad sent out dozens of letters asking about jobs in human relations, criminal justice, even college administration. He said he would especially enjoy teaching or counseling work. I kept my fingers crossed.

As Dad considered leaving the Alabama Council, he also closely followed the progress of the Civil Rights Bill in Congress. First proposed by President Kennedy in June 1963, the legislation faced strong opposition from Southern Democrats and conservative Republicans. Kennedy's assassination changed the political climate. As Dad and other civil rights advocates had urged, President Johnson stated in his first address to Congress in November 1963: "No memorial oration or eulogy could more eloquently honor President Kennedy's memory than the earliest possible passage of the civil rights bill for which he fought so long."

Despite threats to keep it bottled up in the Rules Committee, the Civil Rights Bill finally came to a House vote in February 1964. It passed easily and went to the Senate. A southern bloc of eighteen southern Democrats and one Republican initiated a fifty-four-day filibuster to prevent a vote. Finally, a compromise bill with fewer federal protections for enforcement passed the Senate on June 19 and then gained approval of both houses of Congress.

In a White House ceremony, President Johnson signed the Civil Rights Act of 1964 into law on July 2, 1964. Eight civil rights leaders, including Dr. King and Rosa Parks, stood behind LBJ during the ceremony. The Civil Rights Act outlawed racial segregation in schools, at the workplace, and in public accommodations. It banned voter registration restrictions and most common forms of discrimination against racial, ethnic, national, and religious minorities and women. It met many of the principal objectives of the civil rights demonstrations during the previous nine years, and marked the most important legislation protecting citizens' rights since Reconstruction. However, it did not solve all legal problems for blacks and other minorities. Continued voter registration discrimination, for example, required a new Voting Rights Act, passed in 1965.

Shortly after President Johnson signed the Civil Rights Act, a *Washington Star* article entitled "Uneasy South Awaits Test of New Civil Rights Law" by Reese Cleghorn quoted both my father and Leslie Dunbar, executive director of the Southern Regional Council. Cleghorn began: "The States of the Deep South, now that the civil rights bill has become law, face the most uncertain and probably most dangerous period of probing and testing of recent years."

"The summer and early fall will be a period when we finally have to confront all the problems," Dunbar stated. Cleghorn wrote that Dunbar hoped the Civil Rights Act would be accepted more readily than was the Supreme Court's school desegregation decision ten years earlier, but others were less hopeful:

> From his vantage point in a city besieged last year in civil rights conflict, the Rev. Norman C. Jimerson of Birmingham assessed the dangers in Alabama. "Violence remains a very real possibility," he said.
>
> Mr. Jimerson, a white minister who is executive director of the Alabama Council on Human Relations, cited the leadership of Gov. George C. Wallace as a major factor in his state's prospects. Gov. Wallace has pledged repeatedly to maintain order. But Mr. Jimerson observed: "Alabama is tightening up. People are already less likely to be taking a public stand for law and order or compliance with law than they were in the past few months."

This sentiment echoed what Dad had been saying for several months. In May 1964 he wrote to an Alabama Council leader, Montgomery architect Moreland Smith: "Looks like storm clouds are coming over head . . . and I hope people either dig in or get out, or are fully committed to put everything on the line. Do I seem like an alarmist or just one who is alarmed?" For nearly three years Dad had been putting everything on the line. Now he seemed ready to get out.

As summer approached, Ann and I learned that we would get to return to Camp Merrowvista in New Hampshire. Ann attended girls' camp in July, and I went to boys' camp in August.

Paul and Susie still didn't meet the Merrowvista minimum age of eleven. But Mom and Dad arranged for them to attend a three-week summer day-camp. Held at the all-black Miles College campus, this summer program may have been Birmingham's first interracial day camp. Susie said, "One time I was the only white kid in my group." This stood out because we all went to segregated schools. None of us had much acquaintance with black kids. Susie said she got along fine with the other girls, both black and white.

Paul and Susie rode to day camp in a carpool with other white kids from Homewood and Mountain Brook. Most of them had parents involved in civil rights, particularly with the Alabama Council. As with my introduction to interracial activities at an integrated party, this day-camp experience gave Paul and Susie a feeling of participation in the civil rights movement that so fully engaged our father. They felt connected to the important things going on around us.

The children enjoyed typical day-camp experiences—games, sports, arts and crafts, and music. Instead of swimming in a cold mountain lake, as Ann and I did in New Hampshire, they changed into bathing suits to play on a Slip 'n Slide on the grass lawn. It wasn't as refreshing as a swimming pool or mountain lake, but it helped beat the heat in Birmingham. Susie learned a French song and enjoyed other good experiences. "I really enjoyed it!" she said proudly.

While Ann headed north for girls' camp, I decided to take a summer-school class at Shades Valley High School, which I would enter in the fall. By taking second-year Latin, I would be able to complete three years of French before college. We read Caesar's account of the Gallic wars. This was the summer after Cassius Clay claimed the heavyweight boxing title from Sonny Liston, proclaiming "I am the greatest!" Clay also had announced his conversion to the Nation of Islam and adopted the name "Muhammad Ali." I learned two phrases in Latin II: Caesar's famous statement *Veni, vidi, vici* ("I came, I saw, I conquered"), and the sentence *Et Cassius dicit "Ego sum maximus"* ("And Cassius said, 'I am the greatest.'"). Who knew that Cassius Clay was a Latin scholar?

Ann and I enjoyed Camp Merrowvista that summer almost as much as our first year. Ann returned from camp just as I was heading there. Before I left for New Hampshire in late July, Dad told us about some of the jobs for which he had applied. Nothing definite, but he had his hopes set on two positions at colleges in Michigan. He later explained that his reasons for leaving the Alabama Council had been: "To pursue a longtime interest in teaching, and give my family a respite from the constant harassment of Alabama."

While I settled in to my Camp Merrowvista hogan—no more teepees this year—Kalamazoo College offered Dad a job as director of the Career-Service Program. John Thomas, with whom Dad had arranged to supervise student interns for two years, had retired, and Dad would succeed him. In addition to finding internship opportunities for students to learn more about their chosen careers or to provide community services, he hoped to be engaged in counseling and teaching.

On July 31, 1964, exactly three years after arriving in Alabama, Dad sent his resignation to the Alabama Council Board of Directors: "Please accept my resignation as director of the Alabama Council on Human Relations effective September 15th, in order that I may accept a position at Kalamazoo College as director of the Career-Service Program. It has been a real honor and privilege for me to work with each of you on the Board, and the members of the Alabama Council. I am deeply indebted to each member and contributor to the Alabama Council on Human Relations for making it possible for me to work full time in the area of race relations in the State of Alabama."

Nat Welch, one of his closest friends among the council leadership, replied: "I wanted to express to you my deep appreciation for the great work you have done in Alabama for the last three years. You have demonstrated tremendous dedication, courage, and compassion. These virtues have made you much more influential than you perhaps realize. We are mindful of the great sacrifices you and your family have made and are grateful for this."

After announcing his resignation, Dad wrote to Paul Anthony of the Southern Regional Council that he would talk with Dr. Pitts, ACHR president, about a possible board meeting in August. But he said, "At this point, I feel as if I need some vacation even if it interferes with the Board meeting."

While our family took a vacation trip to Beaver Falls to see Mom's family, and to visit Dad's friend Reverend Elwyn Brown at the beach in Delaware, Anthony wrote to a Birmingham minister who inquired about how to assist the council: "Norman Jimerson is on vacation and thereafter is going to Kalamazoo College in Michigan. This move has come none too soon since Jimerson and his family have been under great strain with much harassment." Anthony noted that Bob Hughes had also suffered from the strain of the Alabama Council position, adding, "Hughes and Jimerson did good work under impossible conditions."

Avoiding a long hiatus like the one during the search to replace Bob Hughes, the Alabama Council quickly found a new director. Reverend J. Edwin Stanfield, a young Presbyterian minister who had been working briefly at the SRC offices in Atlanta, accepted the position of executive director on August 15, 1964. His official employment began on September 15, by coincidence the first-year anniversary of the Sixteenth Street Baptist Church bombing. On the same day, the Alabama Council moved its office to Huntsville, which would be a more hospitable environment than Birmingham. Dad's secretary, Myrtice Hubbard, secured a teaching position in Tuscaloosa and left the Alabama Council.

By the time the Jimerson family—without me, since I was still at Camp Merrowvista—returned from vacation, they faced the daunting task of packing boxes and preparing for a new adventure. This time, at least, Mom was happy about moving. She would be closer to her family, and she would leave behind a huge burden of stress, fear, and anxiety.

As Dad prepared for yet another move, he continued his work with the Alabama Council. He met with Ed Stanfield to discuss current and proposed activities, and to help him prepare for taking over leadership. Dad continued to seek outside funding sources for the council. He requested a grant of three thousand dollars from the United Church of Christ (UCC) to enable the new executive director to do the added traveling necessary for providing support for local councils. Writing to the UCC Committee for Racial Justice Now, he highlighted recent accomplishments: "The Alabama Council on Human Relations has contributed significantly to compliance with the Civil Rights Act, peaceful desegregation of schools, and bringing Negro and white leaders into face to face relations to resolve local problems on a local level."

The renovation of Sixteenth Street Baptist Church in June provided a symbol of healing and progress for the black community of Birmingham. In late August 1964, almost a year after the bombing, my father participated in the re-dedication services for the church building. His good friend Reverend John H. Cross invited him to share the pulpit on Sunday August 30 with Reverend Joseph Lowery of St. Paul's Methodist Church; Reverend Oley Kidd, director of Missions and Promotion for the Birmingham Baptist Association; Reverend Allix B. James, dean of the Virginia Union School of Religion; and Reverend Ed Stanfield. This interracial service marked one of Dad's final official events as the retiring executive director of the Alabama Council on Human Relations.

Within a few days, with all of the Jimerson family furniture and boxes safely packed on a moving van, they began the drive to our new home in Kalamazoo, Michigan. As they crossed the state line into Tennessee, Dad stopped the station wagon and honked the horn in celebration. Everyone stood on the highway shoulder, turned around, and waved good-bye to the sovereign state of Alabama. Our family's three-year endurance test had ended.

Everyone waved good-bye except for me. I was still at Camp Merrowvista in New Hampshire. When I left for camp, we did not know that we would be moving. At the end of the four weeks, I took a long series of bus rides to our new hometown, Kalamazoo. I never had a chance to say good-bye to my friends, to help with the packing, to be part of the family's journey to Michigan. For me leaving Alabama became abstract, unresolved. I was glad to leave, especially going to my home state. But I wished I could have waved good-bye to Birmingham.

After assuming his new position as director of the Kalamazoo College Career-Service Program in September 1964, Dad continued to take an active interest in civil rights and social justice issues. He kept in touch with his former associates in Birmingham, through letters and visits, when his search for internship opportunities for K College students allowed him to return to Birmingham, Atlanta, or Washington, D.C. His ongoing connections included Paul Anthony and Leslie Dunbar of the Southern Regional Council, Chuck Morgan, David Vann, Reverend John Cross of Sixteenth Street Baptist Church, James Head, Dr. Charles Gomillion of Tuskegee Institute, and photographer Chris McNair, whose daughter Denise had been killed in the church bombing. He and Mom kept up a correspondence with Eileen and Jim Walbert, Peggy and John Fuller, and other friends with whom they continued to exchange Christmas cards.

As Dad settled into his new community, he heard from many of the people he had worked with in Alabama. Father Albert S. Foley wrote to Dad in September 1964: "I want you to know that I admire your courage and fortitude in taking the job with ACHR and in sticking with it as long as you did. I really did not believe that a person could take that kind of pressure for more than a year or so without screaming for relief and removal." He added: "I trust that our minor differences of opinion and our mutual upsets over the Birmingham situation last year will not leave permanent wounds on our relationship but I hope that we can still be considered comrades in arms, having endured, you to the fullest and I in a minor way, the burdens of the heat of Birmingham's Bessemer converter."

Reverend Robert Keever, University Pastor at the Presbyterian University Center in Tuscaloosa, wrote: "I am glad, even though you left a fine legacy with your work here, that you can now live at a more leisurely pace and no longer have to worry about whether you and your family will wake up alive the next morning."

Dad replied to Keever from Kalamazoo: "It was a real privilege to work with the Alabama Council on Human Relations for three years, and the kind of privilege that one is also relieved to be away from."

Also in September, Paul Anthony sent a reference letter to Dad's new supervisor, Kalamazoo College Vice-President Lloyd J. Averill, praising his work as director of the Alabama Council. "This position is, without question, one of the most difficult ones in the entire field of race relations in the South," Anthony wrote. "The pressures, difficulties, and intimidation which Mr. Jimerson and his family faced are almost impossible for the mind to comprehend. That he worked and lived under such conditions for so long is a strong indication of Mr. Jimerson's determination and sense of decency and commitment. I think it was possible only because of a very deep faith which he and his family share." He then declared that the Alabama Council not only survived through three tumultuous years, but "was stronger than when he came to it. We are grateful for the part Norman Jimerson had in this."

In return, Dad wrote to Dr. Leslie Dunbar of SRC: "I am having all kinds of strange experiences, such as being invited to speak on two occasions and being part of an organization that is highly respected and held in good affection by many people in the city." This letter reveals both the dark side of his sense of humor, his psychic wounds from the ostracism he had faced in Alabama, and his appreciation for the recognition of being asked to speak to civic and social groups in Michigan.

Reverend Gene Ensley of Hopewell continued to correspond with Dad. "I know that Birmingham must indeed seem like a 'bad dream' and I can imagine how glad you must be 'to be away from there.' At the same time I know that you must have made a lasting contribution to better relations among the races in that turbulent state, the evidence of which will not be fully apparent for generations to come," Ensley wrote in November 1964. "You have given yourself in a truly sacrificial way to a most unrewarding task, and yet one that bespeaks most clearly of the Kingdom which Christ brought to us. And the scars which you and your family bear are not unlike those which the Savior bore. I only regret that more of us do not have the courage and conviction to emulate your kind of Christianity." Nothing would have made Dad happier and prouder than this letter from a close friend.

My father also maintained his contacts with colleagues at the Civil Rights Division of the U.S. Justice Department. In January 1965, John Doar wrote to him: "The people that are really responsible for the progress in civil rights are people like yourself, who worked as ordinary citizens, outside the government, to see that the Constitution was respected." Doar added, "Be sure to stop in to see me when you come to Washington in the spring."

Also in January 1965, Dad wrote to Burke Marshall, with whom he had worked closely during the Birmingham crisis of 1963. "As you leave the Justice Department, I want to tell you that I most deeply appreciated the opportunities I had in talking with you while I was director of the Alabama Council on Human Relations," Dad wrote. "Although at times I had the feeling that I was a thorn in the flesh to you, you gave me great strength and comfort and moral encouragement while I was trying to accomplish things in the area of civil rights in Alabama, operating from an organization that had almost no strength, very few numbers, and even less money."

Marshall replied at once, writing, "You were a great help to us, and especially to me personally, on several very difficult and uncertain occasions. You performed a significant service. I hope you enjoy your new work, which I know you will do well."

Recognition of this kind had seemed scarce during three challenging years with the Alabama Council on Human Relations. But as he started a new chapter in his life, Dad cherished these tokens of appreciation and friendship. The tensions, harassment, and difficulties he had faced gave my father courage and satisfaction as he took on new responsibilities and continued his personal journey seeking to promote human understanding, social justice, and world peace. The three years in Birmingham shaped his life, and the lives of the rest of us in the family, more deeply and longer than any of us could have imagined when we moved to Alabama in 1961.

Having accepted the challenges of directing the Alabama Council on Human Relations only a week before vicious attacks on Freedom Riders in the state, my father left Birmingham three years later, only weeks after President Lyndon Johnson signed the landmark Civil Rights Act of 1964. The civil rights movement had not won the battle—Selma, Watts, Memphis, and many other struggles remained in the future—but some signs of progress could be seen. My father enjoyed the satisfaction of having played a small but valuable role behind the scenes in this epic struggle for justice, decency, and mutual respect.

As I joined my family in Kalamazoo in September 1964, I noticed a new item displayed on the dining-room hutch, along with the usual family photographs and knick-knacks: a large square of twisted leaded stained glass. This memento of my father's engagement in the epic struggles for civil rights in Birmingham became a fixture on the maple shelves of our dining room hutch, through many future moves to New York, Massachusetts, Virginia, Washington D.C., and back to Massachusetts.

❖

After leaving Alabama in 1964, my father worked for three years as director of the Career-Service Program at Kalamazoo College. He then spent one year developing a similar program at Elmira College, and from 1968 to 1970 served as director of the Metropolitan Inter-Church Agency in Elmira. He finally returned to the ministry, as pastor of First Baptist Church in Hyannis, Massachusetts, for nearly eight years. In 1981 my parents became co-directors of Plowshare Peace Center in Roanoke, Virginia. They moved to Washington, D.C., in 1984, where Mom accepted a job as congressional liaison for the Church of the Brethren. Dad worked for World Peacemakers and later Quest for Peace.

In 1992 my father was invited to return to Birmingham for the dedication of the new Birmingham Civil Rights Institute. With an African American mayor presiding over part of the ceremonies, the institute embodied Birmingham's willingness to confront its past and to remember the historical events of the 1950s and 1960s. I flew down from Connecticut to join Dad and Mom for part of the multiday event. I met Fred Shuttlesworth, Andrew Young, David Vann, Deenie Drew, and other civil rights veterans Dad had often talked about.

On November 16, in the Sixteenth Street Baptist Church sanctuary, my father spoke on a panel that included Reverend Bob Hughes, David Vann (by now a former mayor of the city), and Reverend C. Herbert Oliver. The next day's *Birmingham News* began its coverage of the day's events with this account:

> The Rev. Norman Jimerson has spoken with ease before thousands of people over several decades as a minister. Yet his voice choked off and tears fell Monday when he began to recall for a few dozen teenagers the horrors and miracles of the civil rights movement in Birmingham three decades ago. . . .
>
> "It always struck me as a privilege to be in Alabama to work for justice," said Jimerson. . . .
>
> He got as far as "I want to say to you children" when his voice halted and many in the audience joined him in sobbing as the intensity of the conflicts and victories washed again through the historic church.
>
> "Ever since I left Alabama I get choked up when I talk about it," he said amid long pauses. "I want to say to you children not to shrink from doing right even if it brings you harm. Your joy will be greater than any pain you might experience."

This dedication of a new museum devoted to civil rights marked my first return to Birmingham since heading off to summer camp in New Hampshire twenty-eight years before. As Dad finally received public recognition for his contributions to better race relations, I rejoiced that I could join my parents for this celebration.

Epilogue

I have told these stories of my family's experiences during the civil rights struggle in Birmingham from my own perspective as a teenager. Fifty years after these events, it is time to hear from each of the Jimerson children about the impact and meaning of our individual—and very personal—engagement with the three years we spent in Alabama.

RAND JIMERSON, BELLINGHAM, WASHINGTON

My experiences as a young teenager in Birmingham shaped my outlook on the world, my personality, my career choices, and my values in profound ways that I am still uncovering fifty years later.

Three months after leaving Alabama, for a tenth-grade English assignment to write about someone we admired, I wrote about my father and his self-sacrificing role in the Alabama Council on Human Relations. After listing some of the problems he encountered with the council, I wrote that "most important was the sense that he was helping people gain respect." At the end, I acknowledged the complexity of his personality: "My father's worst fault is probably his overpowering belief that he is right. Yet this can be a benefit when trying to put ideas across. I think that my father is a remarkable person. I am proud of him." My parents saved that handwritten essay; it is now in my possession, faded and stained. With all his faults—and he did have his share—I am still proud of my father.

When I applied for conscientious objector status at the height of the war in Vietnam, I wrote of my moral awakening in the midst of the civil rights movement: social ostracism, being forced to leave the church we tried to join, being called "commie" and "nigger-lover" because of my support for justice and equality.

Having taken an unpopular stance opposing the war in Vietnam during high-school debates, I decided to attend Earlham College in Indiana. Part of the influence in choosing a Quaker college came from hearing Dad's frequent tributes to the Quaker witness for civil rights. Dad might have become a Quaker himself if he could ever sit still in silent meeting for worship.

I became a historian largely because of my quest to understand the sectional feelings of difference lying behind such terms as "Yankee" and "Rebel." Moving frequently had early stirred my interest in geography, maps, and history. After completing graduate studies in history at the University of Michigan, I spent eighteen years as an archivist before taking a full-time teaching position focusing on archives, records management, and history.

After joining my parents for the dedication of the Birmingham Civil Rights Institute (BCRI) in 1992, I decided that the time had come to return pieces of the stained glass from Sixteenth Street Baptist Church to the museum, located across the street from the church. In 2002, with my mother's agreement, I delivered the stained glass to BCRI, where it is now part of the museum display.

For me the broken windows of the Sixteenth Street Baptist Church—the twisted fragments that my parents kept for nearly forty years on the hutch shelf in the dining room, wherever they moved—symbolize our family's connection to one of the most complex, inspiring, and heart-breaking episodes of our country's recent past. The civil rights revolution remains unfinished. Perhaps it will always be so, until we imperfect mortals can rise above our self-interest and embrace our fellow beings with love, respect, and humility.

ANN JIMERSON, WASHINGTON, D.C.

At age ten, I was eager for our family to stand up for justice. I had never met an African American family, had no black friends, but I knew I wanted to be on the "right" side. Our Birmingham years have always held meaning for me—and feeling. Fifty years later, I have passed through many stages as I consider our family's small part in America's civil rights story.

Pride. Every time I watch *To Kill a Mockingbird,* I look for Dad in Atticus Finch. A handsome young father, principled, risking it all by standing up for right. Dad's legacy to his children and grandchildren is clear. It's our job to give back, to be on the side of justice.

Mortification. For years, every time our family is invited to someone's home, Dad manages to turn the conversation to Birmingham. Does he think people are interested? Does he need to convince everyone that he was important?

Solidarity. Just home from Peace Corps, I join thousands of my mostly African American neighbors in D.C. on the Capitol lawn. Stevie Wonder sings "Happy Birthday," as we press Congress for a holiday to honor MLK Jr. This is my family, too, I think.

Doubt. Sometimes when I read Dad's correspondence from those days, it seems he was on the opposite side from the movement's main organizers. Was his insistence on dialogue "old school," just slowing down change?

Fury. Twenty years later, reading Paul Theroux's *Mosquito Coast,* I quickly identify with the kids in the family. Fed up with American consumerism, a visionary father drags his family to the coast of Honduras where he plans to save the world. Things fall apart, lives are at risk. I'm furious: Who let Dad move us into the midst of Birmingham's violence? Who said it was okay to send a twelve-year-old girl alone by Greyhound Bus from Birmingham to New England? What were our parents thinking?

More doubt. During Dad's visit to my home, I myself steer the conversation to Birmingham, wanting to interest a friend. Dad starts in on the old "war stories." When he tells about visiting the FBI station upstairs from his Birmingham office, my friend is astonished. She challenges him: Why would he tell the FBI agents, of all people, about insider information he had on the movement? I think: Was Dad that naive? Had he possibly caused harm to someone in the movement?

Wonder. Watching the 1987 documentary series *Eyes on the Prize* with Mom and Dad, now in their mid-sixties, is a revelation. In every episode, they recognize someone. "Jim, we were in their living room!" "Hey, isn't that the guy who . . . ?"

Humility. Why are we, a white family who was just passing through the South, trying to lay claim to this story?

Grounded. My personal collection of Birmingham memories includes key events of the movement. But it isn't until Mom, Sue, and I visit the Birmingham Civil Rights Institute in 2002, and I walk through the timeline on the walls, that I put together what a powerful year 1963 had been: Wallace became governor, MLK and crew came to town, children marched and German Shepherds attacked, thousands convened for the March on Washington, racists killed four little girls at Sixteenth Street Baptist Church, and Kennedy was shot. We were in Birmingham during all of that.

Ready to tell the story. Each January, I ask another young person what she'll do to honor Martin Luther King Jr. on his day. She is astounded by my question and admits she can't imagine that there wasn't always a holiday. I see again that we have reduced the civil rights movement to a few iconic names. I am making the shift from viewing myself as "a child of the movement" to being an elder with a story to tell.

Telling the story. Recently, as part of a workshop on civil rights stories at a local college, I told my own story, including the way Dad scooped up the broken stained glass the evening of the church bombing. That glass had always evoked strong feelings in me. Still, I was not expecting the students' response when I lifted up the beautiful, twisted rosette of glass that we had kept in our home. A collective gasp, tears, and then a reverent silence. It was as though we were all there, almost fifty years back. I want our young people to feel it, to see that we were thousands of foot soldiers for justice. The struggle continues—and they too can be active players in the story.

PAUL JIMERSON, CAPITOLA, CALIFORNIA

Birmingham in the early sixties was not the safest place for a civil rights worker, and it was the beginning of my socio-political awakening. I was still too young to really comprehend the madness of the political situation in Birmingham, but undoubtedly it shaped my consciousness about the world, and helped turn me, years later, into an angry young radical.

My memories of Birmingham are frayed postcards, flashes of light illuminating a few dark corners of my memory. I was seven, eight, nine.

My third-grade teacher was Miz Taylor—not to be confused with "Ms.!" She was tough as Alabama iron. Each morning when she strutted into the classroom, the class stood and cried out in a unified drawl, "Good mornin' Miz Tay-lor."

I was not hassled as much as Randy was, but I was called a "nigger-lover" in the school hallway. One day, I heard my mother yell into the phone and hang up. She was crying. Another nasty phone call from one of dad's enemies. I found out later that one of the people who made threatening phone calls to the house was my Cub Scout den mother.

A young black boy had been shot off the back of his brother's bicycle by two white teenaged boys. My father took me with him to visit the family of the boy, at least his mother and siblings. I can still picture the dirt front yard, the ramshackle house, the large black woman with a long skirt, and the little black faces peering from behind it. Whatever combination of emotions I was feeling—perhaps fear, alienation, curiosity—that visit made an indelible impression on my mind. I realized that there were two Americas: one white, comfortable, middle class, and one poor and black. It was like visiting a strange planet.

I was nine when my fourth-grade class was interrupted by an event that would change everything. A television, that modern window on the world, was wheeled in. Gray images flashed ominously. President Kennedy had been shot. Mayhem whirled into our young lives that day. I saw, from a safe distance, confusion, terror, shock and grief, images that are part of my generation's, and my parents' generation's, consciousness. Three children broke into applause. Three nine-year-old children, ordinary nine-year-old children, children I sat with and studied with every day, actually cheered the death of John F. Kennedy. I didn't know anything about politics, and I'm sure they didn't either, but somehow they had learned that Kennedy was bad, and that bad people deserved to die.

Aside from these few memories, most of my life consisted of being a pretty normal little boy in a pretty normal suburban house. I rode the bus to school, ate with my family at lunch counters, played with friends. The race war raging around me merely brushed the edges of my life. Black people rode on different buses, ate at different lunch counters, played different games.

Dad was a complicated person. On the one hand, he was a courageous, principled man. On the other hand, he was an angry man, who took his anger out mostly on me. I spent much of my life hating the man. As I got older, I could begin to see how a person could embody such contradictory impulses.

I spent much of my life trying to avoid the "family business" of being a social worker. Inevitably, I succumbed, working in the field in various capacities, from social worker to psychotherapist. Dad's positive legacy to me was his belief in social justice, and his courageous action, which have manifested in my life in many ways, from being a young writer of letters to the editor, to founding the Progressive News Service at the University of Massachusetts, writing on social justice issues for *The Daily Collegian,* attending marches, supporting United Farm Workers boycotts, to my current preoccupation of signing online petitions and putting them on Twitter and Facebook.

Martin Luther King Jr. Day always has a special resonance for me. I was just a child when my father gathered up a charred, twisted bit of the stained glass window from the rubble of the Sixteenth Street Baptist Church in Birmingham that was bombed on September 15, 1963, killing four young girls. For many years, that twisted fragment of stained glass graced my mother's hutch, long after my father's death. It was eventually given to the Birmingham Civil Rights Institute, and is a cherished object there.

Stained glass has been used for a thousand years to decorate churches, usually depicting the life of Christ and his disciples, an aesthetic symbol of hope and redemption. Growing up with a twisted and blackened bit of the

Sixteenth Street Baptist Church was a reminder of the violence that twists and distorts the human psyche, the distortion of racism and hatred, but also a symbol of hope. My belief was always that, if people could talk and really communicate about the violence and hatred that is symbolized by that twisted clump of glass, racism could finally be eradicated.

President Barack Obama appropriated the word "hope" in his campaign, and his election was, for many, symbolic of the eradication of racism. Of course, we need more than symbolism to eliminate racism, but talking about it is a start. It is my hope that we can have meaningful national conversations about racism and hatred, so that these evils can come to light and be, once and for all, a thing of the past.

Birmingham is in my blood. How can one not be affected by the close proximity to the violence, the hatred, the insanity of racism? I will always be grateful to Dad for exposing me to the reality of racism and implanting within me the desire to see it ended.

SUE JIMERSON, WEST DENNIS, MASSACHUSETTS

At the time that we moved to Birmingham, I did not understand the impact or importance of what our father was undertaking in his work with the Alabama Council on Human Relations. I saw and experienced events through a young child's eyes and understanding, as I was almost six years old when we moved to Birmingham. I must have heard conversations at home about the events unfolding, about equality and social interactions between blacks and whites. I did take notice on many occasions when my best friend and her brothers would talk back to their maid, who was taking care of them. When they talked back I couldn't believe how they were speaking to her because she was the adult!

I was not conscious of the impact of segregation in school, just learning to relate to other kids as a normal part of growing up. I do clearly remember going to a three-week integrated summer program after third grade. Paul and I carpooled there with several other kids. On the first day of the day camp, I was the only white kid in my class. It was awkward for a while, until I got to know the other kids, then it was a lot of fun.

The time that we spent in Birmingham had a great impact on me in later years. I remember the sadness I felt when John F. Kennedy was assassinated, and watched the funeral procession on TV with the family. In the not-so-distant future, I felt devastated when Martin Luther King Jr. was killed, and

I had a sense of sadness, anger, and loss of hope. It was especially upsetting when some of the kids cheered, because we were sent home early from school. I felt a connection with Dr. King and the sense of hope for social change that he inspired.

Our time in Birmingham has had a major impact on my choosing to go into social work and to try to reach out to help others less fortunate. It made me conscious of the need for social justice. I have often felt a sense of pride in the work that our dad carried out, and hearing stories of his late-night meetings at the Gaston Motel, and meeting Dr. King, Andrew Young, Fred Shuttlesworth—and Dick Gregory, comedian.

I have felt a special connectedness to the civil rights movement, whether or not I have shared that involvement when the topic came up. I have joined strangers in celebrating Dr. King's life and ministry, and when singing "We Shall Overcome" together, have felt a bit choked up in knowing that we were there. I have at times wondered about Dad's role in the movement; as Ann said, why did he talk with FBI agents at all? And I have learned other things that Dad had done that I didn't realize at the time, like being one of the ministers at the funeral for one of the girls who was killed when the Sixteenth Street Baptist Church was bombed.

As the years go by, it sometimes seems like those days were so long ago. Then I read about another incident in the news of racial hatred and discrimination and wonder what we have learned. Why haven't things changed more drastically? I wonder what I have done to affect social justice issues myself. It's one thing to remember and honor the work of our father, who did his small part for the movement. But what have I myself done to follow in his footsteps? Have I spoken up when it was needed, or taken risks that needed to be taken? What can I do even now to help work for equality and speak up when needed?

What happened in Birmingham, and around the country, has inspired so many people to continue to fight for justice, and to never stop. Each time we celebrate Martin Luther King, it is a good time to take stock of what we can do in our own day to work for justice.

One of the reminders of the call of justice has been the stained glass pieces from the church that was bombed. This glass has been a tangible image of the unfathomable violence that took the lives of four little girls. The stained glass has been a stark reminder of the reality of the violence perpetrated against African Americans and others who fought back against daily discrimination and humiliation. It has provided a sense of connection to those important events, and a reminder to continue to work for justice. I feel blessed that our father took the time to gather that glass, to remember not just the bombing, but to remember the sacrifices that were made. May we do our part today.

MARK JIMERSON, SPRINGFIELD, MASSACHUSETTS

I was two years old when we left Birmingham. I grew up hearing stories about our family's experiences there, and fragments of shared memories that didn't have to be told in full, because everyone else could put the pieces together and know what they meant. As time went on, I was able to fit some of the bigger pieces together and form a kind of picture that made sense to me. I saw photos of the house we'd lived in. I sat with my family in a dark room and watched a grainy 8mm movie of snow in the backyard, and kids sliding down the hill on it, laughing and talking to the camera without making a sound. It seemed that there was a normal family there, living normal lives, and I was born into it like any child is born into a family.

But most of the time when my parents and siblings spoke of Birmingham, there was a kind of hushed awe that added weight and wonder to their words. Big and powerful things must have happened there. I owned a book that had a chapter written about my father, and the man who wrote it had penned words just for me near the front: "For Mark, who was born in the middle of it all. Good luck." I read those words long before I ever read the chapter or the book. It made me feel important to think that I had been born in the middle of something big, something historic. But it was hard to understand what it was.

Sometimes guests would come to our house and ask about the broken stained glass on our hutch, and my mother or father would tell about the church that was bombed and the little girls who were killed. In a bathroom, of all places. Flush, and boom, as I understood it. Death was hard to understand. Killing people was harder to understand. I wanted to know everything. I wanted to understand what it was like for those girls, how it felt to die, and what it looked like. There were some things my parents could tell me, and some things that no one could.

My memories of Birmingham are buried deep. As a clinical social worker, I know enough about psychology to understand that the first years of life can have a powerful impact on the development of the psyche. An infant or toddler may not have words to explain what he or she is experiencing, or the means to implant a memory that can be recalled to consciousness in later years; but emotional memory can be built almost from birth. A mother's sense of danger and feelings of fear are easily passed to her baby. A toddler can sense when people around him are nervous or scared.

Though our father moved us from Alabama to Michigan when I was two, the emotional memory of those years has remained with me ever since. I realized sometime around the age of nine that I thought about death more than other kids. It wouldn't be an exaggeration to say that I was obsessed with it. My grim curiosity about the little girls in the church was never completely satisfied. I wanted to know, literally, how it was possible to die. What kind of injury could cause it, and what actually happened to the body? Eventually, in Freudian terms, I was able to sublimate this obsession into a pretty fair knowledge of human biology.

Though it took me many years to realize it, my father's life and work had a powerful influence in my choice of career, and really, in how I live my life. He was a good man. I didn't fully realize this in my adolescence, but I managed to figure it out before he died. He was a Christian man. He was pastor of the church we attended when I was eight years old, until I was sixteen. He taught me that being Christian is more than declaring a set beliefs, it's something active, it's who we are.

I never planned to be a social worker. It felt at the time like it happened almost by accident. When I shared with my father that I had decided to apply to a master's of social work program, he said that the MSW was something he always thought he should have, and at times had regretted not pursuing it. I told him about my interest in psychology, and I shared with him the depth of anxiety that I experienced in my twenties. I wondered aloud if it could have any connection with my first two years of life in Birmingham.

He could have dismissed or minimized such a thought. As a student of psychology himself, he could have given me any number of other plausible causes. Instead, true to form, he said he often felt badly about the things he had exposed his children to during those years in Birmingham. He said he had done what he thought was right, and what God had led him to do. He said he believed that the older kids had learned some important lessons, but he knew too that the experience had been very upsetting to our mother, and in many ways, to us as children. He thought it plausible that my generalized anxieties could have roots in my early life experiences. He didn't think I was crazy.

I was in my twenties and trying to learn how to be a man when we had this conversation. I had spent many years rejecting my father and his beliefs.

But finally, I was learning who he was, and learning how to be proud of him. Even in my rebellious years, he had never stopped telling me he was proud of me. Now I'm fifty, and he's gone from this earth. But the more I learn about who he was, and what he did, the more proud I am of him.

When my mother donated one large fragment of the shattered stained glass window from Sixteenth Street Baptist Church to the Birmingham Civil Rights Institute in 2002, she kept a second rosette of leaded glass as a family memento. In February 2012 I watched live TV coverage of the groundbreaking for the Smithsonian National Museum of African-American History and Culture. As President Barack Obama talked about the value of such a museum, I heard him say: "I want my daughters to see the shackles that bound slaves on their voyage across the ocean and the shards of glass that flew from the 16th Street Baptist church, and understand that injustice and evil exist in the world." I decided then that our family should donate the remaining piece of stained glass, so that it could reach a national audience with its evocation of that tragic event.

On September 9, 2013, Ann, Sue, Mark, and I delivered the stained glass to the Smithsonian during a small ceremony in Washington, DC. Paul was unable to travel from California for this event. Two days earlier, the *Washington Post* carried a front-page story about our donation. As Lonnae O'Neal Parker wrote: "It is perhaps a second tier of civil rights emotion that the country is just starting to get to—the disaffection and alienation felt by families like the Jimersons." The price paid by white people who took a stand against racism she said was being "shunned or name-called."

On the day after our donation, the four of us were invited to attend the ceremony conferring the Congressional Gold Medal on Denise McNair, Carole Robertson, Addie Mae Collins, and Cynthia Wesley, the young girls killed in the church bombing fifty years ago that week.

My family now knows that the shattered glass of Birmingham's Sixteenth Street Baptist Church, which our father saved and preserved, will be a lasting reminder—both in Birmingham and Washington, DC—of the violence and hatred of the past. Yet it will also remind those who see it of the heroism, sacrifice, and persistence of those who continue to fight for human dignity and the rights of all people.

NOTES

CHAPTER 5

62   Morgan paraphrased from *A Time to Speak,* 129.

CHAPTER 6

68   Bob Zellner's father quoted in *The Wrong Side of Murder Creek,* 22.
69   Zellner, "I found out . . . ," paraphrased from *The Wrong Side,* 60, 139.
70   "I shoulda let them . . . ," quote in *The Wrong Side,* 162.
70–71   "Bob said, 'Well, Jim . . . ,'" Zellner comments in these conversations paraphrased
            from Zellner interview, 2012.
71   "Mr. Zellner you are . . . ," quote in *The Wrong Side,* p. 171.

CHAPTER 8

97   *Birmingham Post-Herald* quoted in Jimerson report to SRC, April 5, 1962, Southern
            Regional Council Records.

CHAPTER 9

111–12   "Stars Fell on Alabama" lyrics available at www.songlyrics.com/johnny-mathis/
            stars-fell-on-alabama-lyrics/. Accessed January 30, 2013.

CHAPTER 11

130–37   Portions of this testimony and the conversation in the car paraphrased from "State-
            ment by Norman C. Jimerson [re. *State of Alabama* v. *Norman C. Jimerson*]," in
            Charles Morgan Jr. Papers, Alabama Department of Archives and History; also from
            Jimerson interviews in *Peacemaker in Birmingham.*
139–40   "Morgan later wrote . . . ," from Morgan, *A Time to Speak,* 134.

CHAPTER 12

142   McWhorter quote taken from *Carry Me Home,* 289.

CHAPTER 14

159   "Second Emancipation Proclamation," in "An Appeal to the Honorable John F. Kennedy," May 17, 1962, available at www.thekingcenter.org/archive/document/appeal-honorable-john-f-kennedy-president-united-states. Accessed February 2, 2013.

160   Wallace inaugural address, available at Alabama Department of Archives and History website, digital.archives.alabama.gov/cdm/singleitem/collection/voices/id/2952/rec/5, accessed February 2, 2013.

160   Religious leaders' statement, in Bass, *Blessed Are the Peacemakers,* 233–34.

163   "New Day Dawns for Birmingham," quoted in McWhorter, 320.

165   "most cruel and vicious thing," quoted in McWhorter, 324.

165   "Do you Negroes want . . . ," quoted in McWhorter, 325.

169   Good Friday letter quoted in Bass, 236.

CHAPTER 16

180   "misuse of police power," Alabama Advisory Committee minutes, in James Head Papers, Birmingham Public Library.

185   "Lawyer Vann . . . ," quoted in McWhorter, 353.

187   Thornton quoted in Thornton, 328. Much of the preceding discussion of negotiations in which my father did not participate comes from Thornton, 312–28.

192   Wallace quote available at digital.archives.alabama.gov/cdm/singleitem/collection/voices/id/2050/rec/3. Accessed February 2, 2013.

193   Katzenbach quoted in McWhorter, 443.

193   Kennedy speech available at www.pbs.org/wgbh/americanexperience/features/primary-resources/jfk-civilrights/. Accessed February 2, 2013.

193   Thornton quote in Thornton, 378.

194   "Anti-Jewish Crusader," quote in McWhorter, 200–201.

194–95   NSRP bulletins available in David Vann Papers, Birmingham Public Library.

CHAPTER 18

214   "Get up, Virge" quote in McWhorter, 531.

215   Boutwell quote in McWhorter, 534.

215   Morgan quotes found in "Statement of Charles Morgan, Jr., Birmingham, Alabama, September 16, 1963," Norman C. Jimerson personal papers.

CHAPTER 19

216	Morgan quotes in *A Time to Speak,* 173.
217	"We realize Carole . . . ," quote in McWhorter, 515.
218	King funeral eulogy available at www.drmartinlutherkingjr.com/birmingham-churchbombingeulogy.htm. Accessed February 4, 2013.
220–21	Mary McGrory column, *Washington Evening Star,* September 23, 1963. Copy in Burke Marshall Papers, Birmingham Public Library.
222	Mary McGrory column, *Washington Evening Star,* September 21, 1963. Copy in Burke Marshall Papers.

CHAPTER 20

| 231 | "Blowin' in the Wind" lyrics available at www.bobdylan.com/us/songs#us/songs/blowin-wind. Accessed February 2, 2013. |

CHAPTER 21

| 248–49 | Morgan quotes found in *A Time to Speak,* 127, 132–34. |
| 251–52 | Hoover quotes from *Masters of Deceit,* v, 202–3. |

CHAPTER 22

256	President Johnson quoted in Ted Gittinger and Allen Fisher, "LBJ Champions the Civil Rights Act of 1964," *Prologue* 36, no. 2 (Summer 2004), available at www.archives.gov/publications/prologue/2004/summer/civil-rights-act-1.html. Accessed February 4, 2013.
256–57	Reese Cleghorn quotes found in "Uneasy South Awaits Test of New Civil Rights Law," *Washington Star,* July 1964, in Norman C. Jimerson personal papers.
264	Quoted passages found in Joe Nabbefeld, "1,800 Look at Past at Rights Institute on First Exhibit Day," *Birmingham News,* November 17, 1992, 1C.

EPILOGUE

| 276 | Obama quote found at www.loop21.com/pres-obamas-remarks-national-african-american-museum?page=1 (accessed August 22, 2013). |
| 276 | Lonnae O'Neal Parker quote found in Parker, "Piece of Birmingham Coming to D.C.," *Washington Post,* September 7, 2013, A2. |

NOTE ON SOURCES

A historical era as complex and controversial as the twentieth-century civil rights movement cannot easily be compressed into a single volume, nor understood from one specific vantage point. The "long" civil rights era in the United States surely dates from the first introduction of African slaves into Virginia in 1619, and it has evolved—and continues to evolve—in many forms. Historians can identify a series of civil rights time periods, but such distinctions are necessarily arbitrary. The common perception of the modern movement often focuses on the period between the Supreme Court's 1954 decision in *Brown* v. *Board of Education* (that segregated schools were inherently unequal and unconstitutional) and the rise of the black-power movement in the mid-1960s. This story is a personal account of one family's experiences in a single community during only a three-year period within this brief time.

My account presents the perspective of a family of white northerners living in a suburb of Birmingham, Alabama, from 1961 to 1964. My father, Rev. Norman C. "Jim" Jimerson, served from August 1961 until August 1964 as executive director of the Alabama Council on Human Relations. He was the only white person working full time in the field of civil rights in the state. This is his story. But it is also the story of our family: of my mother's efforts to support Dad and to nurture and protect four (and soon five) children in an often hostile environment; of my coming of age as the eldest child trying to comprehend the powerful social forces at play during the civil rights struggle; and of my younger brothers and sisters as they sought their own understandings of what we were experiencing.

We happened to live in Birmingham during some of the most tumultuous years of the era: the time of Bull Connor's police dogs and fire hoses; of Governor George Wallace's vow to defend segregation forever and his defiant pose blocking two African American students from entering the University of Alabama; of Dr. Martin Luther King Jr.'s "Letter from Birmingham Jail" and his "I Have a Dream" speech during the March on Washington; of the bombing of the Sixteenth Street Baptist Church and the deaths of four young girls; of the murders of other children and civil rights activists; of the assassination of President Kennedy; of the passage of the 1964 Civil Rights Act. Our family's story recounts how we responded to these events, how the daily experiences of life in a segregated society affected concerned white people seeking social justice, how our childhood perspectives juxtaposed adult realities.

This is a family memoir, not a history of the civil rights movement. It shapes and presents past experience in ways that, I hope, remain true to my emotional memory of events. These stories reflect the perspective of a young teenager trying to make sense of momentous events that profoundly affected me and my family. In trying to present this story as authentically as possible from my youthful perspective, I have chosen not to include detailed footnotes and references to each source of information used for historical background or fact-checking.

Most of what I learned as a boy about the South and civil rights came from my father. I remember numerous conversations about civil rights activities and issues during dinner, or during family devotions in the evening. After fifty years or more, I clearly cannot remember exact conversations—with a few memorable exceptions—but I have reconstructed the essence of such discussions based on both my own memory and documentary sources, including oral history interviews, correspondence, my father's reports to the Southern Regional Council, newspaper and magazine clippings, and family papers. In 2003 I transcribed or copied many of these sources in a booklet I compiled for family members, called *Peacemaker in Birmingham, 1961–1964: Rev. Norman C. Jimerson and the Alabama Council on Human Relations*. Copies of this booklet are available at the Birmingham Public Library, the Birmingham Civil Rights Institute, and the Alabama Department of Archives and History.

In writing this memoir I have quoted many of these documentary sources directly; in others I have recast them as conversations. I have taken some liberties in shaping the written language into conversational speech, but I have tried as much as possible to retain the authentic voices, mood, and underlying meaning of these sources.

The notes cite sources of direct quotations taken from secondary sources used in my research. The list of principal sources used for this memoir includes additional sources, both primary and secondary, which have provided general background for the personal stories recounted in this volume, sources for fact-checking oral history accounts and personal memories, and sources for the historical context of the civil rights era.

PRINCIPAL SOURCES

Alabama Department of Archives and History, Montgomery. (ADAH.)
    Charles Morgan Jr. Papers.
Atlanta University Center Archives.
    Alabama Council on Human Relations Records, 1960–65, in Southern Regional
        Council Records.
Bass, S. Jonathan. *Blessed Are the Peacemakers: Martin Luther King Jr., Eight White
    Religious Leaders, and the "Letter from Birmingham Jail."* Baton Rouge: Louisi-
    ana State University Press, 2001.
Birmingham Civil Rights Institute. (BCRI.)
    Interviews with Deenie Drew, James Head, Robert Hughes, Anny Kraus, Charles
        Morgan Jr., C. Herbert Oliver, David Vann, David Walbert, and Eileen Walbert.
Birmingham Public Library, Archives Division. (BPL.)
    Bishop C. C. J. Carpenter Papers.
    James Head Papers.
    Burke Marshall Papers. (Copied from John F. Kennedy Presidential Library.)
    David Vann Papers.
Branch, Taylor. *Parting the Waters: America in the King Years, 1954–63.* New York:
    Simon and Schuster, 1988.
Chappell, David L. *Inside Agitators: White Southerners in the Civil Rights Movement.*
    Baltimore: Johns Hopkins University Press, 1994.
Corley, Robert Gaines. "The Quest for Racial Harmony: Race Relations in Birming-
    ham, Alabama, 1947–1963." Ph.D. diss., University of Virginia, 1979.
Eskew, Glenn T. *But for Birmingham: The Local and National Movements in the Civil
    Rights Struggle.* Chapel Hill: University of North Carolina Press, 1997.
Garrow, David J., ed. *Birmingham, Alabama, 1956–1963: The Black Struggle for Civil
    Rights.* Brooklyn, N.Y.: Carlson Publishing, Inc., 1989.
Hoover, J. Edgar. *Masters of Deceit: The Story of Communism in America and How to
    Fight It.* New York: Henry Holt, 1958.
Jimerson, Melva. Interview by Maria Klein. Washington, D.C., January 1, 2003.
———. Interview by Randall C. Jimerson. Washington, D.C., March 20, 2003.

Jimerson, Norman C. Interview by Andrew M. Manis. Washington, D.C., June 13, 1989.

———. Interviews by Randall C. Jimerson. Washington, D.C., April 14, April 16, April 18, and July 20, 1992.

———. Personal papers. In possession of Randall C. Jimerson, Bellingham, Wash.

Jimerson, Randall C., ed. *Peacemaker in Birmingham, 1961–1964: Rev. Norman C. Jimerson and the Alabama Council on Human Relations*. Bellingham, Wash.: privately duplicated, 2003.

Manis, Andrew M. *A Fire You Can't Put Out: The Civil Rights Life of Birmingham's Reverend Fred Shuttlesworth*. Tuscaloosa: University of Alabama Press, 1999.

McWhorter, Diane. *Carry Me Home: Birmingham, Alabama, the Climactic Battle of the Civil Rights Revolution*. New York: Simon and Schuster, 2001.

Morgan, Charles, Jr. *A Time to Speak*. New York: Harper and Row, 1964.

Samford University Library, Special Collections, Homewood, Ala.

   Maps of Homewood.

   History of Howard College.

Thompson, Jan Gregory. "A History of the Alabama Council on Human Relations, from Roots to Redirection, 1920–1968." Ph.D. diss., Auburn University, 1983.

Thornton, J. Mills, III. *Dividing Lines: Municipal Politics and the Struggle for Civil Rights in Montgomery, Birmingham, and Selma*. Tuscaloosa: University of Alabama Press, 2002.

Walbert, David and Eileen Walbert. Interview with Randall Jimerson and Ann Jimerson, Homewood, Ala., December 16, 2011.

Zellner, Bob. Interview with Randall Jimerson. June 29, 2012, by telephone from Bellingham, Wash.

Zellner, Bob. *The Wrong Side of Murder Creek: A White Southerner in the Freedom Movement*. Montgomery, Ala.: New South Books, 2008.

INDEX

Cash, W. J., 85
Central Park swimming pool, Homewood, 37, 114–15
Chamber of Commerce, 47, 83, 141, 142, 148, 161
Chambliss, Robert, 224
chapters of ACHR: Birmingham, 177, 195; Huntsville, 37–38, 205; Mobile, 205; Muscle Shoals, 206; Tri-Cities, 78
Chattanooga, TN, 31
Cherokee, NC, 30
Cherry, Bobby Frank, 224–25
Children's Crusade, 184–86
Chippewa, PA, 28
Christian Science Monitor, 248
Christmas letters, 157–58, 198, 239
churches: black church bombings, xiii–xv, 162, 207–13; black churches, visiting, 62–63; Dawson Memorial Baptist, 57; First Baptist Church, Beaver Falls, 51; Hopewell First Baptist, 34; Lutheran Church of Vestavia Hills, 62; New Pilgrim Baptist, 220; Pilgrim Congregational, 63–64, 87; Second Presbyterian, 60–62; Shades Valley Presbyterian, 58–59, 63–64, 155–56, 207; Sixth Avenue Baptist, 218–19; St. John's A.M.E. Church, 217; Vestavia Hills Baptist, 52–56. *See also* Sixteenth Street Baptist Church
Citizens for Progress, 142
Civil Rights Act (1964), 193, 240, 246, 256
civil rights campaign (1963). *See* Birmingham campaign
Civil War, 33
Clark, Charles, 112
Clark, Ed, 198, 200, 201
Clay, Cassius (Muhammad Ali), 258
Clayton, Jim, 96
Cleghorn, Reese, 256–57
Cold War nuclear threat, 73
Coles, Robert, 97
Coley, John, 206, 232
Collins, Addie Mae, 212, 218, 225, 276
Collins, Sarah, 212
Commission on Civil Rights, U.S., 120–21, 180, 246

"communist" label: churches and, 58–59, 60–62; Hoover's *Masters of Deceit* and, 251–53; housing discrimination and, 27; NCJ and, 46; at school, 72, 99–101, 245
Congress of Racial Equality (CORE), 39, 75, 253
Connor, Eugene "Bull": Birmingham campaign crackdown by, 180, 185; city-government change referendum and, 142, 145–46; election campaign, 98, 102, 107–8; food surplus program cuts and, 97; as leading opponent of integration, 47–49; mayoral campaign, 161, 163; parks segregation and, 74; refusal to vacate City Hall, 163; SCLC convention and, 143; spies of, 83, 149, 181
Cook, Sergeant Tom, 39
CORE (Congress of Racial Equality), 39, 75, 253
Cox, Annette, 35, 45, 83
Cross, John H., xiii–xiv, 208, 212, 217, 260, 261, *photo section*
cross burnings, 8, 65, 246
Cuban Missile Crisis, 130, 135, 159
Cullman, AL, 78–79

Dabbs, James McBride, 95–96
Davenport, Roy K., 125
Dawson Memorial Baptist Church, 57
death threats, 83
De Graffenried, Ryan, 102, 108, 159
de la Beckwith, Byron, 194
Democratic Committee of Jefferson county, 97
Democratic primary race for governor (1962), 98, 101–2, 107–8
demonstrations: activist vs. moderate strategies, 136–37, 182–83; anti-integration, 206, 214, 218; Birmingham campaign, 126, 164–72, 180–93; efforts to delay Birmingham campaign, 143–48; FBI and, 82; in Gadsden, 205–6; injunction against, 103–4; kneel-ins in Talladega, 127, 132, 134; NCJ on "research and education" vs., 11; restaurant picketing by whites in Mobile, 113; school desegregation and, 206; in Selma, 232; Talladega lunch counters sit-ins, 102–3, 127–29, 130–33; warnings of, 143

move to Virginia and being called a "Yankee," 15–17; music, power of, 152–53; NCJ, complicated relationship with, 120; phone harassment and, 84; at Prince George County School (VA), 17; reflections of, 267–68; at Shades Cahaba Elementary, 41–42, 99–100; in spelling bees, 123; stuck hanging out the window, 210; summer school at Shades Valley High, 258; at Talladega trial, 135–39; visiting Mike in hospital, 90–91; at Wallace speech, 235–36

Jimerson, Susan (Susie), *photo section;* baby Mark and, 117; in Beaver Falls, 115; birthday in New Hampshire, 203–4; .birth of, 15; Halloween costume contest, 66–67; at interracial summer day camp, 257–58; missing, 92–93; at rally with LBJ, 24; reflections of, 272–74; at Shades Cahaba Elementary, 41–42, 59, 65–66; Spitzy (dog) and, 22–23; on swimming team, 115; "What if I marry the wrong person?" 229

Johnson, Don, 203

Johnson, Lyndon B., 23–24, 237, 240, 241, 256

Johnson, Merilee, 203

Jones, Bob, Sr., 68

journalists, NCJ's connections with, 96–97

Joyce, Brice, 49–50

Junior Chamber of Commerce, 174, 186

Kalamazoo College, 177, 247, 258, 261

Kaplow, Herb, 96

Katzenbach, Nicholas, 192–93

Keever, Robert, 261

Kennedy, John F.: assassination of, 236–38, 271; church bombing, response to, 216; Civil Rights Act announcement, 193; Cuban Missile Crisis and, 130, 135, 159; election, 23–24; Emancipation Proclamation centennial and, 159; Hoover and, 252; telegram to Council from, 61

Kennedy, Robert (Bobby), 146, 166, 186, 211, 240

Khrushchev, Nikita, 130, 135, 159

Kidd, Oley, 260, *photo section*

King, A. D., 166, 167–68

King, Coretta Scott, 255, *photo section*

King, Martin Luther, Jr.: American Baptist check presented to, 89; at American Baptist Convention, 255, *photo section;* arrests of, 72; arrival in Birmingham for campaign, 163, 165; assassination attempt on, 190; assassination of, 272–73; Birmingham campaign meetings and, 166–67, 168; Birmingham campaign settlement announcement, 187–88; Birmingham convention and, 143, 147; at Civil Rights Act signing, 256; confrontation strategy and, 183; criticisms of, 165–66, 191; denunciations of, 61; Emancipation Proclamation centennial and, 159; funeral sermon for bombing victims, 218; "I have a dream" speech, 204; Jefferson County Interdenominational Alliance address, 170–71; "Letter from Birmingham Jail," 169, 232; as messiah, 181; NCJ's lunch with, 171; press conference in Birmingham, 189; recruited by Alabama Council, 7–8

King, Tom, 161

kneel-ins, 127, 132, 134

Knox, Helen, 105

Kraus, Anny, 101, 106, 174, 177

Kraus, Frederick, 101, 106, 177

Ku Klux Klan (KKK): after Birmingham campaign, 194; church bombing and, 225; Hughes and, 8; news media, control of, 80; police and, 47; readiness for action, 76; school desegregation and, 206, 214; Shelton as grand wizard of, 70–71; shootings and, 224; in Talladega, 133; in Tuscaloosa, 70, 71; welcome signs by, 69, 70

Lake, Clancy, 238

Landrum, Jack, 131

Laursen, Per Worsoe, 67–72

law enforcement discrimination lawsuits, 149

Leake, Ann, 5

Lee, Herbert, 69

Lee, Robert E., 160

"Let's work together" brochure (ACHR), 108–9

"Letter from Birmingham Jail" (King), 169, 232

libel sheets, 80